PHYSICAL ELOQUENCE
AND THE BIOLOGY OF WRITING

SUNY Series on Literacy, Culture, and Learning:
Theory and Practice

Alan C. Purves, EDITOR

PHYSICAL ELOQUENCE

AND THE BIOLOGY OF WRITING

Robert Ochsner

State University of New York Press

Published by
State University of New York Press, Albany

© 1990   State University of New York

For information, address the State University of New York Press,
State University Plaza, Albany, NY 12246

Library of Congress Cataloging-in-Publication Data

Ochsner, Robert, 1950-
    Physical eloquence and the biology of writing / by Robert Ochsner.
        p.   cm. — (SUNY series, literacy, culture, and learning)
    Includes bibliographical references.
    ISBN 0-7914-0313-0. — ISBN 0-7914-0314-9 (pbk.)
    1. English language—Rhetoric—Study and teaching. 2. Authorship-
-Physiological aspects. 3. Writing—Physiological aspects.
    I. Title. II. Series.
PE1404.O24   1990
808'.042'07—dc20   89-38062
                                                                        CIP

10 9 8 7 6 5 4 3 2 1

808.0420?
Och

TABLE OF CONTENTS

ACKNOWLEDGMENTS

The original title for this book was *A Literacy of Eloquence*, taken directly from Richard Lanham's *The Motives of Eloquence*. As my research progressed the title changed, mostly to express my greater concern for the biology of writing. Since the current title no longer shows an outright piracy of Lanham's title, I want to acknowledge here my fundamental debt to his original and provocative work on language and literacy.

I also want to thank Patrick Hartwell for his acute reading of an earlier draft; Karen Kerr, Stefan Martin, Carolyn Fitzpatrick, Elizabeth Ermarth, and several other colleagues at the University of Maryland at Baltimore County have at various stages of my work contributed their advice. All these readers deserve credit for helping me shape my argument and jettison unnecessary text.

My wife and children have endured another year with me closeted in a study, so for Nancy, Allyson, and Nathan I extend my deepest appreciation.

1

The Biology of Writing

Rather than state what this book is about, I want to start with its omissions. Although I will discuss the teaching of writing at length, this is not a book that deals exclusively with written literacy. Neither do I explore in depth topics like inner language (Vygotsky), learning and acquisition (Krashen), errors (Shaughnessy), nor most other aspects of what I consider to be "mainstream" views on writing. Of course, I recognize that composition studies is an emerging discipline and, as one result, the evidence for consensus on any issue is debatable. Literacy, for instance, clearly is undergoing a change in definition as composition theorists become increasingly influenced by social constructionism; nevertheless, I have used the term *literacy* in a relatively conventional way rather than explore its newer, but less stable, meanings.[1]

This deliberately "dumb" presentation may unsettle readers who want a straightforward exposition of terms like *literacy*. But I have chosen a manner of presenting my ideas that crucially depends on a reader's ability to think as if writing differs from accepted norms. In this sense I have written an exploratory book, one that challenges readers to rethink their own assumptions about writing. In effect, I am asking my readers to consider writing, and writing development, as if both were primarily a physical—and hence biological—activity.

As a statement about the biology of literacy, this book describes an approach to teaching writing that stresses the neurological foundations of written English, mastered almost like a "foreign" language. As a discussion of eloquence, it starts with the axiomatic decline of contemporary print culture, of belletristic writing and the values associated with a Western literary tradition, so that I can promote a *physical* writing curriculum that takes into account the supremacy of popular culture and the emergent ascendancy of its spoken idiom. A lesser eloquence, more physical than metaphysical, thus is joined in this book with a radically different literacy, different because it stresses subconscious processes in the biology of writing rather than planned, rehearsed, and formally practiced activities for learning to write.

Nothing exotic, a *literacy of physical eloquence* is best summed in Alfred North Whitehead's (1929) maxim for educators: Allow that your students have bodies. Certainly high school and college teachers, as well as scholars who study written literacy, can benefit from a similar attention to the biology of writing, if only because a writer's body plays an important role in generating a text, a role that is distinctly pre-cognitive.

Although a writer's progress towards physical eloquence does not necessarily coincide with cognitive development, I am not in this book advocating a literacy of mindlessness; ideas count, even from a biological perspective. I do, however, regard the teaching of ideas as less important for most students than the propaedeutic instruction that enables students to express their ideas fluently. Thus the quality, logic, force, and elegance of ideas—and the apposite characteristics as they take shape in prose— follow from a student's basic ability to put thought in writing.

The biology of writing is "basic" because without it there can be no writing. Over a decade ago Janet Emig made a similar point in her article "Hand, Eye, Brain: Some 'Basics' in the Writing Process":

> Much of the current talk about the basics of writing is not only confused but, even more ironic, frivolous. Capitalization, spelling, punctuation— these are touted as the basics in writing when they represent, of course, merely the conventions, the amenities for recording the outcome of the process. The process is what is basic in writing, the process and the organic structures that interact to produce it. What are these structures? And what are their contributions? Although we don't yet know, the hand, the eye, and the brain itself surely seem logical candidates as requisite structures. (1978, 59)

The hand, eye, and brain. To these I would add the ear. Considered together, all four organic structures constitute the biology of writing. Considered separately, the study of each biological structure complements other research on writing, especially studies of cognitive processes and broader concerns like the social nature of discourse communities or the design of a writing curriculum.

The relative importance assigned to biological or social topics (and scholarly commitment to their study) varies from generation to generation; in this book I engage a biological tradition that differs from the contemporary and more fashionable cognitive and social approaches to writing research. It would be accurate, though perhaps foolhardy, to acknowledge the beginning of this biological tradition with the Sophists of ancient Greece and to trace its lineage through the neo-Sophists of Rome, the courtiers of Castiglione's Italy, the Elocutionists of pre-Romantic England, concluding, alas, with the advertisers of modern America. However accurate this account might be, it would necessarily go beyond the scope of this book—as would even a preliminary discussion of the mind/body controversy.

Instead, in this study I concentrate on the relatively neglected topic of biological processes in composition, a topic that deserves more notice if only to clarify its relationship to other research on writing. As a much stronger claim for studying the biological processes of writing, I can contribute in a practical manner to the effectiveness of writing instruction. For only by recognizing, as Whitehead warned, that students have bodies can teachers of writing succeed in preparing their students to write well.

Relationship to Traditional Rhetoric

This book addresses the last three parts of traditional rhetoric, but in reverse order, a reversal that signals a corresponding shift in the way *delivery, memory,* and *style* are analyzed. In classical rhetoric a speaker could take for granted the quality of a speech in order to memorize it and then deliver it with studied gestures for desired effects. Similarly, a writer assumes the existence of a complete topic or the opportunity to discover one as part of the mental task initiated by writing. If *invention, arrangement*, and figurative aspects of *style* are largely mental endeavors, they contrast with the physical activities of producing a text—or its delivery—and generating the language—from our memory—for this text production. A writer's style also has a physical, mostly spontaneous expression that contrasts with the self-conscious, often edited uses of language.

Besides this division of writing into mental and physical tasks that correspond to the first two and last two parts of traditional rhetoric, I have made a fundamental change, at least from a physiological perspective, as to the significance of these rhetorical terms and their appropriate study.

The most basic change is to reverse the classical order so that arrangement and invention are the last two steps of text production. By this reversal, arrangement overlaps contemporary interest in the nature of argument, especially practical and ordinary means of persuasion as studied by Stephen Toulmin and Chaim Perelman.[2]

Like arrangement, invention retains its classical meaning as the choice and application of a topic. But as a matter of text production, it comes at the end of the writing process when revision subconsciously reveals intended meaning. That placement reflects the difference in training between classical and modern writers. Unlike a classical writer who could choose among *topoi*, contemporary students have no set of learned ideas, topics, and arguments that they can consciously apply to their writing. Instead, they typically "deliver" ideas straight from the subconscious; even reflective writing begins with this inchoate invention.

From this biological premise, the other three categories of traditional rhetoric undergo a more radical change in meaning. For instance, delivery changes from the actual presentation of a speech to become the study of hand, eye, and ear. This attention to the neurophysiology of writing is supplemented by the related studies of normal writing development in college students, and the opposite consideration of writing loss among adults who suffer from agraphia. The definition of memory changes from techniques of recalling a speech to become the subconscious recall of all language, the storage place from which words are chosen and then placed into grammatical sequence. The definition of style changes too, but not as radically, from the study of tropes and schemes to the classification of basic linguistic features that correspond to stages of writing development.

Style probably receives less attention now than in previous decades, the 1960s and 1970s in particular being a fertile period of style studies. During that period Thomas Sebeok's *Style in Language* (1964) and Donald Freeman's *Linguistics and Literary Style* (1970) appeared, as did Stanley Fish's influential critique of style studies.[3] More recently, Norman Holland, David Bleich, and other scholars like Fish have shifted their attention from style in a text to the varieties of discourse that occur in social contexts. Arguably, this change is simply a matter of redefining style studies to emphasize social rather than textual factors in language use. But this change most clearly departs from the classical tradition of limiting style to three or four social varieties (high, middle, low), providing instead an apparently endless range of social contexts. The ancients, by contrast, let the study of figurative language develop into a seemingly unending number of tropes and schemes.

My work keeps style at the center of rhetorical theory, but it is grounded in a biological rather than social or textual analysis of language. This biological emphasis also explains the changes I have made in the order and meaning of terms in traditional rhetoric. These changes are outlined in Chart 1.1.

Relevance to Contemporary Writing Research

Each of these changes has its counterpart in contemporary writing research. The physiology of producing a text, or "delivery" as I have

Chart 1.1: **Changes from Traditional Rhetoric**

Traditional Rhetoric	Biology of Writing
Invention	Delivery
Arrangement	Memory
Style	Style
Memory	Arrangement
Delivery	Invention

redefined this term, clearly overlaps current interest in the writing process, notably prewriting or collaborative writing, but this interest is almost exclusively focused on a student's mental or social preparation for writing, and therefore slights the physical act of writing. Work by Carl Koch and James Brazil (*Strategies for Teaching the Composition Process*, 1978) and Chapter Six of Erika Lindemann's *A Rhetoric for Writing Teachers* (1987) exemplify the cognitive emphasis of prewriting instruction.[4] James Williams reviews the objectives of collaborative learning in Chapter Eight of *Preparing to Teach Writing* (1989).

Until recently, memory has had a strong theoretical emphasis in contemporary studies of writing, there being *de rigeur* attention to differences between written and spoken language. David Olson's seminal article on this topic, "From Utterance to Text" (1977), and F. Niyi Akinasso's extensive review "On the Differences Between Spoken and Written Language" (1982) show the complexities of this research and its implied relevance to writing instruction. Nevertheless, despite extraordinary attention to speech/prose contrasts, there has been relatively little research of a practical bent that would examine how students can recognize differences between speaking and writing and whether it is useful to teach them to make these distinctions. Jeanne W. Halpern's "Differences Between Speaking and Writing and Their Implications for Teaching" (1984) stands out as a rare example of this practical research; in this book I will expand that teaching focus to include the biology of writing.

Equally important, to further highlight memory I will look for basic similarities in speaking and writing, especially to identify the emergence of prose styles. This divided attention to differences and similarities of a writer's linguistic memory enables me to analyze what Deborah Tannen calls the "complex, overlapping, and intertwined" relationships between speech and prose (1987, 85). It also reveals the essential link between memory and style.

Style studies have departed in recent years from the search for an *ur-style*, something invariable about a written text that remains unaffected by changes in topic or the occasion for writing. This transition has coincided with a strongly social definition of written language, based in large measure on the work of Richard Rorty. His views on language, as expressed in *Philosophy and the Mirror of Nature* (1979), have been interpreted by composition researchers to mean that a writer's developmental progress is more a matter of attitude than aptitude. Yet, as I will argue in this book, it is possible to identify biological features of style that uniquely correspond to levels of progressively higher writing ability. The key to this identification is to examine the physical (rather than the mental or social) act of writing.

Physical Eloquence and the Biology of Writing: A Synopsis

Delivery, memory, and style are most appropriately studied as they advance the teaching of writing. To that end I have sought ways to promote the development of physical eloquence, an ability that all capable writers possess for coordinating the neurological functions of hand, eye, and ear.

In this book's next two chapters I will discuss the literacy role of physical eloquence. Chapter Two examines the literacy functions of prose and the sense of biological play that motivates students to write well, even to be eloquent. Chapter Three extends this new literacy of eloquence to the design of a writing curriculum.

Most students, like most people in our society, remain anonymously inept as writers, lacking the motive to write well in a culture that devalues print. As writing teachers we can do little to offset this problem, but we can salvage prose for some especially talented writers, provided they are not taught the wrong way. In asserting that a literacy of eloquence can be taught, I must also acknowledge that schools past and present have a dismal record of teaching even basic literacy. They have failed, and we perpetuate this failure, by teaching writing as a skill to be learned rather than teaching it as a natural gift that someone gradually develops.

By failing to develop the acquisition of prose, we endorse a cognitive and social attitude towards writing that fundamentally denatures a learner's body, as if writing is entirely a mental, self-conscious effort. In fact, in most writing classes all that matters is a student's ability to express ideas, which is why the writing curriculum, especially now, emphasizes writing as a thinking process.[5]

As a corrective to that mind-only emphasis, in the middle three chapters of this book I examine separately the organic functions of hand, eye, and ear in order to identify the contribution of each to the biology of writing. Chapter Four addresses the neurological function of the hand, which establishes a "kinetic melody" that regulates the pace of writing.

Without this control, a mild kind of physiological writer's block inhibits fluent expression. Chapter Five deals with the neurological function of the eye, which regulates the "visual melody" of editing and revision. It may also affect the reader's pace of interpretation. Chapter Six examines the neurological function of the ear, important for speaking and writing, since the "auditory" melody of inner speech attunes linguistic form to an appropriate discourse or register. When all three melodies function in harmony, a writer has developed the ability to write with physical eloquence.

As I explain in these middle chapters, a writer masters physical eloquence by progressing through developmental stages that correspond to kinetic, visual, and auditory styles of expression. Each stage also entails a dysfunctional use of writing that resembles some basic features of neurological language disorders (agraphia, apractic agraphia, agraphia with alexia, and productive or receptive aphasia). Of course, college students do not exhibit the behavioral symptoms of these disorders, and neither are they in any sense neurologically impaired. Yet, because all writers invoke the same networks in the brain to control their writing, a failure or breakdown in any network—regardless of cause—produces related categories of kinetic, visual, and auditory writing problems. Developmental writers exhibit similar problems because they have not yet fully connected (or perhaps not fully utilized) the neurological pathways that control the biology of writing.

Based on this neurological evidence for stages of writing, in the two penultimate chapters I recommend specific techniques for teaching physical eloquence. In Chapter Seven I urge teachers to avoid formal instruction that fosters conscious learning. Lectures, grammar lessons, sentence exercises, even the use of textbooks on writing are among the many unproductive and potentially disruptive teaching practices that I would exclude from the writing *classroom*, but not necessarily from other areas of a student's education. Instead, teachers should promote the subconscious acquisition of prose, starting with a "silent" method of instruction and followed by any traditional or innovative technique that encourages a meaningful exchange between writers and audience.

In one sense, some students may firmly believe that formal instruction is the only appropriate way for them to improve as writers, and this belief in effect dictates that for their own satisfaction they must receive some formal writing instruction. In another sense, those relatively few students who have already acquired the ability to write well may actually benefit from formal lectures on advanced principles of writing. I will address both these exceptions in Chapter Eight and elsewhere, but my basic premise remains that subconscious acquisition surpasses conscious learning for nearly all college students and, by extension, for the overwhelming majority of people who want to improve as writers. Chapter Eight itemizes some instructional options that will encourage this subconscious acquisition.

Although many of the options cited in Chapter Eight are by themselves unexceptional, they nevertheless form an unusual curriculum of methods and techniques for improving a student's writing ability. As I argue in Chapter Nine, the conclusion of this book, not only can writing be enhanced by this special attention to physical eloquence, but biological emphasis may also be the most ethical way to teach writing.

Since I anticipate an audience that already recognizes key terms and issues in composition studies, I will not devote as much space to reviewing pertinent research or defining controversial terms as would otherwise be appropriate for a less exploratory book. However, for my readers who are not familiar with composition studies, I do want to briefly introduce here some terminology and scholarship that recurs in different chapters.

Play:

Richard Lanham is the most outspoken advocate of teaching language *play*, especially to counteract the normative standard of "clear, brief, and sincere" prose. In   *Style: An Anti-Textbook* (1974) he examines the motives for play in bureaucratic, academic, and other forms of "professional" writing. As I will use this term, especially in Chapter Two, it has a fundamentally biological emphasis that differs from Lanham's concern with playful opacity versus purposeful transparency in styles. Perhaps my usage can be best understood by comparing biological play to sexual play. This comparison allows play to be more spontaneous than rehearsed, and more attuned to physical than mental processes.

Learning and Acquisition:

Researchers in evolutionary theory, immunology, and modern generative grammar have increasingly concluded that "there is no such thing as *learning.*" The fullest case to support this claim has been argued by Massimo Piattelli-Palmarini, who defines learning as "the transfer of structure from the environment to the organism" (1989, 2). The demise of learning means that "imitation, induction, analogy, problem solving" and other forms of instruction do not facilitate this transfer or teach anything new. Rather, instruction merely exposes an organism to structures already present "before any encounter with the outside world" (p. 4). In other words, the organism cannot learn what is already there; it also controls the input of anything new.

By contrast, *acquisition* "has nothing to do with . . . structure [learned via instruction] and everything to do with mechanisms of internal . . .

filtering affecting a pre-programmed chain of multiple interruptions and internal switches" (p. 3). In effect, an organism sets parameters within which it filters the environment; these filters or "switches" keep the organism in complete control of everything it wishes to process or exclude.

As applied to writing, the distinction I will make between learning and acquisition does not preclude learning as having some value, but it does strongly emphasize the advantages of acquisition. This strong case for acquisition is taken directly from second-language research, especially the work of Stephen Krashen as reported in *Principles and Practice of Second Language Acquisition* (1982), *Writing Research, Theory and Application* (1984), and *The Input Hypothesis: Issues and Implications* (1985). Learning is the result of formal instruction, as when a teacher focuses a student's attention on linguistic or metalinguistic form. Teaching the rules of subject/verb agreement would by this definition encourage formal learning. By contrast, acquisition occurs spontaneously, albeit slowly, as a result of frequent "meaningful" exposure to language. According to Krashen, what a student learns can be stored in a "monitor" that will then edit prose, but this formal knowledge about language cannot be used to generate prose. Neither can it be assimilated into the acquired store of language that a writer taps to produce a text.

Whether Krashen is right or not in making so sharp a distinction between learning and acquisition—a point that many researchers have challenged[6]—I think we can agree on the challenge he poses to educators who take for granted the value of formal, conscious learning. Following Krashen's lead to de-emphasize formal learning, we may also see that students and teachers barely acknowledge its counterpart—the unrehearsed acquisition of language, including writing that is prompted by the subconscious.

Just how the subconscious mysteriously drives acquisition is another issue that researchers heatedly dispute, yet without an accepted definition of the term *subconscious*, basic disagreements will undoubtedly persist in language studies. For our purposes we can define the subconscious informally so as to avoid the most common difficulties of using this term. Following Joseph Fodor's (1983) influential claim for "modalities of mind," we can regard the subconscious as a multilayered, multifaceted construct that mediates between largely inaccessible mental processes, and that sometimes surfaces to the conscious attention of various states of mind (or "minds"). For language acquisition, a person would be essentially unaware of the subconscious as it functions; we can leave aside the possibility of bringing this function to conscious attention (Pienemann 1989).

From the biological perspective of this book, particularly in the second chapter, the simple dualism of learning and acquisition enables us to regard writing from the perspective of a subconsciously acquired physical activity. It may help as well to consider the standard difference between conscious learning and subconscous acquisition this way: no child develops mastery of a first language through formal instruction. Mere exposure—provided it is meaningful to the child—seems to be enough. Although adults may require more than meaningful exposure in order to master a second language, we can pattern that effort on a child's success so that formal learning serves only a minor role.

The process of acquiring written language can begin well before a child starts school. Whether the child of three understands the printed word *exit* (from Sesame Street) or *on* (for the TV control) is less important than the awareness that surely develops equating print with meaning. This development varies, of course, by social class and by the child's personality and experience, so that some children may actually know the alphabet or even write their own names by age three while others of that age will exhibit little or no ability of this kind.

These differences among very young children probably have no lasting effect on the attainment of writing, but the opportunity to "catch up" deserves special notice, especially after children have begun their formal training in writing, which usually occurs by age seven or eight in the lower grades of primary school. Unlike speech, which children hear constantly and produce spontaneously, the language of print has an intermittent, almost ephemeral time and place for its development. Children practice writing a few hours each day in school; at home they may read the brand names on cereal boxes or glance through a TV guide for their favorite programs, but even the children who read books for pleasure will not engage printed language with anything like the engagement that continuously moves them to speak.

I will discuss the developmental differences (and similarities) between speech and prose more fully in Chapter Five; at this point I want to stress two fundamental points: compared to speech, children *and* adults rarely use print actively, either to write something or to read a text with care, and this developmental lag between spoken and written language underlies some of the problems that college students have when they begin freshman English. Without discussing how these problems are manifested in student writing (I'll save that discussion for Chapter Five), we can attend here to the principle cause of difficulties: inadequate exposure to written language.

Adequate exposure is not, I must concede, easy to define; Krashen argues that reading is the main source of acquired knowledge about writing. While I accept the importance of reading for writing, I do not stress it as a principle factor in prose acquisition, except in the limited sense that writing may also be regarded as a form of reading. At the risk of being circular I will maintain that adequate exposure is whatever type and amount guarantees a proficient writer. If a student does not write well, then he or she has not sufficiently developed as a writer. To make this tautology a workable definition, I must add that input does not necessarily become intake, since no amount of exposure to written language will offset a negative motive to resist prose.

To underscore this issue of motive (which functions as a socio-biological "filter"), consider the same point as it applies to speech. All normal children acquire a first language, regardless of personal motives (or perhaps because the acquisition of speech is more biological than social). Yet as children become older, especially after puberty, they apparently lose the same capacity to acquire a second language with anything like the fluency they had for a first language. Biological factors may account for some of this loss, but researchers have increasingly downplayed this explanation (Dulay, Burt, and Krashen 1982) because it appears to be related almost exclusively to pronunciation (Schumann 1977). As Rod Ellis points out, "There is now general agreement that adults are neurolinguistically capable of learning a [second language] in much the same way as children" (1984, 142).

However, even if there is a critical period up to approximately age twelve for successful language acquisition, no one has proposed a similar period for writing, perhaps because prose is still regarded as a subsystem of speech (i.e., the "first" language) or perhaps to avoid the biological impasse of teaching writing to postpubescent adults. In the first case writing becomes a trivial accompaniment of spoken language, yet the inability of many college students to write well suggests that fluency in speech does not transfer directly to prose. In the second case writing is presumed to have no critical period because adults can obviously benefit from a teacher's efforts. But if social conditions and personal motives underlie a critical period—not biological factors, as is still popularly believed—then writing may indeed be subject to the same limitations that affect second-language acquisition. Krashen apparently endorses this point of view.

Just as meaningful exposure to a second language is the first prerequisite for acquisition, so too a writer must have meaningful exposure to writing based on interaction. This means reading a text to interpret it and producing a text for someone who responds. These forms of interaction may be sufficient for children to acquire prose fully, since their motives for writing are probably similar to their motives for speaking. This claim has been well documented in John Oxenham's *Literacy: Writing, Reading and Social Organization* (1980), Don Holdaway's *The Foundations of Literacy* (1979), and Donna Taylor's *Family Literacy*

(1983). For adults, however, the motives for using speech and prose differ widely, reflecting the attitudes they have developed towards each medium. Writing is, for most adults, hard work with little social reward and usually has no immediate effect on others. By contrast, speaking is relatively easy, socially rewarded, and personally meaningful as an expression of self- and group identity. For children these distinctions between speech and prose are either too abstract or too remote from their ordinary experience to influence how they judge either medium. As a result, children are equally motivated to acquire speech and prose (or to acquire a second language).

This motivation changes as children grow older, a change that coincides with the quantity and quality of exposure to written language. Simply put, most students read little and write less, whereas their facility in spoken language continues unabated because they speak and listen to others constantly. For the relatively few students who do read often, how they read and what they read undoubtedly affects their fluency as writers, but the available evidence from research on reading shows that these students will write more effectively than students who do little or no reading (Krashen reviews the pertinent studies in *Writing*, 1984).

It might follow that having all students read often would make them into competent writers. Unfortunately, the motive to read is not something a teacher can assign to students, and the amount of reading assigned during a single college semester obviously cannot fix ten or fifteen years of neglect. While college students may be exposed to heaps of textbook prose, they can "filter" it to a relatively small amount of meaningful text that is highlighted by their yellow markers. Or they can read entire texts without much interpretation, as if storage and recall for the short term are the equivalent of permanent knowledge and understanding.

Acquisition not only takes a long time, it also requires appropriate or "comprehensible" input, a key principle in Krashen's theory. Even then, the social factors that shape our attitudes towards writing must not impede progress. I will discuss these issues more thoroughly in Chapter Three, where I propose a fundamental change in the writing curriculum and in methods of writing instruction.

On a smaller scale, as I explain in Chapters Seven and Eight, a teacher can facilitate acquisition by controlling the environment—the writing classroom—where a student is most fully exposed to what W. Ross Winterowd calls the "scene" of literacy (1986, 18). The immediate results of control in this scene may not be spectacular or even significant by contrast to other courses, but the long-term effects of acquisition clearly outweigh the short-term gains that may occur through formal instruction. Just as important, because college freshmen are adults, they can be far more efficient than children in acquiring prose. A teacher can augment this efficiency by intensifying the process of acquisition, in part by focusing students' attention on different stages of the writing process and, in larger part, by guiding them through questions and answers about what they are doing.

Because Krashen is not entirely clear on the teacher's role in promoting acquisition,[7] I will assert the unequivocal value of teaching that does *not* promote formal learning. Everything else that a teacher does in the writing classroom potentially helps students to acquire prose. For instance, an "inquiry" method of instruction, as defined by George Hillocks, Jr., in *Research in Written Composition* (1986), will promote acquisition because it focuses students' attention on meaning rather than form. This emphasis differs from formal instruction (what Hillocks calls the "presentational mode") because it engages students in the process of self-discovery. It differs too from the "natural" method of instruction if, by that misleading term, we understand students to be primarily self-taught, by analogy to a child who spontaneously acquires a first language through exposure alone. But as I noted earlier, exposure is not sufficient for acquisition to take place; it must also occur as meaningful input, and a teacher serves the vital role of judging—if only by intuitive means—what comments, questions, tasks will lead to improvement.

To a large extent the teacher in a classroom controls the acquisition of prose, but subsuming this control is the question of motive, which a teacher cannot control, at least not directly, although grades can provide students with a powerful secondary motive for short-term progress. A literacy of eloquence does more, as I explain in Chapters Seven through Nine, by giving students the personal opportunity to excel as writers along with the primary social motive to write for others. Judith Langer (1987) argues for just this change, noting that modern education has denatured literacy, and that progress will only occur when the social and personal advantages of literacy are reintroduced into the classroom. I will go even further to advocate a literacy program that necessarily transcends the classroom, the university, indeed all the domains of education since it addresses what is ultimately a social and biological process.

Literacy:

The study of *literacy* is divided between those who regard alphabetic literacy as conferring a special cognitive advantage to its users, and those who completely reject this assumption, holding instead that social relationships create differing but equally valid literacies. Walter Ong, Eric Havelock, and E.D. Hirsch, Jr., are typically associated with the first group; Robert Pattison, Michael Cole, and Harvey Graff with the latter.

Rather than discuss the relative merits of either side, I have chosen instead to dismiss them both, albeit for quite different reasons. The first group, by far the most influential, holds what Patrick Hartwell (1987) calls a "party line" view of literacy, suggesting their politically conservative or right-of-center efforts to resist change. Since I accept as given the decline of print literacy, resisting this change would simply rally us to an already lost cause.

Print culture sustains the prestige of belletristic writing, and implicitly devalues the prestige of spoken language, especially storytelling and informal conversation. Tannen (1987) makes a similar claim that "conversation is generally thought to be messy, pedestrian and error ridden . . . [whereas] literary discourse is thought to be an exalted use of language" (p. 69). It would take another book to examine the signs of print culture's demise or to cite evidence for the nascent ascendancy of oral forms of literacy. For our purposes I will define print culture as the embodiment of an attitude that makes writing a superior medium for thoughtful and artistic self-expression. As for the decline of print culture, I must ask my readers to draw their own conclusions.

Chapters Two and Three examine social aspects of literacy that clearly transcend the biological perspective of the other chapters. Like the "liberal" view of literacy, a view towards endorsing social or educational change, this discussion serves in complementary relation to a literacy of physical eloquence.

In discussing that literacy I will refer to its oral and written forms without making a broader distinction between orality and literacy. By this usage, oral literacy has the same potential for sophisticated expression in either speech or prose, just as traditional print literacy can also be expressed in either medium, as would occur in a formal speech based on a written text (Tannen 1982b). These two forms of literacy differ to the extent that one has relatively more linguistic features of either speaking or writing.

Of course, linguistic features are only part of a much broader set of relationships binding speech and prose. Although I will analyze these linguistic features in some detail, I also note in Chapter Five other distinctive categories that comprise a *biogrammar* of speaking and writing. These categories include social, psychological, rhetorical, physical, neurological, historical, and technological features, among many other possibilities. In this regard I certainly accept the position of Nancy Torrance and David Olson that "literate competence should not be identified too directly with reading skills, or writing skills for that matter" (1987, 145). Yet for purposes of close analysis, throughout the middle chapters I will examine linguistic features of college writing as the most direct evidence of these students' literacy.

In several other chapters I will also discuss one social aspect of literacy that receives too little attention. Given the changing demographics of language populations in our country, it is becoming increasingly important to retrain writing teachers in order to promote an understanding of literacy that transcends traditional (White, European) print culture. University classrooms of the future—indeed, most urban high school classrooms now—are filled with students whose cultural heritage is non-European (see Williams 1989, 133). For many of these students English is a foreign language—Spanish, Korean, Vietnamese, and a host of other possibilities being the language they first learned and may still speak at home. A similar distinction applies to students who speak a dialect of English that is lexically and even syntactically removed from the standard written English they are taught in school.

Perhaps teachers in previous generations could anticipate having students whose English essentially duplicated how the teacher might write or speak. Or perhaps no Golden Age of literacy has ever existed save in the imaginations of fanciful educators. In any case, we can expect our students today to speak and write a variety of Englishes, different in many respects from the teacher's uses of speech and prose. Despite this self-evident problem of mismatched languages, surprisingly few writing teachers have been trained in methods of teaching English as a second language (ESL) or as a second dialect (ESD). Yet with this training, a teacher can do much to help student writers, and much more to promote a new literacy.

In Chapter Eight I have included a few methods of teaching writing that are based on ESL and ESD instruction. Besides serving a new population of college students, these ESL and ESD techniques can also assist native speakers of English to understand a printed language (and culture) that has become increasingly "foreign" to them.

Writing Across the Curriculum (WAC):

This curricular innovation has many forms but one central premise: "that writing can enhance *learning*" (Kirsch 1988, 47). Students in all disciplines allegedly benefit from "writing to learn," a goal that translates into having students write more often, ideally in all their classes. In effect, as students write more, they will improve in their studies because the increased writing will sharpen their learning skills.

Toby Fulwiler and Elaine Maimon are among the most prolific and successful exponents of WAC, their efforts having resulted in the widespread endorsement of WAC by composition teachers. But, as I will explain in Chapter Two, this movement's goals are not always consistent with a biological view of language because most college students must first fully acquire writing before they can profitably use it to "write to learn."

It is perhaps surprising that claims for the success of WAC programs have been largely anecdotal, appealing to the belief that having students write more often and in more courses will make them better students academically and perhaps better writers too. This position has been most succinctly expressed by Joanne Kurfiss who, in a 1985 issue of the newsletter *Writing Across the Curriculum*, responded to a criticism of WAC by emphasizing these two points:

> 1. Writing can help students learn and think about content in any discipline, thus helping to achieve the goals of the instructor.
> 2. Writing used for learning does not require explicit *teaching* of writing—only *use* of writing as a pedagogical tool. ("Do Students Really Learn from Writing?").

Although these are interrelated points, I will deal with each one separately, beginning with the question of whether WAC improves students' academic performance.

Based on results I have obtained in testing students' writing (reported in the Appendix to Chapter Nine), the answer to this first question is no. Students who did little or no writing for two years after finishing a freshman English course demonstrated the same level of academic achievement and writing performance as those students who did a considerable amount of writing, some of which was expressly assigned in WAC courses. Similar results have been obtained by researchers dating back to the early 1960s when the first comprehensive study of recidivism was conducted by Albert Kitzhaber and reported in *Themes, Theories, and Therapies* (1963).

Besides the issue of improving writing ability (Question 1), there remains the related question of how much writing students should do in all academic courses beyond freshman English or perhaps in upper-division courses that are typically offered through an English department. Nearly all WAC theorists see writing as a responsibility to be shared by all departments throughout the university. On this point Toby Fulwiler, Art Young, Elaine Maimon, and other well-known exponents of WAC theory have argued that writing instruction should be the responsibility of all teachers, not just those in an English department. In other words, if the teaching of writing is not shared by everyone in a university, then students will not necessarily use writing as a learning aid in all their courses. Underlying this objective is the primary reason for establishing WAC programs, which is to have students do more writing across the curriculum so they may learn better in every discipline. And by some synergistic effect, better learning will enable students to become better writers.

To work through the unstated assumptions of this argument, I want to first consider college students who do not typically write well. By applying their limited writing ability to a wide range of subjects, these students will, allegedly, become better learners, and because they will learn better they will write better, too. But that is not the complete picture. According to WAC advocates, students will demonstrate this gain in writing ability without any instruction in writing per se. Indeed, to expand one of the Kurfiss quotes that opened this discussion, "Writing used for learning does not require explicit *teaching* of writing... and most of what a student writes is not graded, and only some of it is even 'examined' by the instructor" (p. 2). Thus, students in a WAC program will become better writers because they will practice writing in all disciplines.

The appeal of this claim notwithstanding, it does not conform to the evidence I have already cited; equally important, it subtly but fundamentally alters the status of the writing profession by making the teaching of writing a secondary objective of the writing curriculum. The first objective is to have students "write to learn" in all disciplines, as if the mere act of writing can replace the expertise and social responsibilities of a writing instructor.

The work of James Britton and his colleagues (1975) is regularly invoked as support for the WAC slogan "writing to learn," which has been so widely accepted as to be used in the titles of books and articles (e.g., *Learning to Write/Writing to Learn*, Mayher et al. 1983). Yet despite its widespread usage, the actual meaning of this slogan is not entirely clear, almost as if it has the status of a "god-term" (Weaver 1953) among composition scholars.

Perhaps because the term "learning" remains essentially undefined, WAC theorists derive support from "writing to learn" by shifting attention to the first part of the slogan, the argument being that "expressive" writing abets learning. Defined as the language "close to the self," expressive writing "reveals the [writer] verbalizing his consciousness" (Britton et al. 1975, 90). As personal and self-expressive records of one's thoughts, feelings, or other reactions, expressive writing is usually kept in a daily journal which a teacher may or may not read or evaluate, and which may or may not show that the student is exploring new ideas, following old interests, refining existing ones, or even making sense. In other words, teachers need not be "concerned with *what* students write in their journals" (Fulwiler 1986, 25). Presumably then, the value of this writing is the freedom it provides for self-expression.

Toby Fulwiler, in particular, has stressed the value of expressive writing in journals, writing which "looks like speech written down" and is allegedly the linguistic form from which other, more elaborated (i.e., presumably less speech-like) forms evolve (1986, 24). In Chapter Five I will question this putative relationship between a speech-like form of writing and its apparent source in spoken language. In several other chapters I will also question the value of any writing that does not transcend an egocentric point of view.

I do not wish to imply that journal writing is without any value. It clearly merits consideration as a form of prewriting that allows students to explore ideas prior to an audience's response. And it may also be regarded as a social (rather than personal and entirely self-expressive) medium if another person—a peer, friend, or teacher—is understood to be the ultimate reader.

However, WAC theorists offer nothing more than a putative link between expressive writing and enhanced learning. Rarely is objective empirical evidence, however obtained, cited to show that students who write journals become "better" writers. Neither is it established, except by anecdotal reference, that students who merely write a great deal will somehow "learn" better in all their courses.

Unless a student is already a capable writer, writing to learn imposes a double burden: a student must not only develop the ability to write but he or she must also use that underdeveloped writing ability to learn another subject. I see no way to avoid this problem, or to avoid the related problem of lack of writing instruction. If we define writing—indeed all language— as fundamentally dialogic, then we must also question the value of teaching students to write for themselves.

I do not expect that supporters of WAC will see these problems as I have just described them; to do that involves untying the knot that joins writing with learning. Certainly some students will write to learn, but—I must insist—only if they write well already. Other students, undoubtedly a majority of those in college, need to learn how to write before they can profitably write to learn. And to improve as writers they must have writing instruction.

Interlanguage:

First proposed in 1972 by Larry Selinker, *interlanguage* refers to distinctive utterances of a second language learner, utterances that are neither identical to first language forms nor to the forms of the target or second language. In this sense interlanguage is an "in-between" language, showing more influences of the first language initially, but gradually evolving towards similarity with the second language. However, some interlanguage forms may "fossilize," as often happens with accents, so that blends of the first and second language become relatively permanent features of the learner's utterances.

Although Selinker does not explain how or why someone advances through stages of interlanguage to the target language (Horning 1987), his theory does stress that "errors" are a developmental sign of progress. If we allow that interlanguage simply manifests the more obvious stages of acquired language, then its importance for the biology of writing is the stress it places on systematic production of errors. As I will explain in Chapters Four through Seven, these errors mark stages in a writer's progress towards physical eloquence. Moreover, because these errors are positive features of a student's writing, I will use the neutral term "writing style" when referring to clusters of related errors.

Inner language:

Also called *inner speech*, this term for the language of thought was first proposed by Lev Vygotsky, who further proposed that a "condensed" linguistic structure distinguishes inner language from other forms of expression. Vygotsky and other Russian psychologists have described inner language as developing after a child begins to speak; they also characterize inner language as being devoid of function words and intensive verbs (notably relying on the copula "to be").

By contrast to the Russian theorists, I will define inner language in Chapter Five to mean a person's ability to comprehend language; it therefore precedes speech (and writing), serving instead as the linguistic source from which all expressive language is derived.

Neurolinguistic melodies:

This metaphorical reference to music is based on Aleksandr Luria's term for neurophysiological control, which he calls a *kinetic melody*. His use of a metaphor suggests the interpretive nature of all research on language and the brain. During the last one hundred years, three competing theories have emerged: (1) a holistic theory that any injury or dysfunction in one part of the brain will affect all of the brain; (2) a localizationist theory that specific sites in the brain are distinctively responsible for neurological functions; and (3) a functionalist theory that networks join different sites in the brain to control separate functions.

Most researchers today discount the first theory but remain divided between the latter two. Early evidence for both dominant positions was usually taken from autopsy reports, particularly to note brain damage due to strokes or bullet wounds. In more recent studies researchers have been able to devise nonintrusive measures of brain activity, such as charting the brain's electrical impulses or monitoring signals that are divided between the left and right ear or within the split fields of vision for both eyes. Surgery, drugs, CT- and PET-scans, and even direct stimulation of the brain have produced other neurolinguistic evidence.

Based on a review of this diverse literature, I have extended Luria's kinetic melody to include two other neurophysiological functions: *visual melodies* and *auditory melodies*. Like the kinetic melody, which refers to the neurological role of the hand in writing, visual and auditory melodies correspond to the roles of the eye and ear respectively. As may be apparent from these terms, I am adopting a functionalist view of the brain, which will underlie the neurological model of writing described in Chapters Four through Six.

Because brain-damaged people are, after all, brain-damaged, conclusions drawn from this review of research need to be carefully qualified. Although the neurolinguistic melodies of hand, eye, and ear characterize all writing, the way a college student uses them will not, of course, duplicate the impaired uses of someone with neurological disorders. Nevertheless, just as discordant melodies in music can be linked to the original score, the efforts of normal (developmental) writers and abnormal (brain-damaged) writers can be understood as having the same neurological basis.

For the study of language disorders, typically three objectives are noted: (1) to localize lesions causing problems, (2) to predict patterns of recovery, and (3) to assist other researchers by reporting findings. To these goals John Marshall (1986) adds that neuropsychological research has a potential value for the study of normal mechanisms in language processing. It is this final goal, less common than the other three, that this study aims to realize, so that pathological conditions such as alexia and agraphia can provide evidence of "broken" mechanisms in language processing. Based on this evidence I can then infer an unbroken or "normal" model of writing.

Writing:

When I refer to *writing*, my reference is meant to be inclusive, incorporating as many forms of academic writing as college students are likely to produce. These forms might include lab reports, lecture notes, letters of application to medical schools, as well as take-home and in-class writings, essay exams of various lengths, and summaries, paraphrases, abstracts, responses to other students' work, and so forth. A writer's progress towards physical eloquence presumably underlies all these writing tasks, but few students will do them all with equal facility.

How then to explain the student whose lab reports in biology receive an *A*, but in literature and psychology the same student receives a *D* for take-home writings and a *C* on essay exams respectively? Motive, as defined by Robert Gardner (1985), might explain some of these differences, so that a student who enjoys one subject for personal reasons might work harder and therefore write more effectively than in required classes that inspire no personal interest. Another student may simply lack the inherent ability to do well in certain subjects, and that student's writing obviously reflects these shortcomings. Poor teaching can also affect a student who has the ability to write well but who lacks the guidance to demonstrate that ability.

Researchers like Patricia Bizzell and Kenneth Bruffee would also explain these divergent grades as evidence of different discourse communities that have separate standards for quality and that demand of their students a correspondingly different form of writing. While acknowledging this "social" interpretation, I want to stress another point of view, one that considers writing ability to be relatively the same across disciplines. I am, of course, de-emphasizing the social view of writing for the greater uniformity of a physical perspective. Thus, I will consider differences in writing tasks—however defined and regardless of cause—as requiring minor adjustments that all *capable* writers can make with little effort. Because less capable writers lack the physical eloquence to support their efforts, they will have correspondingly more difficulty in making these adjustments.

Empirical data:

In a comprehensive review of writing research, Anne Herrington notes the "tensions existing... over the role of empirical studies" (1989, 117). Similar tensions have affected disciplines like psychology, anthropology, applied linguistics, all closely related to composition studies. No surprise that writing researchers are also divided over the merits of quantitative versus qualitative studies, or that the term *empirical* has become a subject of dispute.

George Hillocks, Jr., demonstrates in *Research in Written Composition* (1986) that controlled statistical measures of students' writing can provide helpful empirical data about effective methods of instruction. For instance, he reports the most success in teaching writing when teachers encourage "inquiry" by focusing students on a problem and assisting them in solving it. On the other hand, a naturalistic case study like Lucille McCarthy's "A Stranger in Strange Lands" (1987), using four research methodologies, provides insights about a student's writing, particularly about the foreignness of written texts, that probably could not be obtained by any other means.

Throughout this book I will cite empirical findings, however obtained, that have immediate relevance to the biology of writing. It would exceed the scope of this book to explain the mixed value of emirical data, or to justify my initial efforts at immersion research, which has entailed several years of intensive reading of several thousand writing samples.

In any case, the central argument of this book does not depend on empirical evidence since I am asking my readers to consider writing *as if* it were entirely a biological process. For that reason I have placed an extensive review of neurolinguistic research into the Appendix at the end of this book, enabling me to stress instead in Chapter Six key relationships between biology and style. In this respect I am essentially providing a subjective appraisal, or what Janice Lauer and J. William Asher call a "rhetorical inquiry" (1988, 5), of some of the difficulties students have with written discourse. Similarly, I have put into the Appendix results of a five-year study of college writing. Both appendices remain available to my readers who would like supplemental reviews of research or informal empirical findings to support the book's central argument. Other readers, especially those who do not value empirical data, can omit the appendices as they wish.

Conclusion

A final word of this introduction should be directed to my readers who are unfamiliar with composition studies and its essential concern for theory *and* practice. This book initiates a study of the neurological functions related to hand, eye, and ear in order to examine particular elements in a theory of the biology of writing. A relatively new topic, its importance becomes evident as I also discuss ways to apply theory for the general advancement of written literacy. Thus, because theory and practice are crucially related, I will give them equal attention, with the opening and closing chapters addressing practical literacy and the middle chapters devoted more to theory. Since I introduce in this book a new concept of literacy, of physical eloquence, and of biological processes in writing, it is perhaps appropriate that I also invite my readers to undertake a new kind of reading, one that oscillates between theory and practice. Towards that goal of mutual understanding certainly we can join here in dedicating this book towards the related goal of helping teachers to help their students write more effectively.

2

Towards A New Literacy

In 1983 the Modern Language Association published *Literacy for Life: The Demand for Reading and Writing* (Bailey and Fosheim, eds.), a collection of essays that essentially depicts literacy as a "survival skill—in economic terms, in social terms, and in political terms" (p. 9). Although these essays claim much more for literacy than its practical importance, that claim alone deserves attention since our society has not done well in teaching students to read and write. By various estimates the percentage of illiterate adults in this country is as low as 10 percent or as high as 30 percent (perhaps even higher). These different percentages can be explained, in part,[1] by the standards used to determine basic literacy: Is it the ability to read the want ads in a newspaper? Is it the commensurate ability to write a letter of application for a job? Is it merely these elementary "economic" skills, or should it also include measures of political performance, such as recognizing names of political candidates? And should it include measures of social competence, such as writing a simple telephone message or reading the test for a driver's license?

Regardless of where the line is drawn that separates mere literacy from something more accomplished, and regardless of who is to blame for widespread illiteracy, too many people in our society are unable to read and write. The underwhelming response to this "literacy crisis" tells us more about our society's attitude towards written language than we may care to admit. In any case, teachers of writing, be they in high school or college, can do little to offset this national indifference towards written language, an attitude that is manifested by even the most accomplished students' overwhelming reluctance to write.

Most students lack the motive to write well because our culture teaches them that writing does not matter. Indeed, how can it be valued in a society that claims widespread illiteracy exists (whether or not it actually exists is irrelevant), yet does remarkably little to correct this real (or apparent) problem.[2] I do not pose this question rhetorically, but consider it instead as the prelude to a substantive revision of literacy instruction.

Simply put, in a society that devalues print culture, we must teach students to write anew. A radical shift is needed in writing instruction, if only to salvage prose for the most capable students who, for whatever reasons, may actually come to value written language. The shift I am proposing initially moves students away from writing to express ideas, and begins instead with their nascent ability to generate the *form* of language.

This emphasis on form corresponds to teaching students the physical eloquence of writing. As we move towards this new literacy, writing becomes less a skill to be learned and more a natural gift that someone gradually acquires. As teachers we must move away from a pedagogy that fundamentally denatures the student's body; we must therefore largely discount writing as a mental or cognitive endeavor. In brief, we must try to de-emphasize writing as a thinking process.

In 2,500 years of writing instruction, there are two notable occasions when teachers have downplayed a student's ability to express ideas and encouraged instead the development of physical eloquence. The most recent example of this change occurred during the late eighteenth century under Richard Sheridan, John Walker, Gilbert Austin, and other English rhetoricians of the Elocutionist movement. Supporters of this movement tried to re-establish the moribund art of delivery, being concerned primarily with eloquent speech. Although they regarded this ability as a gift of nature, they nevertheless wrote extensive manuals—textbooks in the modern sense—on voice, countenance, and gesture, which could presumably be learned through careful study.[3]

Having students learn delivery by this formal means did not succeed, yet the Elocutionists did provide a workable theory for joining language and body as part of literacy instruction. The origin of that theory is, of course, found in the educational practices of ancient Greece, a culture that the neo-classical English knew well.

Henri Marrou (1956) describes education in ancient (pre-Sophistic) Greece as being physiologically based; that is, school trained the body and not the intellect. In this regard, sports were the displaced curriculum of a warrior culture. Since a well-trained warrior, a Spartan for instance, could defend himself and his polis better than an amateur, formal education thus helped him and his society to survive. To that end this *physical* education had an obvious worth and purpose.

But physical education gave way eventually to a more technical and professional training; as Greek society became more civilized during its Golden Age (circa 450 B.C.), the schools provided a new service: training of the mind. With civilization came jurisprudence, and because quarrels could be settled by legal means, the battlefield remained evident but less imminent. This change led to a more displaced system of schooling. Not only were students instructed primarily in citizenship rather than martial arts, but they also were removed from the battlefield (sportsfield) and put into the classroom.

It is important, however, to understand that education was, at least for Western culture, incipiently athletic. Body dominated mind. The physically fit were also the victorious. Into this new, agonistic arena—the classroom—young students came to find a different battle zone: mind versus mind. Yet for the Greeks (and later the Romans) the mental discipline of learning retained a fundamentally physical basis. Students copied their textbooks word for word—a necessary task since books were rare, and original copies remained at the teacher's desk. So new editions had to be copied onto bulky, rolled manuscripts.

This copying must have had a profound effect on how students learned to write. Obviously they had ample writing practice in all subjects they studied (the trivium of rhetoric, grammar, and dialectic; and the quadrivium of geometry, astronomy, arithmetic, and music). Modern students, of course, simply buy their texts, and if they do much extended writing, it is usually done in their English or other humanities classes. Compared to the ancients, students today barely practice the *physical* act of writing.

But I would seriously distort educational history suggesting, as I may have, that Greek and Roman teaching methods and conditions somehow balanced mind and body: a fifty-fifty ideal for literacy instruction. This putative balance of course tilts, yet tilts predictably, for no educational system provides the best balance. There are always extra weights and tradeoffs. For the ancients it was discipline and boredom. The teacher's problem then, as much as now, was what to do with a student's body.

This problem was addressed with serious concern. Teachers not only disciplined their students physically, but they drilled them through mind-numbing activities: to write the Greek alphabet forwards and backwards; consonant clusters forwards and backwards; syllables in all the possible combinations; and words—first monosyllables, then duosyllables, and so on. The tedium and the discipline notwithstanding, some capable pupils survived and learned to write. Indeed, one must remember that such a system, bad as it was, produced tragedians, philosophers, poets, and other stylists of enduring reputations.

And remarkable, indeed, is the educational model that the ancients, even now, provide for higher education. To somehow expunge, if not obviously punish, the student's physiological half has remained a basic educational goal. Corporeal punishment is not the issue here; I certainly do not advocate it. But if it were an accepted practice, then by that educational policy we would at least recognize that a college student has a classroom body. If that body obstructs writing, then it shall be dealt with directly.

But today we have educationally removed the body from its student. It no longer exists academically. Instead, there are two educational spheres, two worlds: in one—the social/athletic playfield—students relieve their extracurricular bodily functions; in the other—the academic classroom—students are expected to return empty but attentive.

As body and mind bifurcate into athletic and intellectual curricula, the Great Books become one intellectual ideal with knowledge for-its-own-sake as the goal of education. Or intellectual training becomes, as the cultural revisionists have argued, a program for social cohesion.[4] And in the "same" intellectual curriculum we have machine-shop electives, the service-station idea of a university that every state government endorses.

At the opposite curricular extreme are the students (and faculty members, too) who balance their intellectual studies by a single, extra-curricular activity: sports. Players and spectators are drawn, increasingly it seems, to the rigid athleticism of a football field. Here, inflexible rules determine behavior; moreover, the game has an unsubtle physical logic which amounts (almost) to killing the opponent. Not only does a vicious tackle become the standard for good play, but this behavior is regulated by a more fundamental discipline: players don't choose the team, the coach does.

While it is true that spectators watch from the sidelines, most students have already learned to do that in the classroom, although as spectators they follow events of a game far more carefully than they listen, think, or participate in a typical writing class as students. They also enjoy the game more than their essay assignments. We might judge the ecstatic enthusiasm of spectators as a measure of the writing classroom's sobering artificiality. Extracurricular mindlessness exists, that is, because the schools have ignored, and therefore disrupted, the normal physical *and* intellectual cycles of education.

In his *Aims of Education*, Alfred North Whitehead states this point emphatically: "I lay it down as an educational axiom that in teaching you will come to grief as soon as you forget that your pupils have bodies (1929, 50)." Not bodies only, of course, and certainly not the college athleticism which separates body from mind, football field from the classroom; rather, education is, or at least it should involve, a physical and intellectual balance.

Whitehead cites three stages of education that promote this balance; from romance and precision to generalization, each stage leads to the next in a cyclic fashion. He warns, however, that we not "exaggerate into

sharpness the distinction between the three stages of a cycle (p. 27)."
Whitehead explains:

> The pupil's mind is a growing organism. On the one hand, it is not a box
> to be ruthlessly packed with alien ideas; and, on the other hand, the
> ordered acquirement of knowledge is the natural food for a developing
> intelligence.... Furthermore, there is not one unique threefold cycle of
> freedom, discipline, and freedom; but... all mental development is
> composed of such cycles, and of cycles of such cycles. (p. 30)

In terms of writing instruction, the stage of romance initiates the
biology of prose as a student explores language according to his or her own
interests and abilities. This romance with language becomes whatever
motivates a student to write for an audience. There follows a stage of
precision, the disciplined analysis of language that is based on formal
learning. Generalization ends the basic threefold cycle of freedom,
discipline, and freedom, as students combine skills they have acquired
spontaneously with those they have learned formally. Thus language play
(romance) and close analysis (precision) undergird the development of an
eloquent style, a style appropriate for the varied demands of generalization.

In a humane world, these demands are satisfied by the art of
conversation, an art that Castiglione could take for granted in Renaissance
Italy but one that does not flourish today, especially not in the classroom.
Indeed, this art has little meaning in our current teaching system. The
body/mind confusion, the arrhythmical free/fixed curriculum jars even the
most elementary instruction. I refer now specifically to college students'
writing: half-page essays choked out word by word, or pages and pages and
pages of empty verbiage. Anyone who has graded students' papers
recognizes these antimonies, which I would ultimately explain in curricular terms as the body/mind dualities of literacy instruction. And like
the larger undergraduate curriculum, there exists no system, no program
for joining them.

Most people recognize, in a conversation for example, these choices: a
frown, smile, nod, pause, and so on. Translated from social events into
writing, these are rhetorical soliloquies, doublets, chiasmuses, oxymorons,
the crossing over from style to style that writers subconsciously or
deliberately choose to perform. However, in making these choices our
bodies are twice displaced: once removed from oral to written form, and
further disembodied because printed words exist in stasis. And the
nonverbal exchange does not become, in prose, self-evident. That is,
people talk but words don't. It is the stylistic function of physical

eloquence to reintroduce the body—its intonation, its rhythm, its voice—into prose. To make prose talk.

The art of conversation provides the spontaneous, self-announcing techniques for an eloquent prose style. We know, without thinking really, the rules for speaking up and the penalties, if any, for lying or talking out of place. It is our birthright, conferred by natural and social means: the cosmetics, savagery, competition, pleasure, what, in a civilized world, becomes a crowded room of chattering students. Until they write, that is—as if all their biological history and social experience stops. What unnatural act does writing invite?

Or to ask a better question: How should physical eloquence be taught? Simple to state. I would acknowledge the otherwise dead bodies that inhabit a writing class. Give them time. Let them acquire prose by the same largely subconscious means that everyone uses to acquire a first language. I would also anticipate among these students a painfully strong desire to study language formally, to learn about writing quickly in order to be done with it. But that impulse can wait, or find enough expression outside the writing class in a writing lab, tutorial session, or some other course where writing is formally taught.

No surprise, then, when the biology of prose heals itself, perhaps not completely in a single semester or even a year of writing instruction, but the healing process will have at least started. And that happens because prose originates in a student's body, a body that innately motivates self-expression, and that self-expression is shaped by physical eloquence.

Language Play and Motive: Functionalism versus Eloquence

We write to please ourselves as much as others, since by engaging an audience we call attention to who we are and what we say. Yet too often teachers think of writing in purposeful terms only, as something a student must learn for success in school in order to succeed in business, law, and other professions.

The five-part essay, or any other formula for writing, essentially takes the writer's motive for granted, perhaps because a teacher's assignment obviates the need to consider motivation. In this regard, a student writes for the teacher, for reasons that are externally defined by the teacher. Even in student-centered classes, where students write for each other, the occasion for writing precedes the motivation for expressing oneself.

This functional view of language sets the wrong teaching objectives. It makes practical skills, like clarity in research papers or conciseness in lab reports, a pedagogical dead end. Once students have mastered these skills, why should they learn more? Why should they refine skills that already serve their needs? By setting functional objectives, we therefore motivate the successful learner to stop learning.

Even worse, teachers make learning to write an utterly serious task. The pleasure we all take in speaking well, in just expressing ourselves to someone, has no place in a functional view of language. Students write to get the job done. Nothing else. It is no wonder that students often resist learning to write. The effort dehumanizes them. It also alienates them from their own language.

Just as writing removes the author from the immediate audience, dividing the real person from the one conveyed in print, so too it produces a split between the normal self and the one "staged" by the written text. On stage is the writer's self-image, measured against expectations that others have of a performance. A writer can, of course, pretend to be elsewhere, as the audience cannot actually know for sure if the performance is real or simulated. To complicate matters, the audience can also be distracted, or variously inattentive, which then influences how they respond to the actor's (or writer's) performance.

A writer has much the same opportunities as an actor to invent an identity, as Samuel Clemens and Amantine Dupin did by pseudonym and countless others have done by ghostwriting a text. But signature is only part of a writer's ability to act out—or play with—language; changes in style, or simply a change in audience, can more fully upend the normal response to a writer's work.

As a matter of self-identity, writing adjusts behavior in a way that parallels a disruption of the normal functions of language. In one sense a writer oscillates between a real self and one that is transmuted by print into someone else. In another sense a writer becomes a different person, only real to an audience as the embodiment of a missing author.

Putting ourselves back together suggests that we have a mechanism for this repair and the ability to use it. Gregory Bateson in *Steps to an Ecology of Mind* (1972, 108) calls this mechanism (which all humans use) *schismogenesis*, a biological cycle for the regeneration of body and mind.[5] Each writer begins this cycle as the body adjusts to isolation or temporal dislocation. Indeed, our mental and physical health depends on this adjustment. At the end of this cycle a posted letter, a finished essay, any form of published writing gives us the chance to recover our normal identity and sense of well-being.

This recovery is achieved with varying skill as a writer moves from a self that is inappropriate for a given audience to another self that is chosen deliberately or by unreflective response to circumstances. By the same interplay of audience and self-identity, a writer adjusts language to fit an audience; or in developing an argument, the writer may find it leads in directions unforseen, even contrary to his original intentions, so that the logic of this discovery becomes an impetus for self-discovery and a slightly altered sense of self.

If we define the central (or ordinary) self as a dynamic role-player, then the schismogenesis of roles describes how we know ourselves. As the external world shapes us, factors that motivate our roles interact—as personality alternates from one self to another, using personal history as well as language values, we compare roles and choose a particular identity.

Schismogenesis of Writing

For writing, linguistic conventions may regulate shifts in identity, even through changes as simple as using *she* for *he* to denote generic reference. Or a writer may control the more difficult, largely subconscious transition from producing a text to interpreting it, in this way alternating from the author's point of view to the reader's perspective (Chart 2.1).

Chart 2.1: **Patterns of Identity**

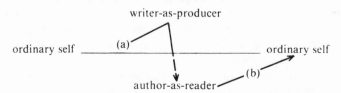

Writing changes us by the physical isolation it imposes, first by making the writer a self-referential producer of words (*a* on Chart 2.1), then, if this creative act has a regenerative cycle, by returning the writer to a sense of self within a larger social context: the author-as-reader (*b* on Chart 2.1). These changes correspond to external versus internal pressures that shape a writer's identity, the external force being a requirement to write, for instance, an essay assigned by a teacher, whereas the internal force fuels a desire to be understood. The same person can, of course, move between these axes of serious and playful writing, though typically one dominates.

A serious writer is imprisoned by words, by the functional motive for producing them or by the reader's need to re-create the text's meaning. One result is solipsistic prose, written as if the author is the only audience—imprisoned within the same textual references (cf. *writer-based/reader-based styles* in Flower and Hayes 1981b). Another result is formulaic writing that supplants the author's identity with a generic one, either for the appearance of objectivity or for the authoritative pose of being invulnerable to criticism (Lanham 1983a).

By contrast, a playful writer takes risks by shifting roles until the right one is adopted; this effort to accommodate an audience further entails an escape from *merely* playing with language for its own sake. As in children, the biological drive to play with language is purposeful, too, as it directs the child towards more sophisticated uses of form. But no child is motivated by this purpose—no child intends to play with language because it promotes acquisition. Similarly, the playful writer does not write solely or primarily to become a better writer. His or her purpose for playing is like any adult's who enjoys games of chance, of risk-taking, of going to the limits of one's abilities. The playful writer also challenges others to judge his or her performance by standards that are not strictly functional; in this respect he or she engages the audience in a game of language play that is won or lost by consensus, according to unstated rules of good taste, style, and eloquence.

A playful writer may initiate this game mostly to achieve the eloquence of a persuasive argument, but sometimes too for the display of language that is skillfully controlled. In either case, the impulse to write has a playful expression that overrides a mere statement of facts or the simple fulfillment of a duty. It is this desire to play with language, to make a game of using it well, that originates in the biology of writing.

Roger Caillois in *Man, Games, and Play* (1961) defines biological play as an activity which must be (1) free, (2) separate, (3) uncertain, (4) unproductive, (5) rule-governed, and (6) unreal/make-believe. Playful writing fits each of these categories:

1. *Free:* Since no one is required to attend college, students are free to go at any time (at least in a legal sense). Nevertheless, many students have the entirely serious task of getting a degree for their parents' sake, or taking freshman composition because their school or major program requires it.

These exceptions notwithstanding, a playful writer is free in the sense that no one is required to be eloquent or to finesse language as a kind of signature. Unlike speech, which everyone must use with some sophistication, writing allows a minimum of fluency without jeopardizing the social status of the marginal, and largely anonymous writer. If, however, a writer chooses to become fully fluent, that choice must be reconfirmed at each level of achievement, until the writer accepts an obligation to play with language and to achieve the physical eloquence of a personally distinctive style. But the writer can, at any time, decide to stop this unending game of self-improvement.

2. *Separate:* A playful writer addresses a specific audience who can participate in the writer's game; he therefore implicitly excludes other readers as nonparticipants. Of course, the excluded audience can invite themselves to read a text, but their attention by itself does not qualify them to "play along." This point applies as well to historical changes in style and taste, for only by adopting the perspective of the intended audience can the distinctive qualities of a writer's style (or their absence) be fairly assessed. In this respect a "guest list" necessarily ties the author to a specific audience distinct from everyone else.

3. *Uncertain:* The uncertainty that a playful writer faces is the risk of miscalculation, of not finding an intended audience, of not persuading the one addressed, of not choosing an appropriate style, or of not handling the right one with competence. Few endeavors are more uncertain than the game of writing to an audience that is not immediately present; no writer is ever certain of being fully understood.

4. *Unproductive:* A playful writer gains nothing of commercial value by striving for excellence; even writers who are paid professionally for their work have few financial incentives to be eloquent, especially since the demands of eloquence narrow the audience to those relatively few people who appreciate the effort and join the game. The risk of appearing ostentatious or effete further constrains writers who might otherwise value eloquence for its own sake.

5. *Rule-governed:* There are four games—*agon, alea, mimicry, ilynx*—governing the roles that a playful writer plays. The basic contest (agon) is to get outside a writer-based perspective, to shift from an egocentric to an audience-centered point of view. In making this change a writer may encourage the random drift (alea) of ideas, of new possibilities that only appear by chance. Or a writer may oppose chance by the deliberate imitation (mimicry) of a style, perhaps to refine it, master it, or maybe for the counterfeit refinement in parody. As a final option, between order and chance a writer can work to balance prose, then against that norm suddenly and unexpectedly shift off-balance (ilynx) to achieve what Kenneth Burke (1965, 89) has called a "perspective by incongruity." In each case as a writer plays a game, by that choice he reveals a facet of personality.

6. *Unreal/Make-believe:* For the playful writer, language

itself is a make-believe representation of what really exists "out there." Without straying into a discussion of nominalism, I want merely to emphasize the arbitrary nature of language or, for writing, the graphic symbols that correspond to speech, as these differ from culture to culture (Semitic, Indian, European) and from language to language (Hebrew, Hindi, English).

Conclusion

Play contrasts with serious, functional, purposeful behavior. The latter behavior usually represents what people are expected to do; it is a socially defined attitude. Play, however, seems to originate spontaneously, as a biological activity. *Sexual play* suggests this bodily—as opposed to social—meaning.

Play can also be social, and it often is socialized as sporting events or "games" (Vygotsky 1978), yet these games still express biological drives: aggression (as in football), hunting activities (as in the speed and agility needed for basketball or soccer), display (as in body building), and so on.

So what does all this have to do with teaching writing? To the extent that expressing ourselves is a biological behavior, then it can be regarded as a play-like activity, one that students can use with as much enjoyment when they write as when they speak. But most writing instructors emphasize the purposeful, asocial, individualized uses of writing only. They also exclude the students' impulse to play with language, an impulse that ironically fulfills a learning purpose.

By analogy to someone who is studying a second language, a person who learns it for strictly functional uses rarely masters that language. A common example would be the graduate student who studies French and German to pass a reading test in those languages. Having fulfilled this requirement, most students are also finished with French and German; they typically lack the motivation to continue their language studies, and even if they do continue reading in French and German, they do not in any sense become fluent in either language.

The successful language learner has a more personal, self-generated motivation. That person often strives to be fluent for the sake of self-expression, either to become more like the people whose language is "foreign," or perhaps to convey the "real" person in that foreign language. Or both. Moreover, good language learners typically adopt a child-like personality; they reset the biological clock, becoming open to new experiences and able to experiment with language; playful, in the sense of learning by trial and error, they are also uninhibited about making mistakes.

If these learning strategies transfer to writing, and I think they do, we need to encourage students to play with language as the motivation for successful learning. Simply put, language play makes writing an enjoyable task, and if we enjoy doing something, that satisfaction becomes its own reward. Moreover, quality of writing improves. Students who enjoy writing will practice often, and their work will have a meaningful objective: personal excellence. Thus play becomes its own purpose.

No functionalism here. The motivation to write well comes from within, and quality of writing is the only objective that perpetuates this motivation. It starts with the biology of writing. Students play, in the sense of expressing their identity in prose; they take risks, having developed enough confidence to learn from their failures. Ultimately they strive to become distinctive writers, to express their own physical eloquence.

In the next chapter I will discuss goals of a writing curriculum in terms of a student's (play-like) personal motive to achieve physical eloquence. Because this personal motive emanates from the subconscious, it does not have the immediate visibility or pragmatic (serious) appeal of a social motive that is imposed on students and that encourages a functional, utilitarian role for the writing curriculum. Yet only by guiding students towards a personal motive for literacy, a motive that is self-generated and self-regulated, can we adopt a biological approach to the teaching of writing.

3

A Literacy of Eloquence
for the Writing Curriculum

Most teachers of writing routinely equate thinking with composing, and they discuss this relationship almost exclusively as a mental process; as a result, students are taught to explore ideas in prewriting, they are expected to master problem-solving routines, and they are formally introduced to types of exposition and argumentation in the rhetorical modes of synthesis, analysis, comparison, and so on. The unmothering of prose results, at least in part, from this strange fascination with cognitive processes. By this mind-only emphasis, a student paradoxically becomes a disembodied learner, a system of half-unplugged connections that needs some additional wiring—one hook-up for clarity, another for brevity, maybe two wires for an elegant style. The rest of a student's body just functions as a telephone pole, supporting the good connections and keeping the bad ones safe, presumably not dangling somewhere.

As it orphans the body, this cognitive view of writing also turns away from nurturing values, leaving students with the inert problem of having no shared sense for culture. What they do share, unfortunately, is the anomie of culture-free writing, of words composed in a form of language that is always foreign and disowned.

Care for words, in fact a love for them, is the opposite impulse, a cultural response to prose that is more shown than taught and, for that reason, more difficult to teach. Since the alternative, the unmothering of prose, offers nothing easier nor more rewarding for teachers of writing or their students, what is needed instead is a new literacy, one that invests written language with the same values that are normally reserved for speech.

Solving The Literacy Crisis: Three Stages

Before I can promote that new literacy, I need to define it. Although my definition of *literacy* applies directly to the college curriculum, it works in other settings that my readers can, I presume, recognize as extending through all levels of education, and well beyond.

Chart 3.1 diagrams three aspects of literacy instruction, each corresponding to a stage of the writing curriculum. In Stage One the developmental writer takes a course (or courses) to become functionally literate. This form of literacy means, among other things, that a student works to acquire prose in the most basic sense for its physical production. At Stage Two a writer may take several courses, including freshman English, in order to write well for academic purposes. Stage Three applies to very few students, perhaps 3 to 4 percent in college, who can study writing for the self-conscious improvement of their own "personal" style.

Chart 3.1: **Three-Stage Writing Curriculum**

	Teaching Objective	Writing Course(s)	Social Result
STAGE ONE:	acquisition of prose	developmental English	functional literacy
STAGE TWO:	acquisition of prose	beginning to intermediate composition	educational literacy
STAGE THREE:	formal learning	advanced composition	personal literacy

To show the social importance of each stage, I will discuss each separately according to its relationship to the other stages. Following that discussion, we can examine ways to implement this three-stage curriculum.

Functional Literacy and Citizenship:

Most college students can read a newspaper, fill out a job application form, follow the directions for using a voting booth; they can, in other words, function adequately in our society. Of course there are exceptions. By these strictly functional standards, perhaps 10 to 30 percent of all Americans are illiterate.[1] Immigration exacerbates the problem, especially when adults who learn English as a second language are functionally illiterate in their native languages. My initial teaching experience was with these students, 150 or so, packed each night into a room with enough chairs for 40. A free night school, the enrollment stayed fairly constant, but very few faces were the same from night to night. Conditions like this obviously militate against effective teaching, yet the motivation to participate in society, in this case, to become U.S. citizens, enabled some of these students to attain functional literacy. My inexperience as a teacher only underscores their accomplishment.

In the worst conditions, a motivated student can become literate; in the best conditions, a student who is unmotivated will almost certainly fail. Since most children want to please their parents (or a parent-surrogate, like a teacher), the schools need only reflect values that parents, and a larger society, hold in common. Literacy enjoins a future role with a cultural norm—that to someday be a good (productive) citizen, one must learn to read and write now. Of course this message is more implied than taught; but its presence is quite real, as are the effects of its absence, which can be seen in the widespread failure of literacy instruction in the urban ghetto, the barrio, or the rural, isolated communities of Appalachia.

Educational Literacy and Competence:

Nearly all students, when they arrive at college, have some functional literacy, as shown by their application forms, placement tests and, one increasingly hopes, by their previous schooling. These students can indeed write, but not always with enough fluency or self-confidence to succeed in college. For some students, the ability to (hand)write barely exists in the form of printed lettering only; others can only write using a simplified syntax, essentially in phrases or simplistic clauses. In effect, their writing approximates the ability of a typical six or seven year old, though in all other respects they are, of course, more intelligent and mature than a child.

These basic writers comprise a relatively small segment of the college population, but the majority of entering students are not competent writers either—at least not competent enough to be successful in courses like freshman English. In testing beginning college students, I have found 65 percent fall below the minimum standard (grade *C*) for passing a writing course, at least at the start of a semester.[2] They begin, in other words, at a level below minimum competence, and by the end of a semester, most improve enough to pass, though just barely. This improvement is quite tenuous, so that by their sophomore and junior years they often lose what little progress has been made, even when their coursework involves significant amounts of writing, and even when that writing is primarily within their majors.[3]

Most college teachers already know about this problem of backsliding composition skills; at this point it is sufficient to observe the contrast between functional literacy, which means that a student can read and write, and educational literacy, which means that a student can use English for relatively sophisticated purposes, often of a metalinguistic nature.

This contrast may be clearer if represented in a more general context. A functionally literate person can write a letter of complaint, read a cookbook recipe and, in most respects, function with no difficulty in our society today. But this minimal ability to read and write is not necessarily well developed nor frequently used. For writing, in particular, many people (including college students) have no real fluency; even simple writing tasks require extraordinary effort. Indeed, faced with the option of writing a letter or using a telephone, most will choose the more convenient medium of a telephone for quick, spontaneous talk. Convenience, in this sense, applies to the person's skill as well as the time involved. Like a second language, prose is not easy to generate if it has not been frequently practiced. Even well-developed skills, if not practiced often, will eventually decline. Similarly, a person who speaks German fluently, then stops using it for several years, will experience some difficulties when speaking that language again.

Most college students are, like nearly all people in our society, infrequent writers. Before entering college these students have had little opportunity to develop their writing skills outside of school, and perhaps little opportunity even in school. The latter problem may be changing as high schools require more writing and grade schools prepare students to do it. But the larger social picture has, if anything, become worse.

Consider, for example, the situation of returning students who find themselves, at age thirty, in freshman English after a decade or more of writing nothing, at least nothing like an academic essay. In my experience these returning students do quite well—they are highly motivated, mature learners who typically spend much more time on their writing skills than "regular" eighteen-year-old freshmen do—but they also express surprise, even anguish and despair, at their inability to write well. Perhaps they have overestimated their former talents for writing, but no matter how inaccurate this perception may be, it remains uniformly consistent that writing is now harder for them because they did not practice this skill during the years they were away from school.

Disuse leads to decline. It only takes a moment's reflection to recognize how pervasive this loss may be. Even professional writers must sustain their craft through constant, often daily practice, or they begin to lose their craftsmanship. The point here is quite simple: If professional writers need to practice their writing, then someone at the functional level of literacy requires practice, too. Certainly most students coming to college have either written too little, or were too late in their development of this skill, for writing to be fully mastered. Since educational literacy builds on this presumably mastered skill, students who lack this basic foundation need to construct it while, at the same time, other students are going beyond educational literacy. Yet colleges do not devote enough time to this problem, either by reteaching functional literacy or by re-creating the social awareness outside the schools that would generate more writing instruction coupled with practice.

Personal Literacy and Social Values:

Suppose we could have students write throughout their undergraduate years—even more, that we could have them achieve the educational literacy of a competent writer. Is that enough? For academic purposes it clearly satisfies a basic, if narrowly defined, idea of the liberal arts curriculum. But the same problem affecting entering students applies when they leave the university. If they do not write often, or at all, their skills will decline, though more slowly and in more subtle ways than would characterize students who are only functionally literate. How, then, do we promote a lasting competence, one that transcends the academic world and transforms the purposeful writer into someone who writes for personal ("nonpurposeful") reasons?

At least one objective is fundamental: We need to emphasize the personal motives for becoming a skilled writer. This means bringing students into contact with real writers, not just academics who produce scholarly articles, but lawyers, engineers, insurance executives, journalists, corporate and government officials, doctors, politicians, as pervasive and impressive a list of people as can be arranged. If they can also be encouraged to help teach writing, so much the better, but their main contribution would be to demonstrate that writing is not entirely irrelevant to a student's future occupation.

This series of speakers (or video tapes, essays, and other media when live presentations are not possible) is not meant to be a public relations event. Neither is it an opportunity for recruiters to pitch their own professions. Rather, as emissaries of print culture, these visitors would convey a radically mixed message—a functional, job-related statement on the importance of writing for specific careers, and a personal, in-class presentation by someone other than the teacher who can be identified as a writer. Thus jobs and self-identity intersect, with a strong chance that students will listen to the practical message on jobs before they recognize the significance of someone who actually writes for a living.

I would prefer to emphasize the last point, for students to identify writing with someone other than a teacher. Although salaries and careers may initially get their attention, it is more important for students to see that writers have nonacademic, extremely important roles to perform in our society. Keep in mind that students are largely school-bound writers who, for obvious reasons, identify writing most often with a teacher. They may read popular novels outside of school, but literacy is, in most other respects, a by-product of their education, a diploma of success but not really a mark of their own identity.

In our age of science and technology, language has a hidden value, unrecognized by most people because it is largely unknown or taken for granted. Similarly, our students may have no cultural insights, no mythic sense of awe, for the power of words in print culture. Many have, instead, a strongly visceral response to the amplified power of music, or they have the disassociated ability of a TV listener who controls the volume, but who lacks the power of dialogue within that medium.

Although a literacy of eloquence expresses a writer's individual voice, it paradoxically lacks the obvious practical value of citizenship (functional literacy) or scholarship (educational literacy). Yet without this personal voice, or the opportunity to develop it, literacy becomes an inert sign, a mere license for achievement but no longer a meaningful goal once that license is obtained.

Towards A Literacy of Eloquence: Three Options

Although many options could be advanced, the first two are the most commonly adopted efforts to improve the writing curriculum, while the third option offers the best means for promoting a literacy of eloquence. In each case students would write more often, under the first option by taking a required upper-division writing course, or under the second option by doing more writing in all their courses. While obviously of some benefit to students, these curricular changes nevertheless lack the long-term gains in writing ability that are possible through the tutorial courses of the third option.

The Upper-Division Writing Requirement:

One option is to have students write more, usually in a course for juniors or seniors that picks up where freshman English left off. The ultimate effect of this option is to provide more of what already exists, a course that broadly accommodates each student's major so those majoring in humanities take their own writing course with other humanities students, while those in social sciences or the "hard" sciences have their own sections as well. To simplify the discussion, I'll give this option a comprehensive label: the upper-division writing requirement.

This *advanced writing course* places writing at the center of learning, since all students must establish their "competence" as writers before they can graduate. It signals, too, a university's willingness to upgrade literacy skills or, in a related sense, to guarantee the writing ability of its graduates. These are, of course, laudable goals, but they may be difficult ones to achieve since they essentially represent a rearguard action against a decline in students' writing abilities.

After freshman English, a student typically must wait several years before taking the advanced writing course. During this interim it is unfortunately possible that no one writes much; students may, in fact, deliberately avoid courses that require writing. For many of these students the skills they learned in freshman English will inevitably decline for lack of practice and instruction; even those students who somehow maintain their skills will have no incentive to do so *after* completing the advanced writing course. Educational literacy (especially in courses like technical writing) becomes its own end; once achieved, at whatever level of competence, a student has no educational incentive to do more.

Why bother? Like a traveler's command of French, a basic proficiency may be all one needs to control. Purpose thus sets its own limits: If getting from the airport to a hotel is someone's main objective, then mastery of French is an unlikely goal for that person to seek. Similarly, if writing competency is defined by a course requirement, then what incentive do students have for mastery of writing? Once they pass the advanced writing course, students have fulfilled the educational demands of being literate; they can subsequently forget this peculiarly academic skill or, if they must ultimately write for their careers, these former students can aim for what school has unfortunately taught them to achieve: a minimum level of writing competence only.

This minimal standard is not itself a problem. Obviously a level of ability can be defined that sets a high (minimum) standard for writing. But even the most rigorous program is a pedagogical dead end; its value stops when the writing course does. Although students may temporarily become better writers, few will retain this improvement outside the university; indeed, most will backslide after a few years to their former levels of ability.

If these claims appear exaggerated, consider what the real constraints are for an upper-division writing requirement. Assuming that everyone who teaches writing can agree on uniform standards (a huge assumption), how will these standards be verified? From course to course, a passing grade of *C* may represent (and often does) entirely different levels of writing ability.

Suppose that one thousand students complete an advanced writing course, with half (or five hundred) receiving a *C* as the grade for "average" achievement. If standards for this course have been closely regulated, then a slippage of grades (i.e., the interreliability of graders) would be held to a minimum. But even under the best conditions we should expect some slippage, especially in the *C* range where some instructors will assign a *C* to papers that others will grade as *D*; or worse, *F*'s will become *C*'s, and so on, for all letter grades. If an average 25 percent of the *C* grades will be revised by subsequent readings done by impartial graders, then of these revised grades, we can anticipate nearly 20 percent involving the *C* to *D* split, and most of these (13 percent) will fall below the average grade of *C*. Consider, too, that half or more of all *C* grades are below the mean; that is, about 250 of the 500 *C*'s are in the low *C* range. Finally, if we adjust the *D* grades to allow for slippage, the total of "below average" writers is around 46 percent. Chart 3.2 summarizes these results.

Chart 3.2: **Idealized Results of Initial and Secondary Readings of Freshman Essays**

Initial Grades:	Revised Grades (second readings):*
A = 5% (n = 50)	
B = 20% (n = 200)	
C = 50% (n = 500)	
	C to C- = 26%
D = 20% (n = 200)	
	C- to D- = 15%
F = 5% (n = 50)	
	D- to F = 5%
	46% below mean of *C*

* The percentages for second readings represent the number of essays that *always* remain below the mean grade of *C*.

This 46 percent result, though derived from hypothetical evaluations, is probably close to an accurate representation of students' writing. Nearly half are poor writers, if by "poor" we mean able to satisfy a uniform measure of writing ability. Take away the uniformity of this measure, and the results could be much worse. Indeed, they probably are.

In the real world of declining enrollments—or just the fear of a decline—few universities can establish, then uphold, a rigorous standard for advanced writing. Imagine a school that would actually fail 46 percent of its juniors and seniors! Allowing these students to retake the course would merely postpone the inevitable failure of learning to write *well*; fifteen weeks of writing instruction, or thirty weeks or more, is a relatively short time for anyone to overcome a lifetime's inactivity as a writer.

Moreover, the reason for mastering this skill is too arbitrary.

Certainly a student who cannot graduate without passing this course has a motive for doing well; but the student who finds writing difficult (most do) and who must satisfy an extremely rigorous standard, will have an even more powerful motive to attend school elsewhere, presumably where there is no advanced writing requirement (or where an existing one is poorly enforced).

In fact, this threat of declining enrollment will never become a problem because the standards of an upper-division writing course will guarantee safe passage for nearly all students. If they could manage freshman English, then an advanced writing course will (re)certify the same level of competence. They will then graduate into a society that typically requires nothing more than standards of minimal competence.

Economy will determine this rite of passage. Schools cannot afford to lose their students; students cannot afford schools that make them, in large numbers, retake a composition course. Another problem is the high cost of administering a writing requirement, especially one that upholds uniform and rigorous standards.

Who will teach these courses? Instructors? If so, full-time or part-time? Moreover, should graduate students be hired as composition Teaching Assistants, adding to the numbers in graduate school? If faculty teach writing, should they be trained and observed, then given the time to attend frequent (biweekly?) staff meetings? At large universities should all faculty participate, or just those who volunteer? Without adequate numbers of volunteers, should all faculty be assigned to teach writing? Regardless of who teaches these advanced writing courses, the commitment will interfere with other responsibilities, notably research and scholarship. These are just a few of the administrative problems.

At schools where the advanced writing course has been required, faculty enthusiasm quickly changes to complacency or even active resistance to teaching composition. After all, teaching a writing course is hard work. Although a small group of faculty may continue to teach writing, these are the people (in English or other departments) who would normally require written assignments in courses other than English composition. Ironically, by having these faculty teach writing there would be fewer opportunities for students to apply their writing skills in non-composition courses.

As faculty participation declines, most of the writing courses would be taught by non-faculty—an underpaid, overworked subclass of part-time instructors. Traditionally these instructors have been graduate students who have received teaching assistantships; but the increase in writing courses (i.e. freshman English *and* advanced composition) and the current decline in size of graduate programs means a new type of instructor would have to be hired. These teachers, many with advanced degrees, would have little if any opportunity for research or other scholarly activities; they would, instead, be teachers only in a negative sense: cut off from the professional activities of a department, with little or no job security, without opportunities for advancement or incentives to excel as teachers. In short, they would have nothing to signify the importance of their work.

As a solution to the "literacy crisis," an advanced writing course creates more problems than it solves. While it may counteract the recidivism of writing skills, these effects would be temporary, essentially gone after a student leaves school. Although having a composition requirement for juniors and seniors would signal the importance of writing in curricular terms, this message would apply only to an academic setting, and only to maintain the lowest standards of writing competence. Recruiting teachers, retaining students, and upholding academic standards would be just a few of the administrative difficulties of this required course. Any one of these factors could undermine the success of an upper-division writing requirement; together they almost guarantee failure.

Writing Across the Curriculum:

A related option shifts the teaching of writing from one department, English, to every department as a university-wide responsibility. Referred to as *writing across the curriculum* (or writing across disciplines), there are two arguments for this curricular change: (1) a pedagogical claim that students learn a subject more efficiently if they are required to write about it, and (2) a curricular claim for liberal arts education that is based on the traditional *paideia* of rhetoric and logic.

Writing across the curriculum (hereafter WAC) seemingly appeals to everyone in the writing profession. It serves to rally teachers of writing, in one sense, by bringing them together from all levels of education, grade school to graduate school, and in a broader sense, by reforming the schools so they can (in theory) *counteract* the "writing crisis." Part of its appeal derives from being new, freeing it from charges of having failed in prior decades to stem the decline of literacy. Another part of WAC's appeal is the shared sense teachers have of facing a disaster together, of preserving a valuable language skill while saving literate civilization from the encroaching mobs of illiterate freshmen.

I may be overstating my point here, but it is hard to exaggerate the force of this movement, especially now, when the teaching of writing has acquired a respectability it never had before. Add to this self-respect a deep sense of urgency about declining literacy skills, and the WAC movement has clearly emerged at a most opportune time for widespread support.

That support is, however, misplaced. Let's first consider the pedagogical claim, initially expressed in Emig's article "Writing as a Mode of Learning" (1977), that writing is a fundamental aid to students in learning to learn. As subsequently developed by Toby Fulwiler and Art Young in *Language Connections* (1982) and Elaine Maimon in "Maps and Genres" (1983), this claim for the efficacy of writing extends to a student's motive for writing in an academic discipline, since learning about an academic subject is augmented by the writing task.[4] Thus, the biology student will learn more effectively when writing about biology since that topic serves his or her interest in becoming a biologist.

If this claim is true, its relevance to literacy instruction depends on the value of having students *learn* to write. As I will argue throughout this book, we may actually impede students' progress if they are expected to attend in a conscious manner to skills and strategies of writing as if they can learn a fundamentally biological process. Should we nevertheless expect them to write as a means for learning other subjects? Or to express this question a different way, if writing is not a mode of learning but instead a mode of *acquisition*, then does it help students to *acquire* knowledge in academic subjects like math, philosophy, engineering, computer science? Probably not.

Despite its largely acquired nature, writing may represent the best mode of learning—no one really knows. However, assuming it does assist a student in learning other subjects, we need to consider, too, the difficulty of this double (or triple) task—of learning another subject while simultaneously learning (and/or acquiring the ability) to write.

The neurolinguist Norman Geschwind (1974c) has estimated that only a minute fraction of all adults master writing with anything like the proficiency they have for speaking. For most of us, then, writing is itself something to be gradually acquired, something we can practice using as an academic aid but not as a skill that readily supports all learning and not as a skill to be used for self-teaching.

These limitations become more obvious if we compare writing to a second language. Should we teach subjects like history, physics, or biology, let's say in high school, while simultaneously using a second language, Spanish perhaps, as the medium of instruction? For bilingual speakers this dual instruction makes good sense; for other students, including those who know some Spanish but not fluently, this dual instruction becomes a double burden: they must acquire Spanish while also using Spanish to learn another subject.

A similar double burden applies to writing. Of course, students may benefit from writing about biology; they may even learn more because they had to write. But the reasons for this success may have nothing to do with writing as the *best* mode of learning; rather, for some students their poor command of writing forces them to concentrate, to focus their efforts with extraordinary care, so that biology eventually makes sense through the difficult medium of prose. For other students—the majority I fear—this double burden will interfere with both tasks; they will neither write well nor learn biology well.

For WAC to succeed, either students must be educationally literate or they must be taught in a way that combines functional literacy with a rather basic core curriculum. It would be foolhardy to presume that many college students write well enough to use that medium for educational ends. But WAC advocates implicitly make this assumption in two ways: They view writing as a cognitive task only (or primarily), and they define writing as a learned skill. In both instances these assumptions neglect functional literacy, since students are forced to express themselves in prose before the quality of their thinking can be effectively demonstrated. Lacking this ability, they must compensate for the double burden of learning to write in order to learn another subject.

Conversely, if the subject matter being taught is simplified, then some students may learn to write well, but they will also receive a fundamentally illiberal education. Perhaps in high school, and certainly before then, a WAC approach to writing poses few difficulties because it coincides with a basic curriculum. But in college, to the extent it still differs from high school, students are taught how to think like a biologist, historian, physicist, political scientist, and so forth. They should specialize in subjects, not in the negative sense of excluding other disciplines but in the positive sense of learning why disciplines exist, why they differ, why they require some autonomy, and, if a college education finally succeeds, students should also learn why "extremes meet."

If, as Elaine Maimon argues, WAC advances the cause of liberal education, then it redefines the meaning of this term, implying instead a do-it-yourself education. In a traditional view of liberal arts, one espoused by Whitehead for instance, general knowledge emerges from learning that is highly specialized. But WAC, perhaps inadvertently, restricts learning to a pre-specialized stage (what Whitehead calls "romance"). Here's the problem: WAC creates a new kind of teacher, one who combines roles as, let's say, teacher of history and teacher of writing. In WAC theory these are complementary functions since learning to write should make a student a better historian. In fact, a teacher who devotes time to writing *instruction* necessarily diverts attention from history to language, from one kind of learning to another. To the extent the history teacher stops teaching history, students receive a reduced or "simplified" exposure to history. If this switch were not necessary, then it would be hard to explain why composition classes should even exist. Yet students can be taught to write, regardless of topic, since language underlies this instruction.

I doubt that many history teachers would actually devote class time to writing instruction. Instead, they would be more likely to require writing assignments; in this respect students would *practice* writing. I want to make a sharp distinction between these terms: writing practice and writing instruction. One applies to the do-it-yourself mode of learning—students can become better writers because they will become better historians, or vice versa; either way, the ability to write is taken for granted, or the ability to think is somehow equated with the physical *and* cognitive task of writing. The other term—instruction—presupposes an active commitment to all stages of the writing process, with as much attention given to functional literacy (i.e., the production of language) as to educational literacy (i.e., cognitive processes).

Returning to the history teacher, if that person also teaches writing, then instruction will probably give way to practice. If so, there will be a strong likelihood of students becoming worse writers. Several decades of research show that simply having students write—that is, increasing the volume of language production—has no significant effect on performance.[5] Since WAC complicates the writing task, students may actually decline in ability; or, if they do receive significant instruction in a "non-writing" course, the quality of their education may decline. Either way students lose.

These are, I concede, hypothetical effects, there being no empirical evidence that directly confirms or refutes my claims. But the same criticism applies to all WAC programs I have read about or observed; this entire movement has been uncritically accepted and, in terms of students' performance, remains irresponsibly untested. Claims for its success— Beaver College in Glenside, Pennsylvania has received the most ac- colades—are strictly anecdotal, with most of the praise coming from the teachers who participate in WAC rather than disinterested observers. Yet the appearance of success, even for a well-documented program like the one at Beaver College, can disguise some rather obvious drawbacks.

Beaver College is quite small (about seven hundred students), a size that insures some cohesion among faculty regardless of discipline. This size also represents a basic difference in purpose between a small liberal arts college and a larger, more research-oriented state university. A WAC program depends on faculty from various disciplines who coordinate the teaching of writing throughout the curriculum (Fulwiler and Young 1982). However, the size of a university determines the relative complexity of this program. At a large university the faculty may work together in small groups, but their efforts to teach writing "across the curriculum" would be difficult to coordinate with other groups. Yet without this central control, a WAC program risks becoming a haphazard series of courses, at best a superficial effort to increase the amount of writing that students must produce.

Money is a related problem. A small school can undertake a major reform in the curriculum for significantly less money than a large school. But even Beaver College needed outside funding (a three-year federal grant from NEH) to implement its WAC program; comparable funds for a large school would not buy the same program. As just one example, Beaver College sponsored WAC conferences for faculty throughout the school year, with national authorities on writing as guest speakers, but for the same funds the large school would be limited to a few training sessions, perhaps a two-week workshop, attended by some (but not all) faculty, especially if the workshop were held during the summer or between semesters.

A program modeled after Beaver College challenges the very existence of writing as a profession. Can anyone teach writing after a few weeks of preparation? Are faculty already qualified to be writing teachers because they write themselves or because they took writing courses as undergraduates? Is the teaching of writing a nonprofession?

To each of these questions, the answer is no. Imagine a physicist who was asked to conduct a two-week workshop on "science literacy," with the immediate objective of making everyone on campus a teacher of physics. Or imagine the reaction of a speech instructor who was told that everyone is implicitly qualified to teach that subject because everyone can speak. Or the literary scholar who learns that anyone with previous literature courses in high school and college is qualified to teach literature. These are imperfect analogies but close enough to make my point: the physicist, the speech instructor, the literary scholar would shout "NO!" WAC invites the same response.

If everyone on campus can (and should) teach writing, if a few weeks of "training" is sufficient for this purpose, then the teaching of writing becomes a nonprofession, more a shared responsibility than a discipline based on expertise. Of course, anyone can claim to teach students how to write or simply require that more writing be produced. But quality of instruction, not the quantity of assignments or the divided efforts of a WAC teacher, is the only guarantee that students will become better writers. That's an empirical claim, one that can be confirmed or refuted by research on writing. (The Appendix to Chapter Nine offers some preliminary evidence that strongly supports the value of instruction). Regardless of how the empirical case is made, there remains a compelling political reason to stress instruction over practice as the basic rationale for having *professional* teachers of writing.

Composition researchers can point to relatively few "facts" about writing. This lack of conclusive evidence makes the political case especially important. If students become better writers through more instruction and not through more practice without instruction, then writing must be taught by qualified, well-trained professionals who specialize in this instruction. Yet the emphasis of a WAC program is on quantity—essentially on practice alone—by having students do more writing in all disciplines. This objective may have a limited value, at least within the university, since it makes writing a more integral part of a student's education. But let's not sacrifice the professional contributions of writing teachers for the novelty of an untested curriculum.

Adjunct Writing Courses:

There is, instead, a genuine alternative. Relatively inexpensive to operate, this option combines instruction with the extended practice of a WAC program by means of an *adjunct writing course*. In this course, which is taught by a writing instructor, students receive intensive writing instruction while they complete essay assignments that are based on material from another course, in any discipline, for any topic, and with any emphasis on style. The adjunct model varies to the extent that it remains an autonomous course or an extension of the other content course (or courses) tied to it. Regardless of design, it does meet two conditions that a WAC program cannot fulfill: (1) a writing teacher coordinates all writing instruction, and (2) students must learn the humanistic skill of writing for a general audience.

To the extent testimonial evidence is worthwhile, adjuncting has been a successful experiment (see Robert Cullen's "Writing Across the Curriculum" 1985, and the last chapter in Richard Lanham's *Literacy and the Survival of Humanism*, 1983). There remains, however, the problem of concrete evidence showing that students actually benefit from this additional instruction.

And there is a related question, one that applies as well to a WAC program and an upper-division writing requirement; namely, do these approaches to literacy isolate writing on campus, making it an academic skill that students can largely ignore after they graduate? No literacy program has, as yet, been concerned with this fundamental question.

A Literacy of Eloquence

A *literacy of eloquence* teaches the personal expression of style. It differs from the first two stages of literacy—functional and educational forms—because a writer is motivated from within, the quality of style and self-expression being an author's main objective when writing.

The key point here is motivation. Does one write for the instrumental purpose of being heard, or does the writer want to be someone worth hearing? In the first instance, getting the point across is all that really matters, so there is no incentive to improve a skill that already serves its social function. In this way, success limits the writer's effort. In the second instance, a writer considers the best way to express something and constantly works to achieve that ideal. This attitude produces a quite different kind of literacy, most clearly demonstrated by the writer's constant effort to improve, and ultimately to excel.

All students should receive training in the three literacies (functional, educational, personal) at all levels of their education (grade school through graduate school). Unfortunately, this ideal model has the right parts for the wrong social period; the schools have, in one sense, failed to prepare students as writers, but the schools are hardly responsible, in a larger sense, for a society that disvalues written language. Schools merely reflect, they do not create, this attitude.

As pressure increases to salvage the remnants of print culture, more students will arrive at college with marginally better writing skills. But no amount of pressure will create a new society of writers, all capable of being understood, all functionally or even educationally literate, all motivated for instrumental reasons, all of them "specialists" in written language. As print culture continues to decline, giving way to nonprint technologies such as computer networking, teleconferencing, and electronic libraries, the demand for higher literacy will, I think, change to a demand for better writing specialists, for relatively few people who can write well, in any style, for all occasions.

We can anticipate this need now, by training the "best" students to be fully literate. This means preparing them to be writing specialists, whether or not they actually pursue careers that require much writing. Only an intensive program can offer this training, in three stages, the last stage of personal literacy being the most important. It is this final stage that obviates restrictions on careers, since no one can predict the changes that will occur in each profession and since no career encompasses the social uses of print.

To train these writing specialists, a university would have to choose its best writers,[6] perhaps about 3 to 4 percent of a typical freshman class. These skilled writers can be readily identified on a placement test or by the recommendation of teachers. Once they have been identified, they should write each semester in college, in all their courses, while also receiving the tutorial guidance of a writing instructor. As they progress in talent, they could be assigned as peer tutors in writing courses, with a tangible reward for this service (either a stipend or some other payment through credit hours). But the most important reward for learning to write should extend outside the university.

When a writing specialist graduates, the university should arrange to place him or her in a well-paid, socially important profession or career. All the businesses and government agencies I have contacted are extremely anxious to hire graduates who can write well. The obvious solution is to provide students with the training that would allow them to pursue these careers. I am not recommending that universities become employment brokers; rather, students who become writing specialists should know that specific companies will reserve positions for them if they attain genuine proficiency as writers. Certainly a university can serve the larger community by informing students of these opportunities.

Even more, when these students leave the university they will become emissaries of print culture, an elite group of specialists who could promote literacy by its personal rather than strictly functional or educational forms. Businesses that hire them could also be asked to support the literacy program for all students at a university.

No curriculum reform is free. The upper-division writing requirement entails many new instructors; for WAC, besides new instructors, the universities must select and train nonprofessional teachers of writing with concomitant "expenses" in the quality and quantity of writing instruction. By contrast, an intensive writing program, one that combines adjunct courses for all students and specialized training for a few, offers the least expensive yet most effective solution to the literacy crisis. This program would cost less because the writing specialists (thirty to forty per one thousand undergraduates) could function as peer tutors, thereby freeing instructors for other responsibilities, in particular the teaching of adjunct courses.

The recruitment of writing specialists should also include a special effort to bring disadvantaged students into the program. This policy insures that elitism does not become racism, for no literacy program can succeed if it fails to correct the imbalances of students' prior training. Just what that training should involve—ideally for everyone, but specifically for these student scribes—becomes a matter of funding, at the very least a commitment to shift resources that already exist. Regardless of money, though, it is possible to describe what this program would be like for college teachers of a typical freshman English class.

Starting with the biology of writing, teachers can promote a new literacy, one that stresses eloquence before argument, achieved above all by teaching the physical act of writing. Quality of ideas remains important, as I will explain in subsequent chapters, but that quality is secondary to the physical eloquence that gives students the basic opportunity and essential literacy to be understood.

Conclusion

Most people, one might believe, would choose to write expressively if, perhaps, they only knew how. But should we presume that most people can be taught this ability, assuming first that everyone has the talent to be eloquent? And if so, what stylistic rules, examples, textbooks exist to teach it? To my first question, the answer is yes, we can all be eloquent, though not in equal measure since eloquence is above all a gift of nature that each person receives differently. Yet despite individual variations, everyone has some capacity for being more than ordinary, if just to maintain a personal sense of self. This self-identity is expressed in countless ways through idiosyncratic mannerisms, preferences in clothes, cars, food, and in language through voice quality, accent, vocabulary, sentence patterns, forms of cohesion, and much more. It is not unreasonable to assume that each person can also develop a writing style with some distinctive signs of physical eloquence. A few do.

To answer the second question, I will acknowledge that for a relatively small number of gifted writers—those who already accept the values of print culture—the kind of formal instruction that typically occurs in a writing class may actually enhance a writer's development. For these gifted students, literature faculty and other traditional humanists can offer relevant expertise for the improvement of writing, since by their training and scholarship they can best introduce students to print culture. Intensive critical reading of texts comprises part of this "initiation" into that culture, accompanied of course by extensive writing about literary or belletristic texts.

These exercises are best reserved for students who can genuinely benefit from the classical techniques of imitation, parody, and analysis because they have already mastered the physical eloquence of composing. But they are, it is well to remember, a small percentage among college students.

By contrast, for the majority of college students writing is a developmental task, infrequently practiced and more formally learned than subconsciously acquired. Gradual erosion of their writing abilities is one consequence of this "old" literacy that fails to teach physical eloquence; a more pervasive illiteracy is the social and cultural con-sequence.

Only by teaching the biology of writing can we ensure a genuine literacy of physical eloquence. This means teaching students to acquire prose subconsciously so they can begin to master in their writing the neurological functions of hand, eye, and ear. On the other hand, writing to learn in all academic disciplines, or learning to write for any functional purpose, must not dominate a student's efforts nor shape a writing curriculum. Instead, as the next three chapters will explain, students should be taught a new literacy of physical eloquence, with rhetorical delivery as text production, memory as a writer's knowledge of prose form, and style as the neurological shape of meaning.

4

Rhetorical Delivery As Text Production

Physical eloquence develops as a writer slowly masters the physiology of text production. In this chapter I will discuss crucial aspects of this development as a way to identify the writing progress of college students.

The physiology of writing can be divided into three neurological melodies: kinetic, visual, and auditory. A *melody* results when neurons coalesce into a patterned behavior, that is, when they have "learned" something as an engram and can repeat it. The Russian neuropsychologist Aleksandr Luria was the first to use the term kinetic melody in his discussion of writing. In *The Working Brain* he describes it this way:

> In the initial stages... *writing* depends on memorizing the graphic form of every letter. It takes place through a chain of isolated motor impulses, each of which is responsible for the performance of only one element of the graphic structure; with practice, this structure of the process is radically altered and writing is converted into a single "kinetic melody," no longer requiring the memorizing of the visual form of each isolated letter or individual motor impulses for making every stroke. The same situation applies to the process in which the change to writing a highly automatized engram (such as a signature) ceases to depend on analysis of the acoustic complex of the word or the visual form of its individual letters, but begins to be performed as a single "kinetic melody".... The participation of the auditory and visual areas of the cortex, essential in the early stages of formation of the activity, no longer is necessary in its later stages, and *the activity starts to depend on a different system of concertedly working zones.* (1973, 33)

Implicit in this definition are two related melodies, the visual and auditory, which control what a writer sees and hears during the production of a written text. Thus, the *visual melody* determines how much of a text the eye takes in as feedback; the *auditory melody* regulates the inner voice as it matches subvocalized or, for more advanced writers, vocally suppressed language with the language of a written text. Yet basic to these functions of the eye and ear is the *kinetic melody*, which innervates muscles in the hand, wrist, arm, and shoulder to produce graphic shapes.

These melodies interact to control the physical and mental pace of writing, and their coordinated use signals a writer's complete mastery of physical eloquence. Prior to that mastery, beginning or inexperienced writers must try to manage the complex interaction between hand, eye, and ear, a difficult task for anyone. One reason for this difficulty—arguably the most important reason—is the fragile nature of a superficially encoded neurophysiological behavior like writing. Even experienced writers can have problems writing if they do not write often.

This recidivism occurs because many areas of the brain—frontal, temporal, post-central, pre-motor, occipital-parietal—contribute to the production of a text. Moreover, the act of writing must tie together these diffusely located parts of the brain, making writing perhaps the most difficult neurological task a human can undertake. It comes as no surprise that writers who have mastered the physiology of producing a text can devote relatively more time to the quality of their ideas. Other writers who have not encoded fully the physiology of writing will have trouble expressing themselves well because they lack the physical eloquence to use time efficiently and to express meaning effectively.

Although no one knows exactly how this physical eloquence develops, the neurological evidence points to these stages: At first the frontal lobe of the cerebral hemispheres prompt ideas which, in the left temporal lobe, become propositional speech. During this initial stage the brain has converted inchoate meaning into something that can be understood, though not necessarily in a linguistic form. The next stage occurs in Broca's area of the brain, where meaning is changed into an expressive schema (or structure) for words, sentences, and entire utterances. These stages, it should be noted, precede spoken language, which depends on the intercostal chest muscles, throat, larynx, tongue, palate, teeth, lips, and nasal passage to produce sounds.

An experienced writer can control the physiological system for producing sounds as an aid for writing, but because beginning writers often switch to an auditory melody to guide their kinetic production of form, they actually exercise less neuromuscular control as they alternately handwrite and subvocalize. This occurs as the left angular gyrus transforms an expressive word schema into a graphic letter schema. As a further complication, the beginning writer may also invoke a visual melody to form a mental picture that coordinates the neuromuscular shaping of letters.

Eye, ear, and hand function as three separate systems for producing a beginning writer's text. By contrast, the experienced writer develops the physical eloquence to subsume all three melodies into one system. In *Thought and Language* Lev Vygotsky (1962) refers to this more advanced writing ability as a "condensed" mental process, one that directly triggers grapho-motor engrams in conjunction with the ear or eye. Or, as Aleksandr Sokolov (1972) explains this process, the experienced writer can produce graphic forms without self-conscious attention to that production. Beginning writers, however, must work through more developmental stages because their writing is more diffuse neurologically. Chart 4.1 shows this difference.

Chart 4.1: **Neurological Stages in the Development of Handwriting**
        (adapted from Brain 1965)

Pre-Handwriting Sequence:

Unpracticed Writer	**Practiced Writer**
Stage 1: IDEAS	IDEAS
Stage 2: PROPOSITIONAL SPEECH	PROPOSITIONAL SPEECH
Stage 3: EXPRESSIVE WORD SCHEMA	EXPRESSIVE WORD SCHEMA

Handwriting Sequence:

Step 1: Phonemes to graphemes	
Step 2: Subvocalization	
Step 3: Visual word image	
Step 4: Graphic letter schema	Graphic letter schema
Step 5: Kinetic hand movements	
Step 6: Graphic motor schemas	Graphic motor schemas

Stages 1, 2, and 3 of Chart 4.1 pertain to spoken language as well as to written forms. For the actual production of text, Step 1 of the Handwriting Sequence begins the process that relates directly and exclusively to writing. For the beginning writer at this level there is a learned association between sound and an arbitrary graphic symbol. Step 2 involves a reinforced sound/symbol correspondence. At Step 3 beginning writers picture the shapes of individual letters or of entire words. These first three steps apply only to beginning writers; Step 4 applies to experienced writers, too. For both groups this step involves the production of learned chunks (letters or words) which have been stored as engrams. Step 5 returns again to the beginning writer, who traces out letter/word shapes as a mnemonic aid.

Step 6, the last neurological sequence in the development of a writer's physical eloquence, applies to both groups when they physiologically produce letters and words.

As the beginning writer becomes more experienced, these six steps will condense into a shorter, more efficient, and neurologically more powerful system for producing a text. But this power and efficiency depend crucially on practice, on the writer's willingness and opportunity to encode the neurophysiology of writing. Other factors may further hinder the writer's chances of success. As many researchers have noted, the ability to write depends on the mastery of other language abilities, especially the visual melody of reading but also the auditory melodies of speaking and listening. For instance, a writer who cannot read well normally lacks the ability to spell accurately. Since the visual aspects of text production do not reinforce the kinetic melody, writing becomes a painstaking activity of sorting out shapes and meanings. Similarly, a person who is born deaf finds the correspondence between graphemes and sounds a baffling puzzle. Even some people who are extreme stutterers will experience difficulty in matching written forms to spoken words.[1]

The study of brain-damaged patients who have lost the ability to write—a condition called *agraphia*—provides further insight into just how delicate and complex a task writing is. As I will discuss in a later chapter, lesions in widely different parts of the brain can result in agraphia; and remarkably, the same form of writing loss, say lack of a spatial sense for letters, can develop from widely separated brain lesions.

Experiments with "normal" subjects have also underscored the fragile process of writing. If the visual feedback of our handwriting is delayed six seconds, errors significantly increase (Van Bergejik and David 1959). Even slight adjustments in the air we breathe can make our handwriting falter (Davis and Davis 1939). As Norman Geschwind explains:

> It is possible that writing is readily disturbed because it depends on so many components (motor, praxic, visuo-spatial, as well as kinetic and linguistic). Furthermore, most normal humans exercise their speaking abilities and comprehension of spoken language constantly. Many people, although fewer, exercise their reading comprehension abilities very extensively. It is, however, only a minute fraction of the population, even among the highly educated, who use their writing abilities extensively. (1974c, 495)

For the overwhelming majority of people, writing is not an easily managed or frequently practiced activity. Certainly a prominent sign of this difficulty, perhaps the most "basic" sign, is a writer's control of graphic forms. Although relatively few college students exhibit serious problems in their handwriting or spelling, these aspects of graphic form do often coincide with other evidence of underdeveloped writing abilities. For that reason it is worthwhile to examine these topics in detail.

Handwriting

In her influential book *Errors and Expectations* (1977), Mina Shaughnessy devoted much of her first chapter to handwriting problems. As she explained, inexperienced writers are often "still struggling with basic motor mental coordinations that have long ago become unconscious for more practiced students. And as long as the so-called mechanical processes involved in writing are themselves highly conscious or even labored, the writer is not likely to have easy access to his thoughts" (p. 14). In lesser degrees, the same difficulties apply to many college students who are not typically regarded as "basic writers." In other words, the ability to generate prose form is not itself sufficient to demonstrate *mastery* of that ability. As with all aspects of writing, there are stages of development, and even some otherwise capable writers may not handwrite efficiently.

Since the early 1900s, researchers have analyzed the graphic form of students' writing. In these studies the handwriting variables most often considered have been letter proportion, size, slant, formation, spacing, stroke, alignment, and the speed of text production (Wright and Allen 1975). Despite some inevitable problems with research designs and the comparability of results (Dremen 1977), there are a few general findings from handwriting research worth noting.

In a very limited manner, handwriting opens a neurological window to the mind. For instance, psychiatrists can isolate some very general personality traits (most often assertiveness) in handwriting samples (DuPasquier 1974); moreover, trained graphologists can reliably identify persons from evidence of their penmanship (Alexander 1977). Related studies have demonstrated that signature size often corresponds to social status, with doctors, lawyers, and other highly paid professionals typically producing the largest signatures (Swanson and Price 1972).

Although these results have no legitimate application to the writing classroom, they do help substantiate at least one finding that teachers should be aware of. When teachers grade writing, they tend to assign higher marks to students who write neatly versus those students whose writing is of equal quality except that the handwriting is difficult to read. This bias holds even when teachers are instructed to exclude neatness from their grading criteria (Marshall and Powers 1969). Moreover, graders who are themselves neat writers will assign high marks to essays they think look neat, and they will assign low grades to writing that appears aesthetically less pleasing. On the other hand, messy writers grade more fairly than neat writers (Huck and Bounds 1972).

In considering these results, it is important to note the differences between handwriting production and its conventions. For the latter, a teacher can easily identify and correct errors: *house* must include the sequence of letters *h-o-u-s-e* and not *h-a-w-s*. But it is neither right nor wrong to produce slanted writing, big letters, cursive script, and so on, provided of course that these graphic shapes conform to handwriting conventions. In this regard the neatness of a writer's handwriting, a production variable, may become a convention error if the form produced is unreadable.

Other differences separate handwriting production from its conventions. In recent decades neurolinguists have discovered the importance of the non-dominant (usually right) cerebral hemisphere for language functions. In an excellent review of hemisphericity, Janet Emig proposes several ways the right hemisphere may contribute to writing. Among many possibilities noted in "Writing as a Mode of Learning" (1977), she stresses our sense of a word's appropriateness and intuitions about an unusual meaning; sudden gestalts for expressing a difficult idea; flashes of prose images, and so on. However, she cautions that English script may have misled some neurolinguists into considering only the left hemisphere when studying the brain and language. Emig bases this caveat on the sequential nature of English script. Because sequence is a left hemisphere function, researchers like Karl Lashley (1929) and Aleksandr Luria (1973) have encouraged the misleading interpretation that all text production occurs in the left hemisphere. Not until the late 1960s was this view challenged by Joseph Bogen in his three-part article "The Other Side of the Brain" (1969), and subsequently confirmed by Eran Zaidel a decade later ("Concepts of Cerebral Dominance in the Split Brain," 1977).

In a more recent series of articles (1987-88), Andre Lecours and numerous colleagues in Canada, France, and Brazil have studied the cerebral representation of language among normal people who are literate and among two groups of illiterates, those who are also normal and those who have language disorders as a result of brain damage. Although the left hemisphere typically dominates for language in all people, literate or illiterate, Lecours and his colleagues have found a more diffuse representation of language among illiterates, especially in the right hemisphere. They caution, however, that education and related "socio-historical factors" can explain only some of the greater left hemisphere asymmetry of literate people.

Indeed, for a complex neurological activity like writing, both hemispheres play important roles, as is clearly demonstrated by the sequential nature of handwriting. The left to right movement of English handwriting requires a spatial control that invokes the motor functions of both hemispheres. Also, as a beginning writer carefully shapes letters between lines, this activity will be accompanied by the visual and auditory melodies that reinforce text production. Although located primarily in the left hemisphere, these melodies of the eye and ear have distinct characteristics often associated with one or the other hemisphere.

Although it is impossible to locate precisely where these melodies form, neurolinguists have identified *cognitive styles* that correspond to hemispheric functions. The auditory melody of hearing is an holistic task, comparable to the cognitive style of the right hemisphere, whereas the visual melody of sight permits us to fixate on something, to analyze it carefully. In this regard, looking at something carefully for details is a cognitive style of the left hemisphere.

Efficient handwriting can be defined as the combination of these left and right cognitive styles. This means:

1. A writer can fixate on a written image by invoking the analytic talents of the left hemisphere (LH).

2. Handwriting conventions require this visual attention to form; as a consequence, the writing act becomes, in contrast to speech, a special mode of language characterized by (potentially) slow, careful editing (LH).

3. Handwriting also permits auditory attention to form, a right hemisphere function when rhythmic shape rather than edited meaning is the purpose of subvocal feedback (RH).

4. After spoken elements are reintroduced into the production of prose, the experienced writer's handwriting becomes automatic (LH and RH), unless there is an overriding need to edit the form.

Having outlined these four aspects of skilled handwriting, I will examine each below in samples of college students' writing produced from 1974 to 1984 at the University of California and the University of Maryland. Over two thousand samples were selected at random from forty thousand placement essays written in forty minutes. Each student's writing was contained in a single test booklet, so I was able to note differences, if any, between drafts.

Initially I assumed that skilled writers would exhibit a form of handwriting that differed from unskilled writers, but the evidence did not fully support that assumption. Instead, one subgroup of the population clearly demonstrated this difference, while other subgroups exhibited basic similarities.

Among the handwriting variables that I examined were slantedness, repairs (e.g., cross-outs), type of script (e.g., manuscript or block letters versus cursive or continuous letters), and size. Of these four categories, only the last two—type and size of handwriting—were significant.

Manuscript versus Cursive Handwriting:

Most children first learn to print, and only at age seven or eight are they introduced to cursive script. Considering how infrequently students actually write, the neurological encoding of the writing task is undoubtedly fragile, subject to breakdown or perhaps even significant loss. We may predict, therefore, that some college writers will have regressed to an earlier stage of writing production, a stage characterized by the exclusive or primary use of printed letters. Other, more capable writers will use only cursive because it allows them to generate ideas more quickly in written form (Early 1976). Still other students will switch between these forms of handwriting, perhaps to adjust the speed of text production or merely as an uncontrolled means of generating a text.

To classify these forms of handwriting, I labelled an essay as cursive if more than 60 percent of the letters were conjoined. If 40 percent or fewer of the letters ran together, I considered the handwriting to be manuscript (printed). Anything that fell between the 60 percent and 40 percent range was classified as a mixed form. However, since fewer than 2 percent of the students routinely alternated between half cursive and half manuscript, I have not included this mixed category in my results.

My prediction about the use of manuscript or cursive establishes that speed of text production should match writing ability: the faster a student writes, the more likely it is that the student writes well. In other words, the less capable writers will favor manuscript for its relatively low speed of production. In neurological terms, their prose is interrupted by the time it takes to lift a pen from the page, whereas in cursive the tracing of letters is more continuous (Early 1976). This variable pace of text production determines the writer's congruence with the relatively fast speed of ideation, a speed that is normally adjusted to the quick production of speech. The use of manuscript or the incompetent use of cursive becomes a serious disadvantage for the less capable writer, who not only struggles to generate written form but also must compensate for the differences in fast ideational speed versus slow production speed.

Of the students who do not write well, 30.5 percent rely on manuscript; by contrast, of the capable writers, 19.5 percent used this form. When these results are further analyzed according to students' gender, males constitute nearly two-thirds (64 percent) of the less capable writers who use manuscript. On the other hand, gender is not a significant factor among the more capable writers using manuscript.

From these results it appears that male students who are not capable writers will frequently write in manuscript. All other students use a form of handwriting that has no clear relationship to their writing abilities, although it appears that neatness may explain why some capable writers would use manuscript.

Handwriting Size:

When capable writers are compared to students of less ability, both groups average about 7.5 words per line. However, the capable writers compress their handwriting to produce longer words averaging six letters, as opposed to the script of the other students which averages only four letters a word. As these figures suggest, the handwriting size of both groups differs notably.

For the less capable writers a large script may serve two visual purposes. It visually assists in demonstrating completion of the writing task, as if the presence of words on a page—regardless of their meaning—signals a completed task. Also, these writers may have less to say than other students, so the size of their handwriting compensates for the paucity of their ideas.

Another reason for large handwriting is the kinetic shaping of letters that a student does not feel comfortable producing. This discomfort also becomes easier to manage as the speed of writing slows. In both instances a student provides maximum opportunities for checking and maintaining the accuracy of text production. Even the auditory melody may be invoked as students subvocalize letters and words that they are handwriting.

Spelling

Like handwriting, spelling provides a useful measure of the neuro-physiology of writing. In particular, spelling errors graphically depict the three melodies of text production. The kinetic melody is apparent in reversed letters and similar disruptions of normal word patterns. The visual melody guides the interchangeable use of words with similar spellings but divergent meanings and pronunciations. The auditory melody can also be used inappropriately so that speech directs misspellings.

Unfortunately, most studies of spelling focus on the problems of children. As Jeanne Ormrod has remarked, "Surprisingly little research related to spelling ability and spelling achievement has been conducted at the university level" (1986, 160). For that reason I will not refer to existing research on "normal" spelling, except where comparison between young children and college students is clearly warranted. However, I do want to note briefly here one aspect of "abnormal" spelling disorders that applies directly to adults.

In recent neurolinguistic studies of spelling, researchers have diagrammed the spelling process so that auditory and visual melodies are regulated by an orthographic buffer. According to Argye Hillis and Alfonso Caramazza (1989), if this buffer, or switching device, becomes damaged, a patient suffers a disruption of "attentional mechanisms" to different forms of written language. For instance, Rhonda Friedman and Michael Alexander (1989) have found that a writer may completely lose the ability to recognize correct visual forms while still preserving the ability to spell correctly aloud.

These findings suggest a close parallel between the graphemic buffer and a "normal" writer's attempts to spell by coordinating the kinetic, visual, and auditory melodies. Obviously this coordination—or physical eloquence—is not easily achieved, so it may be more appropriate to imagine numerous buffers and interconnected switches that regulate the physical activity of writing. Extending neurological evidence this way is entirely consistent with the goals of researchers like Karalyn Patterson and Alan Wing, who note that "neurological patients with writing disorders inform us about the components necessary for a process model of writing and spelling skills" (1989, 1).

As a simple measure of their spelling problems, I have divided college writers into six categories that correspond to their writing ability, beginning with the least capable writers. It is also pertinent to emphasize that spelling was not a specific category that a reader noted when evaluating an essay. Instead, all the essays were judged holistically by independent readers who were asked to gauge a writer's overall ability. I then used those ratings to group writers for purposes of analyzing their spelling.

Type One Errors:

Not surprisingly, writers of the lowest ability do not transcode well from phoneme to grapheme. Ten percent of all writers who were classified at the bottom for ability made these type of errors. Although these students made nearly all other types of spelling errors, they uniquely produced those errors classified as Type One. A representative sample of these misspellings follows:

dicusted	(disgusted)	welled	(welded)
apllys	(apples)	fitious	(vicious)
intransing	(interesting)	bight	(bite)
fammon	(famine)	achomplished	(accomplished)
bacically	(basically)	file	(fill)

Significantly, 69 percent of these Type One errors are written in manuscript, a result that strengthens the importance of handwriting as a diagnostic measure of writing ability. Or to phrase this point in terms of text production, a writer's kinetic melody can be so poorly developed that it will dominate the task of writing. In this regard, 60 percent of the Type One errors occur near the beginning or middle of words. This incipient breakdown of form suggests a corresponding problem with the visual melody, as if a student can edit only the end of words because so much attention is focused initially on the kinetic difficulties of producing them. Also, the shorter Anglo-Saxon-based vocabulary poses as much of a problem for these students as polysyllabic Latinate or Romance vocabulary; each comprises about half the Type One spelling errors.

The wide distribution of these errors across many linguistic categories, their iterative frequency and problematic interpretation, belies the claim, often made by writing teachers, that spelling errors are trivial. Indeed, some types of errors may be insignificant, but these Type One spelling errors are better understood as representing a writer's fundamental difficulties in generating a text.

Type Two Errors:

These errors also characterize writers of limited writing ability, in this case, a slightly better group representing seven percent of all writers. Their marginal superiority can be established by classification, at least in terms of spelling, because they do not produce Type One errors. Thus each level of classification excludes errors from the preceding one but encompasses all subsequent types of errors.

Students producing Type Two errors will conflate graphemes by confusing similar words or their parts; that is, they will generalize features of one word as being appropriate for others. Some examples of these errors follow, with an accompanying analysis of their causes:

reasponsible	(responsible/*rea*son)	degry	(degree/sala*ry*)
intereaction	(interaction/*rea*ction)	mediochre	(mediocre/*ochre*)
earasing	(erase/*ear*)	chemicles	(chemicals/pick*les*)
courently	(currently/*cou*rage)		

Since these errors occur as often in cursive script as in manuscript handwriting, and since they are equally distributed through initial, medial, and final word positions, a disruption of the kinetic melody does not appear to be the problem. Instead, these writers are apparently reaching beyond their visual and auditory competence to use a largely Romance-based vocabulary that is identified with a formal style of writing (or an *elaborated style*, a term Bernstein proposed in "Elaborated and Restricted Codes," 1971).

The word *mediochre* demonstrates this attempt for greater sophistication that becomes an exotic spelling with the hard *ch*. This student's error reveals a knowledge of variant ways to spell a voiceless velar stop (*k, c, ch, ck*) as well as the British *re* reversal of *er*. Given the student's effort to choose a sophisticated word and to spell it in a logical manner, the mistaken spelling should be regarded as a "good" error, if only because it confirms development of the visual and auditory melodies.

Type Three Errors:

About 12 percent of all writers misspell words by adding extra letters, and half of these errors are improperly doubled consonants. The other half are redundant or conflated forms, usually two words that are fused to convey a single idea or two sounds that are improperly expressed by two letters. In both cases, these Type Three errors typically occur at the middle or end of words, with more than 72 percent of these misspelled words having a Latinate derivation.

Like Type Two errors, these misspellings have no apparent relationship to the kinetic melody of producing them. In this regard, Type Three errors are as likely to occur in cursive as manuscript. The doubling of some letters might be interpreted as a handwriting error, but that interpretation would depend on the random occurrence of these duplicated forms. By contrast, Type Three errors are highly systematic in that they are frequently repeated by the same writers. Many are also obvious examples of misapplied spelling rules. Some representative Type Three errors are shown below:

candidatency	(candidate fused with candidacy)
successfuld	(inflected adjective from verb to succeed)
exscused	(phonologically accurate / s/)
flant	(nasalized vowel for the word flat)
envioronment	(extra syllable from mispronunciation)
becomming	(analogy to swimming)
begginners	(analogy to beggars)
accelleration	(analogy to excellence)

The first two examples reveal an auditory confusion of forms that results in an accurate if also mistaken visual shape. The writer has heard the word candidate and knows it has an abstracted, agentless variant, but does not know for certain how this variant is said or spelled. A similar though more egregious error occurs in the transfer of an inflected past-tense ending from the irregular verb *to succeed* to its adjectival form. The resulting word *successfuld* probably would not be used in speech, which suggests that the writer has relied entirely on a visual melody of text production.

The auditory melody appears to have dominated the next two errors, as the writer hears sounds in *excused* and *flat* that prompt misspellings. The pronunciation of *environment* is a closely related problem since the writer either does not know the word's correct pronunciation and therefore adds an extra syllable, or, like most people, the writer says this word with fewer syllables than its written form requires, and realizing this difference, he then overcompensates by inserting the troublesome *o* in two places.

The remaining examples depict a visual confusion about the doubling of consonants. Since the rules governing these forms are sometimes inconsistent and often difficult to remember, they can lead to errors that we might best regard as trivial. The other instances of Type Three errors are more serious because they indicate potentially significant disruptions of the visual and auditory melodies. A student who relies too often on spoken language to generate spellings will most likely transfer a wide range of other inappropriate features from speech to prose. Even more problematic is the opposite dependence on visual cues to producing form without an auditory "inner voice" to monitor them.

Type Four Errors:

Among the final developmental stages of children's writing is their ability to recognize backwards images (Gibson 1965). Although few college writers are appropriately compared to these children, at least 18 percent of the writers in this study did produce spelling errors that suggested a breakdown in the visual melody of constructing words. Among this group of students, undoubtedly some may have a mild form of strephosymbolia, or even a more severe problem with dyslexia (Dinklage 1971). But when most students misspell, it is likely that they make reversal errors of a nonpathological sort. Carelessness or haste may explain some of these "normal" mistakes, as will a student's confusion about how to spell certain words. When these reversals persist, however, we must consider among the nonpathological causes of this problem the student's lack of experience as a writer.

In this regard, fewer than five percent of the Type Four errors are made by accomplished writers, and their mistakes are rarely repeated. By contrast, the least capable writers comprise nearly 60 percent of those students who make Type Four errors, and they routinely produce the same reversal errors. Some typical reversals are listed below:

phyiscal	beigns
buisness	perscribe
gaurd	techincal
marraige	certian
owerneship	preformances
asile	complusion

Except for *owerneship* all these examples involve two adjacent letters, suggesting that students are having their biggest difficulties within syllables or between syllable boundaries. Transposed vowels in diphthongs, as occurs in *gaurd* and *marraige*, are perhaps the least significant of these spelling errors because the combined sound of the vowels can lack any correspondence to the sound of each vowel used independently. In this respect the auditory melody offers no help for spelling, especially if one of the vowels is "silent."

Another apparently minor spelling error involves the reversal of prefixes, for instance, when a student switches *per-* and *pre-* in *preformances* and *perscribe*. Despite the simple substitution of like forms, the frequent occurrence of this error does signal a potentially major disruption of the visual and auditory melodies since the writer may not be hearing the reversal or seeing its individual parts.

Probably the most serious Type Four error breaks (or adds to) the normal syllable boundary of a word. This problem occurs in *aisle* and most notably in *beings*, leaving a reader with a visual puzzle that contextual clues do not always resolve. Since 65 percent of Type Four errors are found in the middle of words, this location also implies a fundamental problem with word roots rather than affixes. The Latinate derivation of these root words further suggests an undeveloped sense for "elaborated" writing.

Although handwriting is not a significant factor in Type Four errors, the kinetic melody may nevertheless be important for students who are reaching beyond their competence to produce new or unfamiliar words. In this sense reversals show the stress or awkwardness of students as they generate new forms. In any case, the visual and auditory melodies that underlie these errors indicate a writer's developmental status.

Type Five Errors:

Students of all but the highest ability will delete letters and sometimes whole morphemes, writing words that have a compressed form. This problem admits several explanations, carelessness and haste being the most obvious reasons for deleted parts of words. In other cases the reasons could be attributed to a dysfunction of any of the melodies. Indeed the scope of explanations must embrace the wide-ranging occurrence of Type Five errors throughout ability levels. Some examples of these errors follow:

more throughly	(thoroughly)	conviences	(conveniences)
inabiliy	(inability)	diaster	(disaster)
deam	(dream)	possibilites	(possibilities)
fatasy	(fantasy)	critism	(criticism)
tak	(take)	strugges	(struggles)
thes	(these)	wich	(which)
nubers	(numbers)	rase	(raise)
discoved	(discovered)	attude	(attitude)
advnage	(advantage)	cites	(cities)

Most Type Five errors (70 percent) involve Latinate words, and most (62 percent) are written in cursive script. These results show the presence of more accomplished writers, whose errors I generally dismiss as being trivial. More significant errors are made by the less capable writers, who almost exclusively produce the letter deletions in one-syllable words. The auditory melody appears most often to cause these monosyllable errors, especially when students spell *wich* and *rase* as these words might be pronounced.

Like Type Four errors, about 81 percent of Type Five errors occur in medial or final positions of words. But unlike most Type Four reversals, these deletion mistakes rarely impede a reader's effort to recognize the correct (or intended) form. Only when a word-final vowel is deleted, as in *tak*, does a Type Five error seriously disrupt a reading, perhaps because the unfinished form allows so many alternate readings (*talk, tack, tank, take*). Even when context rules out these alternatives, a reader must question the writer's ability to control the visual melody of spelling, especially if these errors are repeated. Not surprisingly, all one-syllable errors of this type are made by the least capable writers.

Type Six Errors:

In these misspellings students extend the loops of letters, usually *n, m, u,* or *w*. Very few students make Type Six errors, and among the five percent who do, the distribution from skilled to unskilled writers is almost even. Extended loopings are, in terms of the kinetic melody of producing them, closely related to insertions (Type Four errors) and deletions (Type Five errors), but unlike these related mistakes, Type Six errors have no apparent relationship to the auditory melody of "hearing" them. And since these errors almost never appear twice, they have only a slight significance for the visual melody of editing them. Like many Type Five errors, they are probably best explained as the product of careless handwriting. Some examples follow:

mapsacks	(napsacks)
mearly	(nearly)
im	(in)
begimming	(beginning)
amswwered	(answered)

Since students of all writing abilities produced these looping errors, and since they occur so infrequently, I have dismissed them as being unimportant. Of course, if a student repeatedly made these looping errors, then it would be imperative for a teacher to investigate what may be a pathological problem of text production.

Summary of Results

These six categories of spelling errors comprise an ascending order of writing sophistication and a descending order of exclusive categories. In other words, the least capable writers will produce all six categories of errors, and they will produce the highest percentage of errors in each category; by contrast, the most capable writers will make relatively few spelling errors, and their mistakes will be limited to the last two categories.

These results could be stated to support a misleading generalization that good writers will make fewer spelling errors than poor writers. That claim misleads to the extent that all spelling errors are considered to be equally important; but the evidence I have reviewed suggests that writers of different abilities will produce up to six categories of spelling errors, and within each category these writers can be further identified by specific disruptions of the kinetic, visual, and auditory melodies. Depending on the nature of these problems, even a few examples of spelling errors can indicate fundamental differences among writers that correspond to their writing abilities.

When the neurological melodies do not coalesce, as Chart 4.2 shows, a writer will produce a text that lacks some element of physical eloquence. For all three melodies to function appropriately, a student's auditory melody must develop from a strong reliance on spoken English to a more sophisticated awareness of the student's "inner voice" as it corresponds to written language. More sophisticated visual and kinetic melodies follow from this initial auditory (Type 1) development.

Chart 4.2: **Developmental Stages of Spelling Errors**

Spelling Errors	Example	Neurological Melody	Essay Rating
Type 1: (phoneme/ grapheme correspon- dence)	beleev	auditory, visual kinetic	6 (lowest writing ability)
Type 2: (conflated grapheme schemas)	beleave belive	visual, auditory	6,5
Type 3: (grapheme insertions)	bellieve	visual, auditory	6, 5, 4, 3
Type 4: (grapheme reversals)	beleive	visual, kinetic	6, 5, 4, 3, 2
Type 5: (grapheme reductions)	beleve	kinetic, visual	6, 5, 4, 3, 2, 1
Type 6: extra loopings)	bellieve beelieve	kinetic, visual	6, 5, 4, 3, 2, 1

Students who produce Type One and Type Two spelling errors rely far too much on the Anglo-Saxon vocabulary of ordinary speech as it carries over into their prose. When these students try to introduce more formal, polysyllabic, often Latinate vocabulary into their writing, it not only "sounds" wrong, but it also betrays their legitimate goal of achieving greater sophistication.

Despite the sometimes egregious nature of these errors, a teacher should recognize them as signs of progress that deserve no penalty. Just as important, all three melodies must be taught together if students are to improve further. For instance, even the best intended efforts to make students "see" all their mistakes will necessarily fail because the underlying problem is not always visual (e.g., Types 1, 5, and 6 in Chart 4.2). Having students memorize spelling rules or asking them to identify misspelled words addresses only one neurological melody, as if visual recognition of forms can be an adequate substitute for producing and hearing these forms.

Type One and Type Two errors, of course, are sometimes caused by a disruption of the visual melody, a problem that can be easily identified when a student routinely misspells any part of a word—beginning, middle, end. Lacking a visual vocabulary for most Latinate words, the same student will generalize from a few well-known words to produce others that are unfamiliar to him.

The kinetic melody of handwriting is the final cause of Type One and Two errors. Manuscript, which is normally learned before cursive script, predominates among male students who are also inexperienced writers. This use of manuscript has a developmental basis in that a rarely practiced writing ability will remain constant or will regress to its earliest stages. By contrast, few accomplished writers used manuscript, and those who did probably chose it for neatness.

At a somewhat higher developmental stage we can find another group of students who will not make Type One errors (students at each level will misspell words in all subsequent categories). Unlike students at the lowest level of ability, these writers do not use manuscript often and do not exhibit any obvious problems with the kinetic melody of text production. However, they do make errors that clearly show disruptions of the other two melodies.

Perhaps because these students neither read nor write often, their visual vocabulary includes only enough Latinate forms for imprecise guesswork when they spell unfamiliar words. These students also seem to generalize from a few spelling rules like doubling certain consonants or placing *i* before *e* in order to spell all Latinate words. Type Three errors are the result.

The next developmental stage includes the reversals of Type Four errors. A majority of writers, save the most capable ones, make these errors. In contrast to the prior stages, students who make only Type Four errors (or subsequent types) appear to know the affixes and root derivations of most words. As a result, they do not repeatedly confuse similar spellings or overgeneralize the spelling patterns of words they know. Their mistakes are, instead, a matter of arranging the right parts of a word in the wrong order.[2]

These reversals may also involve anticipation errors that are caused by a disruption of the kinetic and visual melodies. While the hand produces the graphic forms of a word, even a slight break in coordination with the visual recognition of these forms can lead a writer to reverse letters or, as happens with Type Five errors, the writer may ultimately delete them. These anticipation errors probably occur most often while a student is writing under stress, and since all the essays I examined were produced in class, I have not emphasized this problem.

Instead, I will reiterate my basic argument that students make Type

Four errors (and preceding ones) because they lack experience as writers. This inexperience creates difficulties as students attempt to coordinate the three melodies. Only as they develop this coordination through constant practice will they achieve the physical eloquence of a mature writer.

In the penultimate stage, good and bad writers reduce words by leaving out certain parts. Of course, a writer's anticipation of a specific form may account for some of these errors, as will carelessness and haste. These explanations are best reserved for the more accomplished writers.

Among the less capable students who produce Type Five errors, the causes for these mistakes are undoubtedly varied. Some of these students may have learned to spell a word up to something like a neurological blank spot, a point at which they routinely stop. In this way part of the word is always spelled correctly.

For other students Type Five errors may result from incorrect visualizations of a word. For instance, the mind's eye of a writer sees a *believ* rather than *believe*. The same spelling could be analyzed as a Type One error if the student, not "hearing" the silent *e* of *believe*, wrote the word as it sounded. Thus, Type One errors result from a student's acquired knowledge of speech, whereas Type Five errors exhibit a separate knowledge of written shapes.

The final stage of development includes Type Six errors (extra loopings), which returns us to the kinetic melody of handwriting. The simple fact of finding these errors among the most capable writers, indeed, among writers of all other abilities, demonstrates the physical demands imposed by text production. Although these looping errors are not significant indices of writing ability, they do show the persistent difficulties and neurological complexities of physical eloquence. In other words, even the best writers will make these mistakes.

As Chart 4.2 shows, to achieve physical eloquence a writer must control three neurological melodies: all but the worst college writers will begin with an auditory melody (spoken language); as these students develop in writing ability, they will rely on a visual melody (encoded graphemes); and when they have progressed to physical eloquence, the most accomplished writers will balance kinetic, visual, and auditory melodies in complementary positions as they generate a text.

Chart 4.2 also presents one word, *believe*, to show the writing stages that can precede its proper neurological encoding as an engram. At the early stages of writing achievement, students may write *beleev* because the word sounds this way.

The next level of error is *beleave*, which has two explanations: (1) *-leave* is the same as the verb *to leave*, so by analogy to this root word students could anticipate the same spelling joined to the prefix *be-*; (2) a more likely explanation is that students know the word's second syllable has two vowels, yet because the students cannot remember what these vowels are, they guess that *ea* is the correct form.

At the next developmental level students will write *bellieve*, an error that has three interpretations. Some students may double the *l* by analogy to another word like *college* or *bell*. Others may insert an extra *l* by misapplying a spelling rule for doubling consonants. Still other students may have carelessly generated an extra loop (a Type 6 error).

For *beleve* (Type 2) or *belive* (Type 5) there can also be three readings. Students may presume that *e* or *i* can function in this word to represent the vowel sound of the second syllable. Others may have remembered equivalent sounds in others words (e.g., *Eve*) and overgeneralize from that word to spell *beleve*. Or some students may have accidentally omitted the *i* or *e*.

The last two spellings in Chart 4.2 are probably due to reversal and reduction, in that order. Of course, all the misspelled words in this chart can be explained in other ways. For instance, a student's dialect or a teacher's mistakes are among other explanations that I have chosen not to discuss because these sources of errors are idiosyncratic, and clearly redundant to my purposes of showing the neurophysiology of writing.

Conclusion:

In handwriting and spelling, a writer's physical eloquence is shown through his or her control of hand, eye, and ear. The next two chapters continue this discussion of physical eloquence by examining other physiological signs of writing ability, starting with punctuation, in order to demonstrate the biological relationships between rhetorical delivery, memory, and style. In each case, a similar pattern of development emerges as stages of writing ability correspond to a writer's control of all three neurological functions.

Without initially looking for a specific pattern of development, I have consistently found six levels of writing ability; indeed, regardless of empirical evidence, the neurological functions of hand, eye, and ear must necessarily fall into these six permutations:

kinetic, visual, auditory	kinetic, auditory, visual
visual, kinetic, auditory	visual, auditory, kinetic
auditory, kinetic, visual	auditory, visual, kinetic

These permutations also parallel the six steps of text production that are listed in Chart 4.1 for handwriting and Chart 4.2 for spelling.

Based on these findings, I can define rhetorical delivery as normally expressing one of these six possibilities; a writer's "memory" of prose can also be defined as the cumulative knowledge of as many combinations as a writer has previously delivered. Similarly, a writer's neurological style potentially develops in six stages prior to the condensed, unitary form of physical eloquence.

The exact sequence for these stages of development will vary, of course, among individuals; college students will also exhibit greater mastery of the more advanced stages than one might anticipate for children and most other adults. Taking this variation into account, I will postpone to subsequent chapters a full discussion of developmental progress in college students' writing. At this point, however, I want to emphasize the biological limits to writing progress, at least among normal writers, limits that correspond to six ways a writer controls hand, eye, and ear.

Since the biology of writing also entails the partial failure or complete breakdown of neurological functions, the six possibilities for styles and their delivery are more than doubled in abnormal writing. Yet, before considering these dysfunctional uses of hand, eye, and ear, we should first establish the normal writer's memory—or subconscious ability—for using these functions in prose, and, among college students, the corresponding six (or fewer) stages of development they are most likely to exhibit.

5

Memory: A Biogrammar
of Speaking and Writing

Memory is what we retain by conscious effort or by subconscious processes that are seemingly effortless. An example of *conscious memory* would be rules of punctuation that are learned by careful study or, lacking immediate recall, any rules that we might feel compelled to find in a usage handbook. In this regard a handbook becomes a displaced storage for rules that we must remember to consult.

Internalized rules, or any forms of language that we produce without thinking about them, comprise the *biogrammar* of our memory. In this chapter I will be concerned foremost with a writer's subconscious recall from this biogrammar. Since much of what we write emanates from the subconscious, the teaching of writing is largely an effort to expand a student's biogrammar so that a more sophisticated memory will underlie subconscious recall.

Punctuation

Among many features of writing that a student may learn by memorization, rules of punctuation are especially troublesome because instruction in these rules usually ignores the biogrammar of speaking and writing. In effect, there are few punctuation rules that a student does not know in some basic sense subconsciously (Davies 1986); while this knowledge may not be expressed in the arbitrary symbols of prose, each student nevertheless understands the significance of pauses, interruptions, emphasis, closure, and other ways to punctuate speech.

These rules of spoken punctuation are never taught and never learned by conscious mnemonics. They are, instead, acquired by subconscious means and subject to immediate recall from the biogrammar. By the same means, and from the identical memory, a student can begin to punctuate most writing, provided that differences between speech and prose are not ultimately obscured.

For instance, George Dillon (1976) has shown that clause length in speech often coincides with a speaker's pauses. Although these pauses vary by occasion and speaker, an invariable constraint on all speech is the speaker's requirement to breathe, and pauses allow this vital physiological activity. Clause length in writing becomes a special problem when students punctuate entirely as they would pause in speech; sentence fragments are one consequence. Conversely, if students write without any allowance for the constraints of breathing, the length of their clauses can extend well beyond tolerable limits; the inflated prose of bureaucratese is a predictable outcome.

Too often the teaching of punctuation fails because students are misled to believe that spoken language can guide their efforts to punctuate correctly. To some extent, of course, speech can provide a model for students to follow, but because this model subordinates writing it obscures two fundamental relationships between speech and prose: (1) it implies that writing is a secondary system derived from speech, whereas both speech and prose are secondarily derived from the primary biogrammar; and (2) it suggests that writing can be mastered by conscious means through direct imitation of speech, whereas both forms of language are best assimilated indirectly and spontaneously by the subconscious.

Barring common but misleading forms of instruction, students will develop the ability to punctuate correctly; indeed, they need only one contribution from their teachers: the opportunity to make punctuation a part of the biogrammar. The same goal can be expressed in neurological terms as the kinetic, visual, and auditory melodies operating together as they guide a student's writing. For punctuation, this concerted effort becomes a single rhythm within each melody: the kinetic rhythm of pace, the visual rhythm of symmetry, and the auditory rhythm of emphasis.

Like rhetorical releasers, each rhythm expresses an automatic signal that is subconsciously released by a writer. These signals have a largely subconscious effect on the reader, an effect that corresponds to time (space), size (symmetry), and weight or gravity of significance (emphasis). Of course, both reader and writer can achieve these ends through deliberate and conscious effort, particularly when a writer has achieved the physical eloquence to manipulate these signals and a reader has developed the critical abilities to interpret them. But few college students have achieved this sophistication for either interpreting or embellishing prose. In this respect, the rhetorical signals that most students send are naively delivered and uncritically received.

The kinetic rhythm of pace perhaps most clearly demonstrates this naiveté. As students punctuate their clauses, they establish for the reader an implied speed of interpretation. Long distances between punctuation marks will encourage a reader to read quickly. Short, abrupt, frequently interrupted phrases and clauses will tend to slow down the pace of interpretation. The writer's own speed of producing a text becomes a factor, too, as the pauses signaled by punctuation correspond to the writer's original flow of ideas. If the writer attunes the speed of writing to the speed of thinking, his prose will likely demonstrate that ideational pace. On the other hand, a writer who thinks at a speed that outruns the speed of writing will often omit key words and ideas. These thematic gaps can also be signaled by sentence fragments, generated as the most convenient way to punctuate the rapid flow of ideas.

Like the pace of kinetic rhythm, visual symmetry depends on size, signaled in different dimensions, for instance, as either layout or repetition. Layout entails line spacing, paragraphing, and headings for different sections, to mention just a few of the more obvious symmetries in a text. As these examples suggest, the "size" or shape of textual layout follows rigid conventions, and for that reason I will not consider it further. On the other hand, because repetition expresses the writer's own choices, it warrants further consideration.

A writer's repeated use of punctuation to signal clauses of the same length creates a pattern of expectation, and when this pattern is sharply disrupted, a reader will take notice to determine why the change has occurred. If it has no apparent justification, the reader may provide one arbitrarily or, as can easily happen, the reader may even begin to question the writer's competence.

The opposite problem arises when a writer is too repetitive. Aristotle expressly warned against too much repetition in writing since, among other problems, it signals the artifice of poetry (*Rhetoric Book III*). A text that repeatedly breaks into the same punctuated segments also conveys a writer's inability to arrange prose into other symmetrical patterns. By this absolute regularity it appears that one pattern is all that the writer can control.

Complicating this visual presentation is the paradoxical need to follow the absolute symmetry of writing conventions. To misuse a punctuation mark, a writer should be well prepared to justify this change; otherwise, the reader who expects absolute adherence to these conventions has no recourse but to challenge the writer's use of other punctuation marks.

That challenge can easily extend to the auditory representation of emphasis. A writer who stresses words by underlining them, or by using other punctuation devices like capitals, exclamation marks, inverted quotes, dashes, and so on, must adhere strictly to their conventional significance or risk signaling the wrong meaning. Being misunderstood results as well from too frequent emphasis, a strategy that dulls the reader's response to these signals.

Advising students to emphasize their important ideas, but not too often; telling them to keep their clauses in parallel structure, but not always; asking them to abide strictly within the conventional uses of punctuation, but admitting that accomplished writers will sometimes break these conventions—such advice and qualification really does not offer students much help. Fortunately, the biology of writing offers an alternative to formal training of students and the memorization of punctuation rules.

Above all, students must be taught the rhythms of producing, seeing, and hearing written language. One simple, enjoyable, and truly ancient means towards this objective is to have students read aloud. This technique not only helps students to hear prose—their own and other students'—but it also assimilates this sound as the students' inner voices. They begin to hear patterns of stress that correspond to patterns of meaning; they can also develop an intuitive understanding for the pace of a reader's interpretation. Antithesis, balance, and the visual symmetries of emphasizing ideas become auditory clues to understanding a writer's work. In short, all three neurological melodies coalesce in one teaching strategy.

To establish more fully the value of oral readings and to discuss at length the details of this teaching technique, for the remainder of this chapter I need to examine the critical role of the biogrammar as it underlies speaking and writing. I can then address in subsequent chapters how a writer's physical eloquence emerges from the subconscious memory of prose.

A Biogrammar of Speaking and Writing

In conventional theories of writing, speech is generally regarded as a primary system of language, with writing classified as a secondary system, derived from speech. Though accurate in a trivial sense, in other respects this classification needs to be revised: it lacks predictive value, it fails to explain common writing problems, and it may even obscure them.

As I briefly outline a biogrammar of speech and prose, my goal is to summarize information teachers should know about written language, about its origins and development within individuals, about the broader social and rhetorical contexts of its uses, and, of course, about its more narrowly defined linguistic features. Although aspects of this biogrammar may be suitable for teachers to present to students, that pedagogical function is neither necessary nor essential. Instead, its overriding utility is to explain *why* college students write as they do and to show *how* teachers can diagnose students' strengths and weaknesses in order to classify levels of writing ability.

Before discussing these uses, I want to consider first a widely accepted explanation for how someone successfully acquires a second language because, with a few adjustments, this explanation applies equally well to the acquisition of writing. Called the *Interlanguage Hypothesis*, it was first proposed in 1972 by Larry Selinker ("Interlanguage") for the study of second-language acquisition, and for composition research it has been adapted by David Bartholomae ("The Study of Error," 1980, and "Inventing the University," 1985), Eleanor Kutz ("Between Students' Language," 1986), and most recently by Alice Horning (*Teaching Writing as a Second Language*, 1987, 31-41). In much simplified form, the Interlanguage Hypothesis is depicted in Chart 5.1.

Chart 5.1: **Interlanguage Hypothesis**

Interlanguage

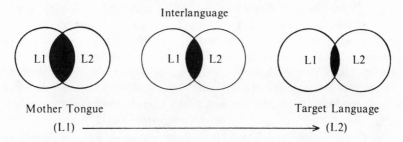

Mother Tongue   Target Language
(L1) ⟶ (L2)

The overlap (shaded area) between the Mother Tongue *(L1)* and the Target Language *(L2)* is *interlanguage*, which begins heavily influenced by *L1* but progressively approximates *L2*. At all stages of its development, interlanguage includes features that are identical in each language plus "new" forms that the learner generates independently of *L1* or *L2*. As the learner becomes more proficient in *L2*, interlanguage becomes relatively less important, though it may still persist in "fossilized" forms (e.g., when other features of *L2* are mastered, an *L1* accent may remain).

This model, with some adjustments, also explains the writing process. Speech serves a function that is similar to interlanguage, though we must qualify the model as it represents *L1* and *L2*. The pedagogical objective of someone learning to write should be a complete linkage between *L1* and *L2*. In writing, *L1* is propositional language, or ideas expressed in words that are largely free of syntactic relations, and *L2* equals the form of written language with all its organizational and syntactic complexities. Simply put, ideas become prose as the writer tries to join thought *(L1)* with form *(L2)*. Speech, as I will explain shortly, serves as the interlanguage of prose.

For someone learning a second language, *L1* already conveys ideas in the mother tongue, so the learner must block or otherwise ignore prior connections between ideas and *L1* in order to join thought with the new linguistic form of *L2*. Interlanguage assists the learner, serving as a temporary bridge between *L1* and *L2*, but its purpose has been fulfilled when the bridge is no longer needed.

In terms of the writing process though, the bridge must remain intact, an essential link between idea and linguistic form. Intermediate links are possible, and sometimes helpful, but only a direct span between *L1* (in this case ideas) and *L2* (prose form) will enable a person learning to write to achieve full competence as a writer.

In contrast to interlanguage, we could label this permanent bridge of the writing process *intralanguage*, though I have chosen the more common phrase *inner language* as it has been used by the Russian psychologists Lev Vygotsky in *Thought and Language* (1962) and Aleksandr Sokolov in *Inner Speech and Thought* (1972). Like these researchers and others in this country, notably Janet Emig in her 1977 article "Writing as a Mode of Learning," I am using this term to imply an irreducible form of language, a view that is currently labeled *foundational.* My usage therefore rejects an exclusively social definition of (inner) language, as Richard Rorty has argued for in his *anti-foundational* books *Consequences of Pragmatism* (1982) and *Philosophy and the Mirror of Nature* (1979).[2]

Unlike Rorty, and exponents of his views in writing research, especially Patricia Bizzell, I accept a foundational basis for language in the sense that linguistic form structures meaning. The neurological evidence for this position amounts to the fundamental distinction between language comprehension and its production. Although many other points could be cited to counter the anti-foundational position, not the least being the evidence for language universals, I will only note a few self-evident "facts" as support. Obviously I do not intend to provide here a full analysis of this complex and important topic; rather, my effort should serve only to demonstrate how an argument against anti-foundationalism might be constructed.

As Bizzell presents her case in the 1986 article "Foundationalism and Anti-Foundationalism in Composition Studies," the current approaches to writing research are "coming under a truly rhetorical theory of language and knowledge, one that sees all language-using practices as determined by social consensus" (p. 38). Significantly, after she disconnects the social uses of language from the biology of language and knowledge, Bizzell can putatively reject "absolute certainty... because the individual mind can never transcend personal emotions, social circumstances, and historical conditions" (p. 40).

Two questions arise from these assertions. Is not the anti-foundational view of rhetoric a type of certainty, one that encompasses "all language-using practices?" Implicit to this global assertion is the absolute rejection of biological constraints that would determine how language is used socially. And as a second, related question: Is the "individual mind" completely trapped by circumstances, *never* able to escape a solipsistic world that mirrors itself? Besides the unresolved paradox of this radical skepticism,[3] I would question the peculiar and singular allowance for social constraints as if the individual's mind did not rest atop a body.

Perhaps biological constraints—like the limitation that breathing imposes on the length of spoken utterances[4]—can be dismissed as something trivial that all speakers happen to share. But the same constraint has a rather important effect in writing, since it literally disappears, resulting in language uses that clearly differ from speech. I will discuss this effect in more detail later as it relates to the biogrammar. Presently I am only concerned with establishing the validity of a foundational view of language.

That validity depends, to the limited extent I have discussed it so far, on the meaning of certainty. Against Bizzell's assertion that the foundational position seeks "absolute certainty," a goal that no one can truly achieve, I would rephrase this objective to be approximate certainty, which is apparently what advocates of the opposite position must endorse. Indeed, as I have tried to show already, the anti-foundational perspective starts from two absolute premises: (1) the certainty of relative viewpoints, and (2) the social foundation of language uses. If these premises are based on some measure of certainty, then the rationale for anti-foundationalism begins to be ironically foundational.

In any case, the terms themselves already show the essential dependence of one viewpoint (the "anti-" perspective) on the prior existence of the other viewpoint. Perhaps it is sufficient here to establish that the practical goal of most research is to accomplish something. In some basic sense that accomplishment adjusts our understanding of the topic being studied. I have deliberately avoided saying that research improves our understanding of something, because of the positivism implied by that claim. Nevertheless, I will argue that most researchers try to achieve a level of confidence in whatever they are studying that is greater than preceding levels. Or to phrase this point negatively, few researchers are in the pursuit of ignorance.

As Kenneth Burke's well-known dictum reminds us, any way of seeing is a way of not seeing; yet any perspective, if one looks intensely enough, also leads to something else (1965). For instance, the anti-foundational perspective, because it embraces variant viewpoints, must theoretically include its foundational opposite. In any case, there is a way to achieve a balanced position approximately midway between them.

This balance can be achieved by recognizing the complementary duality of biological and social factors in language use. With social factors there is a lesser degree of certainty about language, but a greater allowance for the particular variant, the idiosyncratic option; conversely, with biological factors a researcher can with greater confidence find evidence that points to language universals, but this way of seeing necessarily misses related factors because it idealizes a single (exclusionary) point of view. The study of inner language demonstrates the tradeoffs of a largely biological perspective.

Inner language structures a writer's psychological flow of ideas, in whatever form that progression may take. This thinking process includes the ability we all have to understand something without necessarily being able to express it in written or spoken form. In this sense, inner language precedes linguistic expression and corresponds neurologically to Wernicke's area of the brain (the center of language comprehension).

To develop the inner language hypothesis more fully, I have divided it into four developmental stages that correspond to four levels of writing ability.

The Four Stages of Inner Language

Although it is fashionable now to presume that language is socially constituted and, therefore, that meaning is established through consensus, in my research I have adopted a more traditional position allowing for inherent, clearly biological bases for the production and interpretation of language. Thus, while I recognize the importance of social context in determining how a person will speak or write, underlying the speaker or writer's options is, I believe, a linguistic system that structures meaning and that anchors all discourse.

Notably at odds with composition researchers who assume a social definition of language, I have found consistent linguistic patterns in writing that correspond to levels of achievement.[5] These patterns hold regardless of a student's major or, to borrow a term popularized by Bizzell (1982), regardless of a student's "academic discourse community." In other words, the social contexts of different departments have had no significant effect on certain key linguistic features in students' writing. And these features are, as I will explain below, the basis for identifying four generic styles (or "registers") that correspond to four developmental stages of college writing.[6] They also clearly fit into a contrastive grammar of speech and prose.

My results can be summarized as follows. The first generic style is produced by students who are consistently identified by their instructors as being weak writers. To confirm this assessment, I had two independent readers judge writing samples without knowing how the samples had been previously evaluated. My results apply only to those texts where there was full consensus about the quality of a student's writing. I then analyzed the samples to determine what linguistic features, if any, they all shared.

For students who produce the first style, it is not surprising to find that speech apparently guides their efforts to generate prose. We need only observe children subvocalizing as they learn to write and this extreme dependence on speech, which may persist well beyond initial stages of learning to write, becomes obvious. Although recent research has shown that writers of any ability may subvocalize, the *amplitude* of this activity is greatest among beginning writers.[7] In this regard, for beginning writers to acquire the ability to write well they must go beyond the priority of spoken language.

As I have already defined it, inner language underlies speaking and writing. It encompasses them, too, as the following diagram shows:

Chart 5.2: **Four Stages of Inner Language in Writing**

	Stage One	**Two**	**Three**	**Four**
Primary Language System:	INNER LANGUAGE	INNER LANGUAGE	INNER LANGUAGE	INNER LANGUAGE
Secondary System:	SPEECH	SPEECH PROSE (Interlanguage)	PROSE	PROSE
Tertiary System:	PROSE			SPEECH
	Oral-Based Prose	Mixed Prose	Text-Based Prose	Spoken Prose

Stage One of inner language occurs first, in a developmental sense, as language acquisition. The link between inner language and speech then serves a beginning writer (or a developmental writer in college) as the combined system for generating ideas and for expressing them textually, in an *oral-based style*. In effect, the writer will "talk on paper." Stage Two elevates prose to the status of a secondary system that competes with speech for a direct link to inner language. One consequence is a *mixed style*, randomly comprised of features from speech and prose. A related consequence is interlanguage, marked by errors that cannot be attributed directly to either speech or prose, instead uniquely blending characteristics of each. When a writer develops beyond this form of interlanguage, Stage Three occurs, with a direct linkage between inner language and prose. Bypassing speech creates different problems, especially for readability, since a *text-based style* essentially ignores an audience. At the fourth and final stage a writer reintroduces speech as a complementary system of inner language and uses this system for its rich intonational and rhythmic qualities. The most distinctive quality of this *spoken style* is that it reads well aloud.

This four-stage developmental sequence consolidates evidence that all literate people have observed or experienced themselves.[8] Although everyone acquires speech (or sign language) before learning to write, it is inner language, not speech (or sign), that should be represented as a primary system of language. In this regard, before a child actually talks he or she will exhibit the capacity to understand language, and this comprehension skill will continue to develop at a much faster rate than speech production. Thus spoken language is a secondary system that follows the primary system of language comprehension—or, as I have defined it, inner language.

Prose develops initially as a tertiary system. As long as speech provides an intermediate link between inner language and prose, the system of writing is derived from speech and is, therefore, tertiary (Stage One of Chart 5.2). But when prose and inner language are directly joined, the system becomes secondary, parallel to speech (Stage Two and Stage Three of Chart 5.2). Finally, when speech becomes tertiary (Stage Four of Chart 5.2), the acquisition of prose is complete.

In terms of the writing process, speech can help a student learn to write, initially and temporarily, but after the connection with inner language has been established, prose should become a secondary system, independent of speech. If prose remains a tertiary system, with speech serving an interlanguage function, then students will be likely to transfer features from speech to prose that do not belong there. Many writing problems, perhaps the majority of those produced by unskilled writers, result from these speech-to-prose transfers. Although this problem has been thoroughly documented by many researchers, explanations vary as to why it occurs.

Perhaps the most frequently cited explanation is that proposed by Linda Flower in her article "Writer-Based Prose: A Cognitive Basis for Problems in Writing" (1979). In distinguishing between writer-based and reader-based prose, she maintains that inexperienced writers will write for themselves, which makes it difficult for others to understand a text (hence, a writer-based style), whereas the more experienced writers will shift perspectives from the self to an audience, allowing for different responses to the same text (a reader-based style).[9]

The social conventions of speech implicitly define these types of prose. Because a speaker's audience is usually present, immediately available and responsive, the author of writer-based prose may unknowingly anticipate this situation by addressing the text to the only audience immediately present: the writer-as-reader. As students learn that writing entails a displaced audience, one beyond the self and removed from the normal conventions of speech, reader-based prose will (or should) develop.

Although this explanation has much to recommend it, the inner language model provides a more complete analysis of the writing process. Not only will problems arise when students retain the interlanguage of speech, as might occur in writer-based prose, but even students who block interlanguage to make their prose reader-based (and therefore different from speech) will have difficulty expressing themselves well in writing. This dual problem involves on the one hand idea production, and on the other hand text production.

Because we speak far more than we write, nearly everyone learns to express ideas at the relatively fast pace of speech. Thus idea production attunes spoken language to inner language; without this synchrony between speech and thought, the ideational flow of inner language would never match the form it needs for expression. A writer must somehow overcome this habit of spoken language by adjusting idea production to the relatively slow pace of producing a text.

A reader does not normally have direct access to the author's inner language (unless the reader happens to be the writer). Instead, the reader depends on the text to signal how prose should be interpreted. Of course, the pace of reading is not invariably determined by the text; a reader may "construct" from the page any number of possible interpretations, or speedread the text with very limited attention to aspects of form.

I won't consider these alternate readings as important exceptions to my argument. What does typify all reading is the extreme difference between the reader's speed in processing a text versus the time an author spends creating it. Thus, twenty hours of writing may condense visually into twenty minutes of reading. By contrast, note the near simultaneity of speaking and listening.

Without developing an elaborate theory of readability, we can assume that a text becomes more readable as the signals for interpretation are adjusted to match the relatively fast pace of reading. In this regard, text-based prose fails completely as it signals the slow, frequently interrupted pace of text production. One sign of this arrhythmical style is its "unspeakableness" when read aloud.

Prose that reads well—the spoken-prose style—aligns a text with speech for ease of interpretation, for the faster, more speech-like timing of language processing. Of course, the complexity of an argument may slow down the pace of reading, but in spoken prose a reader may proceed at a pace that is relatively faster than would be possible in other styles. In asserting this point, I should anticipate a possible misunderstanding. I am not referring here to objective standards of readability that, for example, Rudolph Flesch outlined in *The Art of Readable Writing* (1949); neither am I recommending something like the relative readability that E.D. Hirsch, Jr., proposed in *The Philosophy of Composition* (1977). Their standards essentially define what exists in the text (Flesch) or in the reader as he/she responds to the text (Hirsch). I want to emphasize both perspectives, how the author's inner language becomes the text and how the reader's point of view shapes its meaning; then after the text is constructed by author and reader, I am only concerned with how it guides similar or disparate interpretations. Thus, in my view readability begins with a text's linguistic form, then develops from this biological source towards a socially constructed meaning.

Aligning the author's production of a text with the reader's pace of interpretation is the final (readability) component of the inner language model. As it defines the writing process, this model depicts four writing styles, in four developmental stages of acquisition. As an expanded version of Chart 5.2, all four styles are diagrammed and summarized in Charts 5.3a, b, c, and d.

Chart 5.3a: **Inner Language and Oral-Based Prose**

Stage 1.

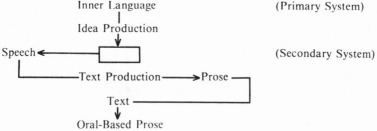

Speaking and thinking are, in terms of production speed, closely matched processes. Indeed, we use spoken language so often to express our ideas that it becomes a simple matter to substitute a speech-like pace for the relatively slow, unfamiliar, and frequently interrupted pace of writing. This strategy may speed up the kinetic production of writing,[10] but it also sacrifices meaning for the quicker (more automatic, basically talk-write) production of form.

By adopting the pace of speech production, writers will generate speech-like vocabulary, with few Latinate derivations but many examples of short, concrete, Anglo-Saxon-based words. They will produce a text too quickly, without adequate time to pause *during* composing to plan ahead (Matsuhashi 1981). They will also use a speech-like syntax, marked by coordinate structure and Subject-Verb-Object word order, with syntactic subjects matching semantic agents. Discourse will focus on the *I* point of view as a writer presumes a self-evident context. These characteristics of speech, and many others that could be cited, become serious problems for freshman writers who depend on spoken language to express their ideas. This dependence is signaled by inappropriate speech-to-prose transfers, including a simplistic diction, often too informal for academic writing, and a repetitive syntax, too often accompanied by the run-ons and fragments of spoken discourse. A style of this kind not only lacks sophistication, it also depicts an autodidactic writer who lacks self-awareness; at its worst this style has the unintended effect of sadly comic prose.

Chart 5.3b: **Inner Language and Mixed Prose**

Stage 2.

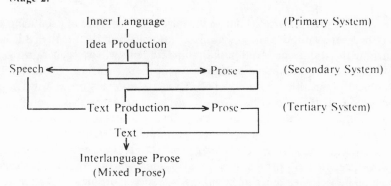

Interlanguage Prose
(Mixed Prose)

The production of a mixed style (Chart 5.3b) exhibits other speech-related problems. As writers of this style generate form, the relatively fast pace of thinking and speaking will eventually outdistance their ability to record ideas in prose. Nearly all students experience this problem and are taught editing skills in order to correct it. But writers of mixed prose will, when editing a text, often apply the same speech-based strategy that produced it. These students will think faster than they write or alternately write without thinking. Or what's more important, they will fill in thematic gaps psychologically but forget or otherwise fail to write down the complete thought process.

As these writers become more experienced, they begin to recognize that speech and prose require different production speeds. In applying this recognition though, they may interchange systems almost randomly; or, as if they cannot choose a production pace, their writing will be extremely brief, perhaps no more than a paragraph, with numerous false starts and cross-outs. Like a temporary form of writer's block, these one-paragraph essays may represent nothing more than intermittent lack of pace (Chart 5.3c).

Chart 5.3c: **Inner Language and Text-Based Prose**

Stage 3.

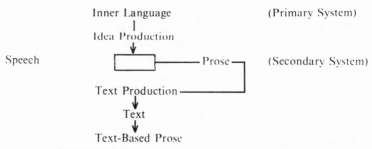

A writer must learn to control the relatively slow pace of producing a text because, without this control, it is difficult to write fluently. But in learning this unique production skill, some students will overgeneralize the differences between speech and prose, as if these forms of language are completely separate and unrelated. Thus, as students slow down the thinking and writing process, they will use ten words where five would do. They will recycle meaning without developing it and explain ideas in so much detail that a false precision is the unintended result.

A text-based variety of freshman prose stands at the opposite extreme from speech-based production. It also represents a more advanced developmental stage of writing, with its own special problems. As students attempt to exclude speech-like influence from their prose, their syntax becomes too elaborate, too complex, a tangle of embedded clauses and modifiers. Similarly, the diction is too often Latinate, pseudo-scientific, and derived from textbook jargon. More general features include excessive use of the passive voice, an overly impersonal style, and the unwarranted use of authority.

These features of text-based prose reflect its manner of production which transfers, as a slow interpretive pace, from writer to reader. Reading this style is difficult because, at least for someone other than the writer, the text signals the wrong pace for interpretation. In other words, the relatively slow physical pace of writing works against the faster psychological pace of reading.

Chart 5.3d: **Inner Language and Spoken Prose**

Stage 4.

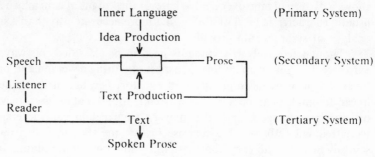

By contrast, spoken prose (Chart 5.3d) is easy to read (silently or aloud) because it highlights patterns of meaning. Indeed, spoken prose reads well because it sets a relatively fast pace for interpretation. It does this in several ways: (1) by the visual symmetries of metaphor or the paratactic reductions of metonymy; (2) through structural cues for organization and appropriate uses of cohesion for developing a topic; (3) with attention to register, manner, and style, in order to meet the needs of an audience; and (4) without apparent effort, while conveying instead an author's sense of control and self-confidence.

Spoken prose is, of course, an idealized style, based on freshman essays and limited to in-class forms of writing. I should add that no style, including spoken prose, is best for all occasions, superior to all other styles, used by every gifted writer, admired by all perceptive readers; in short, no style is supreme. But for the limited purpose of diagnosing a student's writing ability, this style conveys a strong indication of significant talent. In descending order from text-based to mixed to oral-based prose, the other styles reliably characterize writers of less ability, giving a teacher the means to classify each student's development as a writer and, for those below spoken prose, signaling the next stage of achievement.

As with any diagnostic tool, the more it is supplemented by additional measures, the more useful it becomes as a pedagogical aid. By the same reasoning, a teacher gains more confidence in a diagnostic measure when it includes several essays written by the same student rather than one essay as a student's only effort. However, with several writing samples to classify, a teacher may find the same student appropriately assigned to more than one category. Although a mixed style covers the developmental range from oral-based to text-based prose, there are always a few cases between text-based and spoken prose, and even times when a student appears to exhibit all four styles. What to do?

As a practical solution I reserve a fifth classification for these anomalous writers, taking care to analyze their subsequent work until it shows a pattern of improvement. Whatever these signs of gain may be, they usually characterize level of ability in a more accurate way than a similar analysis of errors would provide.

Though relatively few students need to be classified this way, their existence does reveal an important aspect of writing development, one the inner language model must inevitably distort because of its sequential, linear design. Researchers have consistently found that progress in written or spoken language is sporadic, marked by irregular gains interspersed with frequent setbacks. No surprise really—the student who tries consciously or not to do better must attempt something new, unfamiliar, and slightly more difficult than his or her present achievement would support. The same uneven pace of improvement characterizes second-language acquisition, as Stephen Krashen has shown in *Principles and Practice of Second Language Research* (1982). Like the foreign language learner, the writing student experiments, makes mistakes, perhaps learns from those mistakes, and ultimately consolidates the new ability with other strengths already attained. It's this consolidation of strengths that most clearly indicates a level of writing ability; weaknesses, because they can accompany nearly any attempt to improve, are best seen as precursors to gain.

Any system for diagnosing a writer's ability will affect the evidence, distorting it sometimes, making accurate placement of a student's work impossible except by arbitrary means (as my fifth classification of style must do). Despite this problem, the inner language model can show the balance between a student's strengths and weaknesses; it can, for example, explain why the gains a student makes in a writing course may quickly dissipate after a course is finished so that the student actually regresses to a prior stage of development. This recidivism occurs, in part, because a writer's strengths are tenuously maintained in the best of circumstances; even with frequent practice, the supervision of a teacher or mentor, and the genuine desire to improve, a writer must offset at least some pervasive influences of spoken language, which everyone has mastered after years of constant and spontaneous use, which everyone can modify automatically and appropriately for different audiences, and which everyone values so much that fluency is pursued and attained without question.

In terms of the inner language model, recidivism is a matter of relative strengths: the model's central distinction between speech and prose allows that some strengths are complementary where features of speech and prose overlap, but other strengths are either autonomous or mutually exclusive, and where this happens, spoken language displaces the most recent or the most tenuous gains in a writer's development. By analogy, the foreign language student who stops using that language will typically regress to prior levels of achievement. As the student continues to neglect the foreign language, it may be permanently lost except for a few memorized and often meaningless words and phrases.

A complete loss of writing ability would be extraordinary and very likely pathological in origin for any but the most remedial college student, and those exceptions would typically occur only at an open-admissions campus. Nevertheless, any writer who stops writing for a long period will, I presume, experience some loss of ability. In making this claim I need to stress the importance of time as it affects the rate of decline. The more developed a writer's skill is, the longer that person can put aside this skill without incurring a significant drop in ability. Conversely, a person with less developed writing skills is more likely to experience a quick and extensive loss of ability. I can reasonably add that most college students lack enough development in their writing to be unaffected by even short— one or two month—stays from the writing classroom.

In any case, the inner language model helps to explain how the writing process develops and how it breaks down. Since this explanation depends crucially on speech/prose contrasts, I have summarized a few of the more important ones in Chart 5.4. Those at the beginning have a special importance for the acquisition of prose, and those at the end—particularly linguistic contrasts—have more value for a diagnostic reading of students' essays.

Physical Contrasts

The key point here is the diffuse medium of air waves for speech versus the one-dimensional and flat medium of a printed page. Each medium determines the shape of language as negotiated between a writer or speaker and the audience. Because speech constantly fades, the kinetic melody of speaking develops according to the brief temporal existence of spoken words. But there is no corresponding spatial limitation. In this sense a speaker can literally encompass the audience in sound (of course, spatial

Chart 5.4: **A Contrastive Grammar of Speech and Prose**

	SPEECH	**PROSE**
Physical:	acoustical vibrations	print (ink/lead)
	temporary medium	permanent medium
	diffuse medium	localized medium
Physiological:	internal process lungs pulmonary air- stream vocal cords articulators pharyngeal/oral/ nasal cavities	external process fingers wrist hand forearm arm shoulder(?) handwriting/typing
Neurological:	localized areas of left hemisphere (Wernicke's and Broca's areas)	no Exner's center diffuse and localized areas of left hemis- pheres (visual and spatial zones of occipital and parietal areas/Wernicke's and Broca's areas)
	ictal speech (swearing, pro- fanity, phatic language)	left angular gyrus motor cortex (left precentral convolution) diffuse and localized areas of right hemis- phere
Perceptual:	ear (primary organ) 25,000-30,000 receptor cells eye (secondary organ) auditory process	eye (primary organ) 130,000,000 receptor cells ear (secondary organ) visual process
Perceptual:	multi-directional input (paralanguage)	unidirectional input (no paralanguage)

	SPEECH	PROSE
Psychological:	informal context	formal context
	context-dependent	context-free
	socialization motive	aggrandizement motive
	spontaneous	planned
	acquired ability	learned skill
	inner language condenses from speech	inner language condenses from prose
Developmental:	vocalization	subvocalization (suppressed)
	fully encoded ability	infrequently practiced skill
	robust ability	delicate skill
	Piagetian stage: concrete operational	Piagetian stage: formal operations
	parallels acquisition of sign language	parallels second-language learning
Social:	basic communication	educational literacy
	immediate audience	removed/displaced audience
	society's unqualified support of skill	society's support of skill varies
Rhetorical:	self-evident persona	displaced persona
		prescriptive grammar
		extensive citations (bibliography/ references)
Historical:	original form of language (approximately 100,000 years old)	recent form of language (appoximately 6,000 to 7,000 years old)
	evolutionary: susceptible to language change	reactionary: resists language change

Chart 5.4 con't.

	SPEECH	PROSE
Technological:	telephone	handwritten text (pencil/pen)
	taperecorder/ cassette	printing press (books/pamphlets/ journals)
	television	typewriter
	voice-activated computer	word processor
Linguistic:	short breath groups (consistent length)	extended breath groups (variable length)
	regular stress patterns	unregulated stress patterns

limitations apply to the range of a speaker's voice, but this range is usually irrelevant for informal conversations, since the interlocutors must be proximate).

Expressed in the neurological terms of visual and kinetic melodies, we can mark in spoken language a relationship between size and speed of production. Although size can vary widely, as measured by the number of speakers or the length of an utterance, speed remains a relatively constant feature because it controls rhythmically the production of new utterances to follow those fading in the airstream.

The kinetic pace of generating written language inverts this size/speed relationship. Prose does not expand beyond the visual gaze of a reader, who normally sees print only by excluding a much broader field of vision in order to maintain the narrow, specialized focus of reading. The size of print literally excludes everyone but the reader (unless a text is read aloud, but that performance introduces speech). Print also reduces language to a size that is encompassed by the reader, making it possible for someone to "own" language, in a book for example, whereas speech is shared communally and, in this sense, it remains larger than the individual speaker who uses it (cassette tape recorders are an exception, but not a significant one since government, business, and industry still use written language for most recordkeeping).

Although the economic and social implications of print have been thoroughly discussed,[11] most scholars who join this discussion have essentially ignored the literacy implications of teaching the biology of writing and its controlling rhythms. There are a few exceptions, notably those scholars who are concerned with literacy instruction and who recognize that a writer generates prose by various temporal means—slow, fast, interrupted, delayed, speech-based, and so on. As scholars like Mina Shaughnessy and Janet Emig have observed, a large part of learning to write involves learning to control these production rhythms, that is, by subconsciously knowing when and how to use them.

Physiological Contrasts

Just as walking involves physiological movement—pelvic thrust, heel strike, striding movements—writing, too, involves shoulder, arm, hand, wrist, fingers, and neuromuscular networks of the eye and ear to control movements. Such dissimilar activities as walking and writing have in common a single control: kinesthetic rhythm. It not only coordinates exterior movements, the observable motion of walking or writing, but for writing it also adjusts the psychological rhythm (or inner language flow of ideas) to the much slower physical rhythm of recording ideas (i.e., their textual production).

A writer must learn to adjust thinking, which is normally based on the pace of spoken language, to the relatively slow pace of producing a text. Without this synchrony between prose and thought, the ideational flow of language will never match the form it needs for complete, fluent expression. We can consider this point most clearly in terms of hand-writing.

For most college students the ability to handwrite is self-evident, but this obvious skill does not mean that handwriting is unimportant. No matter how well a student handwrites, that form of language production imposes a temporal constraint that uniquely characterizes prose. It takes longer to generate a written text than a spoken message of "equal" length because writing entails a largely external system of production. If we consider production time only, then neither handwriting nor typing can equal the pace of spoken language.

In contrast to prose, speech is an often-practiced neuromuscular skill, and for that reason it may influence how a student generates prose. If we assume that the most-practiced form of language production is, in neuromuscular terms, the most efficient and therefore the quickest, it follows that students may use speech production as a model of efficient writing. Yet basing text production on the pace of spoken language creates numerous problems, the most obvious being idea production that races ahead of text production. One consequence I have previously noted is the typical "freshman English" problem of ellipted expressions (i.e., syntactic and logical gaps in meaning). What the student thought when writing does not physiologically transfer to the written page, and similar gaps of meaning will persist in rewrites if the student continues to use a speech-based rhythm for generating language.

A related problem is automatic rhythm, expressed through prepositional strings (of...of...of) or empty fillers ("What it is that is..."), to name but two. These forms allow a writer to generate form quickly, in predictable sequences, and with a minimum of effort. In terms of language production, they are efficient forms, though typically dysfunctional ones, because ease of production does not necessarily make a text easier to read.

Neurological/Perceptual Contrasts

Writing is a neurological task that innervates large areas of the cerebral cortex without any single location that controls it. In this regard it resembles abstract cognition, which also has no localized center. Speaking and writing, however, do share Wernicke and Broca's areas, which are essentially responsible for comprehension and production of language. Speech differs from prose to the extent we can isolate most of spoken language in these two areas. Stating this point another way, no cognitive task is potentially more complex, involving more neuronal activity throughout the brain, than writing.

As a way to manage this complexity, a writer must learn to coordinate two rhythms, one for producing a text and another for interpreting it (keep in mind that a writer also simultaneously reads prose). The first rhythm, for text production, may comprise twenty hours of on-again, off-again writing. The second rhythm, though, may compress a reader's interpretive effort into twenty minutes, or however long it takes to read a text carefully.

These are crucial differences, especially since the reader's interpretation of a text parallels the listener's role in spoken language. Normally a speaker, listener, and reader will produce or perceive language at nearly the same speed. Even a careful reading will typically proceed much faster than the actual production of a text. In this regard spoken language does model a pace for writing, but it applies only to the rhythm of interpretation.

Without this interpretive rhythm, a text becomes difficult to read, as if the slow pace of its production adheres to the text and slows down the reader. Bloated language is the immediate problem, often due to Latinate morphology, deverbal nouns, passive voice, or uncontrolled syntax, and so on. Most composition handbooks are filled with these examples, but little else that would explain what causes them.

Half the explanation is that speech and prose differ in their production, so it is important for students to understand (at least intuitively) the problem of using a speech-based rhythm for generating prose. However, the same rhythm enhances readability because it establishes a relatively fast, familiar, and predictable pace for interpretation. Thus, speech and prose contrastively define one rhythm and potentially share the other. This dual characteristic, which is the second half of the explanation, deserves special notice because it fundamentally affects how writing might be taught.

Psychological/Developmental Contrasts

I have noted these contrasts already in the discussion of inner language. To continue here I want to clarify my definition of this term, first as it differs from the Russian psychologists' use and then as it relates to Piaget's theory of cognitive development.

Russian psychologists typically regard development of inner language, what they also call "inner speech," as a condensed form of ordinary language, derived from already developed language skills. Thus, Sokolov writes in *Inner Speech and Thought* that "inner speech, far from being an independent entity, is a secondary phenomenon derived from external speech" (1972, 1). Similarly, Vygotsky states in *Thought and Language* that "[oral speech] precedes inner speech in the course of development, while written speech follows inner speech and presupposes its existence (the act of writing implying a translation from inner speech)" (1962, 99).

By contrast, what *I* mean by inner language is the ability we all have to understand something without necessarily being able to express it as an explanation. This ability to understand something is, to a large extent, reflected in our receptive vocabulary for prose, which normally exceeds by far our productive vocabulary for speech. But the distinction involves more than lexical items. Our awareness and expression of forms have a similar disparity in syntax; that is, most people do not talk the way they write.

Obviously, context will affect our use of language; it will also "explain" some words that would not be otherwise understood out-of-context, for example, if words were randomly chosen from a dictionary. Some speakers, too, may appear to talk the way they write. Henry James was said to do this: "He talked, as he wrote, in long involved sentences with a little murmur—mum-mum-mum—standing for parentheses, and with those rhetorical hooks he seemed to be poking about his mind, fumbling through the whole basket of his conversational vocabulary, to find the exact word, which he used in talking about most ordinary matters" (White 1966, 171).

These exceptions notwithstanding, most people have developed unequal skills for understanding and producing language. In simplest terms, most of us think more than we speak, speak more than we write, and our ability to do each of these tasks declines in efficiency as we do them less often. A parallel distinction has been repeatedly noted in studies of child-language acquisition. A five-year-old, for instance, may fully understand adult speech without actually producing more than 80 percent of the lexical forms or syntactic constructions that typify an adult's spoken language.

As the child becomes an adult, language remains unevenly mastered, with written forms being the least developed and inner language forms being the most developed. Speech has an intermediate position. Piaget evidently anticipates this three-part sequence in his own theory of cognitive development. As an infant begins to develop intelligence (which precedes language), rhythm structures the basic operations of thought (Piaget and Inhelder 1969, 19-20). After this prelinguistic intelligence has formed (i.e., the sensory-motor stage), a child begins to use language for its inherent speed, range, and simultaneity of representations (i.e., pre- and concrete operations). The final stage is characterized by the ability to think in abstract, nonrepresentational terms (i.e., formal operations). Each stage builds on the preceding one, with formal operations being the last and usually least developed. Similarly, speech evolves from inner language, and writing evolves from speech. In this way, inner language represents our ability to understand the world; speech and prose serve to "translate" that understanding.[12]

Social/Rhetorical Contrasts

To a large extent writing removes us rhetorically from the social event, an event the reader completes—hours, months, years later—when he or she reads the text. But we are never completely absent—removed from the text—because the rhythm of our prose characterizes us. How we string words together; how we arrange these strings into arguments, images, facts; these linguistic products (or "footprints") convey our physical presence through (among other things) the rhythm of a text.

Although the act of writing conveys our physical presence, the same activity removes us socially from our audience. It is not paradoxical, therefore, to say that words disembody us, for we cannot in prose express ourselves as speakers do in a conversation. A writer lacks the same physical presence of a speaker; or more precisely, a writer presents himself or herself uniquely through rhythm. A speaker, by contrast, can add all the potential nuance of gestures and nonverbal communication.

When a speaker pauses in a conversation, this break frequently signals the opportunity for someone else to respond. A rhythm of dialogue evolves, important not only for the turn-taking it controls, but also for the cognitive processing it allows during each pause. A similar function characterizes prose, especially as an aid to memory (Williams 1987, 311).

The exchange between writer and reader has few overt constraints, since at any point a reader can simply put the text aside, then subsequently pick it up as if no break had intervened. But there is in the text a patterning of language that potentially guides a reader's interpretation. This patterning is the length of clauses, as measured by punctuation or by major syntactic boundaries.

Each pause in a text signals to us—the readers—the pace we need for interpretation. If the pace is slow, marked by long durations between each pause, then a reader may find the text difficult to interpret because the semantic "load" becomes too burdensome. Conversely, a rapid pace can misguide a reader, and disrupt interpretation, because the text signals too little information per pause.

It is a social amenity to guide the reader by signaling a consistent (and appropriate) rhythm for interpretation. In a metaphorical sense, that rhythm reintroduces the writer as physically cuing a conversation. Students can acquire this skill by practicing the conversational rhythms that we all use for speech; this skill, when applied to prose, is relatively easy to develop through practice reading aloud. In other words, students can learn to read aloud with emphasis, attentive to the pauses that different authors require, and ultimately to the interpretive rhythm of their own prose. I will have more to say on this point in a later chapter.

Historical/Technological Contrasts

Most authorities agree that speech evolved at least 100,000 years ago, whereas prose is a quite recent (6,000 to 7,000 years old) technological development—with print, as we recognize it today, being only a few hundred years old. In this historical context, written language has done remarkably well, at least in technological societies, where large numbers of people have become literate. But the technology that underlies this literacy is, and has been, changing.

Before the advent of word processors, print remained essentially different from speech because a written text was almost permanent. Now, even print fades, not only when a text is scrolled or deleted on a monitor, but also when it remains stored on a floppy disk (hard disk, tape, etc.), unprinted and impossible to read in its miniaturized form.

The rhythm of producing prose will be fundamentally altered by word processing. In effect, writing will become more speech-like, at least in its production, as the static qualities of print become more fluid. Moreover, the need to spell, punctuate, or even organize prose will gradually diminish, being replaced by programs that already exist for "correcting" these skills. With the development of voice-activated computers, even the need to write or type will decline, returning us almost completely to a speech-based literacy.

We need to anticipate these changes (along with concomitant problems); in later chapters I will have more to say about the curricular implications of speech-based literacy. At present, however, most students continue to write via the "old-fashioned" technology of pen or pencil; we can anticipate a long, perhaps indefinite, reliance on these tools, especially in the classroom. For that reason I have limited my discussion in this chapter to the old-fashioned mode of writing.

Linguistic Contrasts

By noting the diverse linguistic features of speech and prose, I have already identified four developmental stages of college writing: oral-based, mixed, text-based, and spoken prose. The first three stages represent a writer's progress towards mastery of physical eloquence, but not the complete mastery of all writing abilities. Obviously, a writer can be logical without being in full command of text production, just as the illogical writer can fully control the biology of writing. These exceptions notwithstanding, progress towards physical eloquence does mark an essential gain in writing ability that typically represents progress in all aspects of writing.

The final stage of spoken prose signals a writer's ability to control the biology of writing. Given that control, a writer may express him- or herself distinctively, with competence, and perhaps in clear, well-reasoned, persuasive prose. Or the writer may lack the natural ability or intellectual training to go beyond physical eloquence. In either case, a writer must first achieve the basic literacy of physical eloquence, enabling the expression of ideas to the best of his or her ability.

Part of that achievement is shown in a writer's subconscious control of linguistic features like breath groups and patterns of stress. Like any other linguistic contrast between speech and prose, these two demonstrate a writer's ability to control kinetic, visual, and auditory functions. Breath group length, for instance, can be regulated by the kinetic melody of handwriting, to generate automatic, flatulent, or vapid prose, depending on the match between a writer's ideas and the speed of text production. Or, based on the visual melody of reading, a writer can extend breath groups well beyond the biological limits of speech. Conversely, a writer can attune breath groups to the auditory melody of spoken conversation.

Stress patterns fall into three categories as well. A writer can rely on the visual cues of punctuation, especially devices like dashes, underlinings, and exclamation marks for highlighting meaning. A writer can call attention to prose by auditory cues that suddenly disrupt the text's linguistic or ideational rhythm. And a writer can enliven prose by the kinetic—physical—transformation of implied authorship into personal expression: "this idea" becomes "my idea."

These options correspond to the six stages of writing ability that were introduced in the previous chapter. The least capable writers will typically adopt a kinetic melody for emphasis: "I think, I believe, my feeling is . . ." are typical manifestations of this developmental stage. To a lesser extent they will stress ideas through auditory or visual cues; whichever they favor determines the overall style they produce: kinetic-auditory-visual, or kinetic-visual-auditory.

At a low-to-intermediate stage of development, college students will use the auditory melody *as if* prose has the same means for emphasis as speech. Since voice quality, inflection, and most nonverbal cues are only available in speech, these writers will hear in their prose intended meanings that other readers cannot discern. All that remains evident to a reader is the secondary emphasis of kinetic-visual or visual-kinetic techniques, which may explain why the ideas of beginning writers so often appear under-developed or vacuous.

More advanced writers will most often rely on a visual melody to stress meaning. Their secondary patterns of emphasis will be either kinetic-auditory or auditory-kinetic. Thus, as punctuation serves to highlight their prose, these writers will suppress or infrequently use the personal reference of a kinetic melody or the rhythmic nuance of an auditory melody.

The most capable writers will use all three primary systems without restricting their options for emphasis. In other words, they will develop the physical eloquence of one integrated system,[13] comprised of all linguistic features for emphasis, subconsciously available in the writer's memory and immediately recalled from the biogrammar of speech and prose. With the same fluency as speech, these writers will achieve the biological sophistication of spoken prose.

Conclusion

There are two conclusions I would like to draw from this speech/prose biogrammar. The first concerns its relevance to style studies in the general context of social versus biological views of language. The second concerns the implications of using a contrastive grammar for writing instruction. I will discuss them in that order.

In using a contrastive grammar to examine students' writing, I have obtained results that appear to challenge a strictly social explanation of writing achievement. Although these results could be interpreted as supporting a broader definition of the *academic discourse community*, that interpretation depends on redefining academic discourse community to mean a single unit rather than a diverse group. Also, there remains an unanswered question as to how much any discourse community overlaps another.

One answer to that implied question is the pervasive role of inner language in all discourse, written or spoken. From this inner language starting point, we can begin to see the interrelatedness of all discourse, and the logical possibility of finding universal features that would characterize all styles of writing. In this regard the four styles I have identified—oral-based, mixed, text-based, and spoken prose—may qualify as universal types, albeit limited to college writing pending further study of other prose.

Their universality does warrant notice in the biology of writing, since all writers must engage the neurological functions of hand, eye, and ear. At the very earliest stages of development, a writer will produce an oral-based style with handwriting, spelling, and punctuation problems, all related to the kinetic melody of text production. Later in this development, the oral-based writer will invoke the auditory melody as a way to overcome these initial problems, but that creates new difficulties, the most obvious being inappropriate transfers of linguistic features from speech to prose. As a writer becomes aware of these speech-like errors, he or she begins to experiment with auditory and visual characteristics of writing, producing a style that is randomly mixed in terms of neurological functions. Near the end of this development, a writer concentrates on the visual aspects of prose, and generates a text-based style that is nearly devoid of speech-like features. Finally, when a writer achieves the physical eloquence to coordinate all three melodies, he or she is employing spoken prose.

As a related point, there may be a limited pedagogical value to stressing these styles when teaching students to write, though I must add the caution that all formal instruction belongs outside the writing class. In a writing center or writing lab, in a teacher's office, in the cafeteria or in the halls—banished somewhere outside the classroom—formal instruction may actually help those relatively few students who have already mastered the biology of writing. For them, conscious attention to form is fully supported by their subconscious ability to generate a text. For most students, however, formal learning displaces the biology of writing by substituting conscious attention for subconscious awareness. As one result, a writer's physical development is sacrificed for intellectual or cognitive development. Another result, discussed more fully in a later chapter, is the relatively limited gains of formal learning versus the long-term gains of informal acquisition.

The main advantage of formal instruction—albeit outside the class-room—is that we can anticipate serving students who would be otherwise unhappy without formal instruction of some kind in writing. One means of providing this instruction would be to teach the contrastive grammar(s) of speech and prose; exactly what aspects of this grammar should be taught as part of a generic style remains for writing teachers to determine through trial and error. Obviously it would be counterproductive and most likely impossible to teach every contrast for all four styles.

However it would be done, the attempt to teach these contrasts may enhance the *formal* teaching of writing. As even a cursory review of current composition texts will show, if some basic features of speech and prose are noted at all, they are not examined in any detail. Of course, many rhetorics and handbooks devote considerable attention to grammar and usage, but the teaching of grammar as a supplement to writing instruction makes little sense if it fails to explain or demonstrate how speech differs from prose, and how they resemble each other, too.[14]

Whereas writing researchers like George Hillocks, Jr., and Patrick Hartwell have argued against grammar instruction because it fails to improve students writing,[15] their arguments (and related ones) may only indicate that researchers have, for most of this century, examined the wrong grammar, one that is based on the priority of speech rather than inner language. These speech-based grammars provide but half of what a student can profitably learn about the grammar of English, and basically the wrong half. For instance, teaching students the major and minor form classes—or parts-of-speech—begs the question as to why they need to learn these forms. Only a contrastive grammar of speaking and writing, as I have tried to indicate so far, begins to answer this crucial question.

Based on that grammar, a teacher could explain that in speech the major form classes (e.g., nouns, verbs, adverbs, adjectives) typically receive a degree of stress that signals their relative importance for conveying content. The minor form classes (e.g., prepositions, articles, conjunctions, and most pronouns) receive a lesser degree of stress that corresponds to their minimal semantic value. These distinctions, of course, can be heard in speech through intonation and patterns of stress, but the mostly silent and static nature of print obscures them. In other words, a student who is also an inexperienced writer probably does not intuitively understand the semantic value of these grammatical forms in writing. A contrastive grammar may augment the start of that undeveloped intuition.

While I remain skeptical that formal instruction has any positive, lasting effects, I do not rule out the likelihood that it helps students temporarily and perhaps psychologically, too. Another chapter will discuss these points in more detail; for now it is sufficient, for teaching purposes, to locate a student's memory for prose in the biogrammar of speaking and writing.

A full contrastive biogrammar would examine all the categories cited in Chart 5.4, and possibly more. But as I have already noted, a pedagogical version of this grammar would be necessarily selective and incomplete. Thus, in the final category for linguistic features I have listed only two contrastive items, breath groups and stress patterns. Obviously more items could be included here, but these two provide a fundamental contrast that is almost universally neglected in writing texts.

Simply put, people breathe when they speak, and this physiological activity, this ingressive and egressive flow of air, necessarily constrains how much language can be produced between breaths. Writing, of course, can potentially override this constraint so that potentially neither the writer nor the reader is affected by the pace of breathing. But when this breath group constraint is removed, all sorts of stylistic problems can potentially arise. One immediately thinks of inflated prose, the bureaucratese, Engfish, official talk, and gobbledygook that has been lamented since antiquity. In fact, it was Quintilian who first commented on the relationship between breathing and writing; our modern approach to teaching grammar has lost this basic insight.

Just as important, we could usefully teach the linguistic basis of stress, something that students know intuitively in speech but have no intuition for in writing. How many students know, for instance, that major form classes like nouns and verbs typically are stressed because these "content words" convey basic meaning? Without this knowledge, be it intuitive only, they cannot begin to structure meaning carefully in prose because they cannot understand how patterns of meaning are constructed *silently* in a written text. Indeed, their intuitions developed from speech may actually misguide them—again, an obvious point of contrast, but the nature of stress is rarely explained in composition textbooks.

I have chosen these two linguistic examples merely to demonstrate the possibilities for a more detailed contrastive grammar of speech and prose. Once such a grammar is produced, a project only introduced in this chapter, it can be used to determine if grammar instruction really does help students become better writers. Also, it should provide a useful tool for evaluating prose.

6

Agraphia and Style

The term *agraphia* was first proposed by William Ogle in 1867 and has come to mean the neurological inpairment of writing ability, ranging from partial loss of this ability (called dysgraphia) to complete loss (agraphia).[1] The comparable disorder in speech is called *aphasia*, which can be divided into two main forms: *Broca's aphasia*, the inability to produce speech, and *Wernicke's aphasia*, the inability to comprehend speech. In *Human Neuropsychology* (1978) Henri Hécaen and Martin Albert cite two other language disorders that are pertinent to the study of dysfunctional writing: they are *alexia*, the visual loss of reading ability, and *apraxia*, a kinetic disruption of the neuromuscular system of motor control.

The relationship between these four language disorders and style is mirrored in the neurological functions of hand, eye, and ear. By examining the linguistic signs of breakdown in writing ability, I can identify components of physical eloquence that are basic to all writing, and I can isolate linguistic features of normal development in writing that correspond to kinetic, visual, and auditory dysfunctions.

In making this comparison between normal and abnormal writing, I do not mean to equate college students with patients suffering from cerebral injuries. Rather, I am comparing their writing as a product of the same neurological functions. Patients with agraphia, aphasia, alexia, or apraxia do not have these functions fully intact, whereas most college students have normal functions that are not fully developed. In both cases, the connections between hand, eye, and ear are incomplete, and this incompleteness directly causes specific writing problems.

These problems will not exactly correspond so that subgroups of abnormal writers are matched with normal writers. Too many additional factors influence that congruity, not the least being a person's level of writing ability prior to a pathological condition, a point emphasized by Hécaen, Angelergues, and Douzenis (1963, 205). Yet a general pattern of

107

errors can be attributed in both normal and abnormal writing to dysfunctional kinetic, visual, and auditory systems. For instance, the severe spelling disorder of a literal alexic results in consistent reversals or deletions of letters at the end of a word, problems first discussed at length in Hinshelwood's *Letter, Word, and Mind-Blindness* (1900) and more recently corroborated by Hécaen ("Aspects Sémiotiques des Troubles de la Lecture," 1967) and Dubois-Charlier ("Les Analyses Neuro-psychologiques," 1976). This visual "blindness" to word-final position may also characterize a group of normal writers whose developmental errors point to other visual dysfunctions. These normal writers may then be said to produce a deficient visual style, by analogy to the linguistic disorders of alexia. As I will explain in the rest of this chapter, similar comparisons can be made between stages of writing ability and kinetic or auditory forms of language disorders.

Mapping The Ability To Write

Based on neurological evidence of language dysfunctions (see the appendix to this chapter for a review of this research), I have adapted from Luria's work (1970b), and from Fergusson and Boller's adaptation thereof (1977), a general model of normal writing. Other studies as early as Wernicke's "Ein Fall von Isolierter Agraphie" (1903) and as recently as David Roeltgen and Karl Heilman's "Review of Agraphia and a Proposal for an Anatomically-Based Neuropsychological Model of Writing" (1984) have proposed similar models, but the one I have developed is distinctive because it excludes mental processes that precede the writer's neurophysiological activities. In this regard it differs from the neurological map of handwriting that I introduced in Chapter Four. Consistent with my goal of identifying physical eloquence in the biology of writing, this map also more directly parallels the kinetic, visual, and auditory functions with their related prose styles that I reviewed in Chapter Five.

According to Luria, three general areas of the brain control writing. The first area that a writer may invoke is located in the central (kinesthetic) region of the left hemisphere. Use of this auditory melody apparently depends on a writer's need or desire to subvocalize as a way to evaluate speech sounds or to recognize a word, phrase, or sentence. Children, many developmental writers, and even some accomplished writers who are uncertain about a word or other segment of text will begin here.

The next location, actually the initial one for many writers, bridges the visual and spatial zones of the occipital and parietal lobes. In effect, the writer creates a network for the visual and kinetic melodies, a network that codes phonemes into graphemes and enables the writer to see a word's shape. Parts of the prefrontal region may also join this visual/spatial network as a writer monitors spelling for the sequential order of letters.

The final location for writing is in the frontal lobes where ideational analysis takes place. This analysis depends crucially on a writer's ability to hear his or her inner voice as it expresses meaning; from this logical expression of ideas a network can also extend to the right hemisphere, where a writer attends to the visual and auditory aesthetics of prose form. Once this network has been established, perhaps also linked to other networks, a writer may begin anywhere in the writing process and work his or her way through all three neurological melodies.

A similar three-part sequence is presented in Fergusson and Boller's model of text production. At some point a writer must attend to motor (kinetic) feedback from the neuromuscular apparatus as words are being formed; he or she must analyze visual feedback to check the shape, spelling, punctuation, and syntax of prose; he or she must also monitor auditory feedback for sound, sense, and aptness in meaning and style. The sequence a writer follows for producing a text probably does not matter, yet the recursiveness allowed by a fully developed writing ability should not disguise the fundamentally linear progress of someone learning to write. That step-by-step progress may bring a developmental writer two steps forward and then one step back; nevertheless, the writer's progress is linear, aimed towards creating neurological networks, discovering what to connect and how to make the connections.

However developed, each network has the idiosyncratic mark of the person who uses it, a mark that potentially becomes the signature of a writer's style. Although some styles are highly distinctive, they all emerge from the same neurological functions of hand, eye, and ear, and can be classified accordingly.

No style is best, as if a single means of organizing language could accommodate every audience and be appropriate for all occasions. Neither is any style good nor bad intrinsically, though some may have a more limited appeal or greater utility than others. Despite these qualifications, styles can be classified by their provenance among the three neurological melodies and then arranged to show the developmental abilities of college writers who typically produce a generic style.

Developmental Progress in College Writing: Four Stages Preceding Physical Eloquence

Although the vast majority of college students obviously show no evidence of having abnormal writing disorders, most do exhibit problems—like patients with agraphia, aphasia, alexia, and apraxia—controlling the same linguistic networks and neurological functions that determine a writer's physical eloquence. By noting these problems and related signs of developmental progress, I have identified four stages of writing ability that directly correlate with five generic styles.

The least capable writers will have unusual difficulty in generating prose, a problem attributable to their lack of practice and inchoate development as writers. Following this *kinetic style*, other students will adopt a generative strategy for "talking on paper," a practical but also dysfunctional use of the auditory melody that produces an *auditory style*. As students begin to develop a more sophisticated inner voice for prose, they may have difficulty regulating the temporal pace of writing. A dysfunctional kinetic melody seemingly stops and goes, as if colliding with other language functions to produce a random, confused, arrhythmical sequence of styles. The result is a *mixed prose style*. More advanced writers, perhaps to control this prior linguistic chaos, disconnect the inner voice from speech, and disconnect the kinetic melody from temporal constraints, in order to focus their attention exclusively on the visual representation of ideas. As the visual melody dominates this effort, a writer may produce imagistic, highly metaphorical prose, but the most common result is simply a *visual style* that uses print reductively to mirror ideas. At the highest stage of writing ability, students achieve the physical eloquence to connect and control all three neurological melodies. Because this control approximates the fluency of speech, these writers can choose the appropriate register for their topic and audience; they can also express ideas in a visually enhanced prose that is attuned to the reader's pace of interpretation. In speech the equivalent mastery of these skills is normal, but in writing relatively few students achieve this *melodic prose style*.

Besides these interlocking melodies, differences between speaking and writing provide another way to classify all five styles. Thus, oral-based prose is the linguistic equivalent of apractic and some agraphic styles; mixed prose corresponds to the majority of agraphic styles; text-based prose shares linguistic features with an alexic style; and spoken prose exhibits the same physical eloquence as a melodic style. By using these two systems of classification, one for linguistic features[2] and the other for neurological functions, I have been able to analyze more accurately in students' writing the evidence of progress as it has occurred over a four-year period. At least two experienced writing teachers then confirmed my analysis through independent and impartial readings of the same (unmarked) texts. Chart 6.1 summarizes these results across a neurological range of styles, from the kinetic melody of apraxic prose to the physical eloquence of all three melodies.

Of these five classifications for style, the least common is a kinetic style, with 2 to 3 percent of the 1,190 students I have reviewed demonstrating this type of writing.[3] The remaining four styles are distributed as follows: auditory style is 21 percent; mixed style is 50 percent; visual style is 23 percent; and the melodic style is 3 to 4 percent.

Chart 6.1: **The Neurology of Style**

Neurological Disorder	Symptom	Style	Characteristic
apraxia	lack of muscular coordination	kinetic	lack of text production
aphasia	inability to produce or understand meaningful speech	auditory	talking in prose
agraphia	disrupted or inefficient text production	mixed	random or disorganized blend of styles
alexia	verbal blindness	visual	elaborate syntax
none	none	melodic	physical eloquence

A different population of college students would undoubtedly have produced a different distribution of styles, affected by such obvious factors as open admissions or selective recruitment, students' ages, their social and economic backgrounds, to name just a few variables. With these qualifications in mind, I can state that the results I have obtained are probably close to the distribution at other medium-to-large public universities. More importantly, these results establish a principle for classifying writing styles by the three neurophysiological processes that can generate them. In that sense these results apply to any college setting.

What follows are examples of each style with a brief analysis of its linguistic characteristics. While not all students will exhibit the same features in their writing, in general they all follow a consistent pattern of development. Of course, over time some may bypass a style entirely or, lacking the opportunity to write often, they may backslide to a prior developmental stage. Still other students may generate prose that does not apparently fall within one of these five classifications. Nevertheless, all students must develop some ability in the use of hand, eye, and ear for writing. These basic biological functions are also necessary, though perhaps not sufficient, antecedents to the quality of ideas in students' writing.

Linguistic Features of Neurological Styles

Without equating pathological disabilities with a developmental writer's partially formed capabilities, I want to examine in these quite different sources of writing the same biological functions of hand, eye, and ear. Similar comparisons could be made between normal writers and those who are blind, deaf, or in some other respect physically disabled. But these latter cases do not provide the same neurological insights as provided in studies of aphasics, especially when these patients progress towards full or partial recovery of writing. It is precisely this developmental aspect of both normal and neurologically impaired writers that interests me, and that I will examine below as both types of writers exhibit similar neurological styles. Consistent with my previous observations, these styles divide into five developmental stages, each with its own unique linguistic features.

Apraxia and Kinetic Style

Like the patient with apraxia, a student who writes a kinetic style will have difficulty generating even a small amount of text, lacking the coordination between hand and brain to write with any comfort or fluency. An hour of composing may result in a few sentences, or maybe a paragraph, often written in large script to inflate the appearance of length. Repeated false starts, frequent cross-outs, and erratic spellings are among the more obvious signs of visual and temporal dysfunctions. Quality of ideas may, however, show much promise. The passage reprinted in Figure 6.2, representing the entire effort of a student during a 45-minute in-class writing, exemplifies the characteristics of a kinetic style.

Figure 6.2: **Kinetic Style**

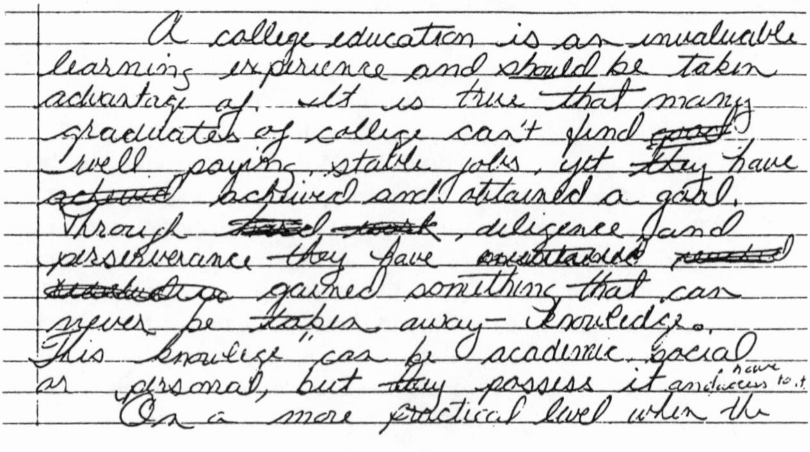

graduate begins to seek out a job. ...ve employers are impressed by the fact that one has attended a school of higher learning. If the student did well and excelled in his classes than it is all the more impressive to the employer. Good academic standing may say a lot about someone. It demonstrates that he/she is capable of hard work and takes pride in his endeavors.

The other aspects of attending aspects of attending a university or college are many. Among them is the understanding of one's self and where he/she belongs. Schooling opens doors and greater positions to the individual. A person bent on becoming a plumber might enroll in a college and find (through his studies) that settling for becoming a plumber is pointless because his real interest lies in art. Through the process of school one is exposed to numerous fields and directions of the job market. There are diverse and varied courses offered at college that can guide a person to what they would like to become in later life. Without the experience of attending a facility of higher learning one is denied this choice.

Considering this style in developmental terms, the writer has a poorly encoded neuromuscular ability for text production. Since infrequent practice in composing may create problems as basic as shaping letters, the writer of this style needs extraordinary time to coordinate the physical task of putting words on a page. Even when that effort appears under control, the writer must adjust this slow pace of text production to the relatively mature and much faster pace of generating ideas. Lacking the experience to make this adjustment, the writer of a kinetic style becomes frustrated and often despondent, unwilling to continue writing or just content "to go through the motions."

Not just a "psychological" problem or some other cognitive form of writer's block (as described in Mike Rose's "Rigid Rules, Inflexible Plans, and the Stifling of Language," 1980), the kinetic style is primarily a lack of coordination between hand and brain—a physical problem. To correct it takes more than a writer's patience and a teacher's encouragement; especially in college, time for slow developmental progress is not available, and few writing teachers can offset the overwhelmingly negative response of other teachers to this style.

Yet these "basic" writers may show obvious latent ability, surprising determination to improve, and definite—albeit limited—progress after just one semester of writing instruction. That success depends, of course, on ample time and sufficient motivation for a student to close the developmental gap between inherent talent and actual practice. A few students can catch up without additional assistance, but a larger percentage would improve if teachers stressed the development of physical writing abilities. In particular, if a student practices different paces of text production, he or she can encode more completely the physical act of writing. Having attained that basic maturity, a student can then develop a productive, efficient synergy between the speed of thought and the pace of writing.

Aphasia and Auditory Style

As previously stated, neurological speech disorders can be divided into two broad categories: impaired comprehension (Wernicke's aphasia) and impaired production (Broca's aphasia). The writer of an auditory style exhibits both problems by transferring from speech distinctively oral characteristics that do not belong in prose. This attempt to "talk on paper" disrupts the lexical, syntactic, and prescriptive usage rules of conventional writing; simplistic diction, sentence fragments, run-ons, and poor punctuation are typical results.

This distorted output is caused by a writer's inability to hear prose as it differs from speech, a verbal deafness that often coincides with a basic problem in being understood. Attuned to speech, the writer's inner voice does not function as a reliable monitor of prose, either in form or content, a shortcoming related to the visual permanence of prose versus the auditory impermanence of speech. Because errors fade in speech, they are often less noticeable and less disruptive than equivalent errors in prose. With a writer's greater tolerance for errors goes an easier facility for generating words; thus, unlike the kinetic style with its limited output due to the writer's physical awkwardness, the auditory style is often overly long and, it seems, effortlessly produced.

Production Problems:

The writer's fluency in creating prose does not make an auditory style exemplary. While relying on speech does solve the problem of pace, this solution for the kinetic style nevertheless introduces many speech-based errors as the writer attempts to talk on paper. Even when developing an argument, the writer will adopt an informal register:

> I guess, though, that one of the things that attracts me the most is all the pomp and pagentry that went on back then.

> Now a days everyone's always in a hurry to get somewhere to do something and consequently they don't even have the time to apologize even if they run right into you and practically knock you down.

In these examples, the writer's self-discovery becomes an almost stream-of-consciousness form of writing. How the writer experiences the world and reacts to it may be so private that no one else will understand it well. For instance, "pomp and pagentry" are transformed by metynomic fiat into events that "went on," as if the emblems of these events have a temporal span. References to time become further confused by the indeterminate "back then," which potentially embraces all history. Subsequent references do not clarify these ambiguities.

Instead, the writer's spontaneous flow of ideas translates directly to the page. As in speech, there are many active verbs, adverbs, and deictic words to convey this momentary reality where tactile, concrete experiences "practically knock you down." And to keep pace with this immediate rush of words, the writer's kinetic melody of generating prose speeds up to match the speed of thought, creating an almost breathless style "in a hurry to get somewhere."

Comprehension Problems:

The writer of an auditory style evidently presumes that the same deictic functions of speech apply in prose. In a linguistic sense, he or she literally "points" to the evidence in mind, as if the reader can follow the deictic reference:

> When something is against the law, then this creates a black market.

> I hope I have presented an unbias viewpoint because I personally think that.

These writers take for granted a reader's understanding of what *this* and *that* refer to. A similar faith in their personal "viewpoint" justifies whatever claim is made.

As in speech, the auditory melody adopted for this style tolerates a loosely connected string of main clauses that follow main clauses via coordinate *and's, but's,* and *or's.* This syntactic "looseness" results in a constant recycling of ideas that ignores the visual permanence of words on a page. By contrast, an iterative function in prose may refine meaning by interpretive shadings from one reference to another. These semantic adjustments can also be made in syntax to delete agency, subordinate ideas, qualify and rearrange modifiers, among many options that guide the visual melody of interpretation.

Redundancies in the auditory style do not assist a reader; the same repeated words and sentence constructions may even become ambiguous since intonation and other suprasegmental features of speech are not available to clarify these repetitions. They also convey the impression of a writer who is limited in ability, forced to repeat ideas using the few words and syntactic forms he or she knows well.

This apparent incompetence may actually be nothing more than a writer's reliance on speech. In other words, if a writer subconsciously chooses among other possibilities to "talk on paper," he or she may have only made a bad choice, one that does not necessarily indicate latent abilities. On the other hand, if a writer relies on speech in order to compensate for lack of ability, that dependency invariably marks a writer of an auditory style.

The resulting prose exhibits the same "loose" syntax, the same fragments, run-ons, lack of cohesion or development that, among other things, characterize speech:

1. Sentence Fragments

> But most likely the way in which his family, friends, give him the respect he so rightly deserves.

2. Run-On Sentences

> The ring was first made by the dark lord, and it had only powers of evil, which increased proportionaly as the power of its Bearer, then in a war between the powers of evil and good, the dark lord was killed, and the ring was taken by one of the good people, and he was a man, but the Ring betryed him by falling off his finger (the one who puts the ring on this finger becomes invisible), and he was killed by his enemies while he was swimming in the sea.

3. Coordinate (Run-On) Sentences

I drove for two hours this morning, and arrived here with a headache; and it wasn't even rushour traffic and it is no wonder that the nine to five worker arrives home each night after an eight hour day and let's say a total of two hours on the freeway, and plops down in front of the television and remains there all night.

4. Simple, Redundant Sentences (lack of variety, use of exact repetition)

As a kid I have always had an interest in trains. I had to ride trains during my childhood summers. It was an experience to ride a train as a kid. It was not untill the summer of '66 that I received my first train set. It wasn't much of a train set, but I looked on it as a personal treasure. It not only brought me joy of playing with it, but it also brought back memories.

As these examples show, too often the writer of an auditory style takes for granted information that a reader does not, and frequently cannot, possess.

This strategy has many problematic results. As the following examples show, the writer will fail to notice agreement errors and other aspects of anaphoric reference:

There is indeed other answers.

Laws attacking the criminal and not the weapon is a more logical deterent to violent crime.

Although the magazine is quite liberal, the topics that they chose shows a high degree of human interest.

Another typical problem is lack of agreement between subject and predicate:

Back in the Golden Ages ... there wasn't a lot of things to read.

Too much emphasis are placed on the minor crimes.

The assassinations of the last decade has proven the lax attitude of the gang in Capital Hill.

In a single student's work, these errors are often more sporadic than universal, suggesting that the writer intuitively knows most agreement rules but applies them haphazardly. Yet carelessness does not explain all these errors, especially when most writers produce them. By transferring to prose the less formal rules of speech, these writers do not really create agreement problems, at least not from their speech-based point of view.

Expressed another way, the reader's viewpoint is not a speech-based writer's concern, since all that matters to this writer is self-expression. This egocentric attitude leads stylistically to repeated use of first-person pronoun address:

> As a kid I have always had an interest in trains.
>
> I drove for two hours this morning...
>
> I personally believe that it seems obvious to me.
>
> I guess, though, that one of the things that attracts me...
>
> I hope that I have presented an unbiased viewpoint.
>
> I do not believe the film industry effects society to a degree of concern.

In extreme cases the writer will completely lose an audience; the text will be loose, informal, imprecise; it will digress, lack authority, and read like a monologue:

> Back then "civilization" had really taken over so there were alot of places to ride a horse while admiring the beautiful countryside. Another thing I remember along these lines is that since there wasn't so much *civilization* around there wasn't so much pollution. The environment was clean for a change. And *something else* was that since there technology wasn't nearly as advanced as ours is today and there was not need to fear the terrible possibility of a full scale nuclear war. (my emphasis)

By using explicit thematic tags, an author can avoid the loose effect of the above example (which also has many features of a mixed style). These tags are like syntactic tracers or signals to the reader that old patterns underlie the new. Thus "civilization" in the above example would have recurred as a key word conveying the same meaning. What we find instead are three meanings: a widespread civilization (first tag), a limited civilization (second tag), and something else (third tag). In conventional writing a reader anticipates these variations, but will only understand them if they are explained.

In sum, the writer of an auditory style does not address an audience other than himself or herself. In the context of speech this egocentric attitude works because the audience can join in, interrupt, or signal responses nonverbally. Of course, for conventional writing these options do not exist, a fact the speech-based writer apparently ignores. One consequence is the auditory melody of a style that reads as if someone is speaking in print. A related consequence is hyperkinetic prose generated at the spontaneous speed of thought.

These speech-based problems are familiar stuff. Any college teacher will recognize the provenance of many freshman English papers in the auditory style. But the familiarity goes deeper. Every normal person speaks the way these students write, or with a comparable degree of informality. What seems incongruous is the unedited transfer of speech into prose. These students literally write the way they talk. And that strategy, at least for academic prose, does not usually work.

Agraphia and Mixed Style:

Nearly all cases of agraphia are complex rather than pure, with accompanying disorders of reading and speaking. Like agraphia, a mixed style has a developmental etiology that may differ significantly among writers and even differ from time to time within the same writer. One source of this fluctuation is the writer's trial-and-error progress, which may combine two kinds of developmental errors, one being more "advanced" than the other. A second, related explanation for mixed style is the writer's newly developed ability to switch styles, resulting in an "error-free" pastiche of discordant words and syntax.

The composite prose of a mixed style is difficult to represent in short passages. There are, nevertheless, specific features that identify this style. The most distinctive among these features is an overgeneralized "rule," which will produce neologisms like:

> Learn to conquired your own problems.
>
> When the child cannot fulfilled that expectation.
>
> The best way to solved that problems are letting the student do his own thing.

In these sentences the inflected verbs *to conquired, to solved,* and the modal-plus-base form *cannot fulfilled* indicate an overgeneralized application of rules for forming the past tense. Significantly, in the same essays one finds correct uses of past tense and uninflected forms:

> The child cannot work eight hours and study also.
>
> The emotional problems that a student may encounter while attending college: parents expectations of you, how well you do in school and the problems you have to adjust to school.

There are two ways to explain these "mixed" results. In some instances a writer will apply rules to conventional writing that may not be part of his or her dialect (e.g., regular past tense -*ed*). However, this dialect interference accounts for a relatively small number of mixed-style errors, so it cannot explain the frequent occurrence and wide distribution of these syntactic neologisms in students' writing.

There is a more comprehensive explanation. Unlike the writer of an auditory style, in this case a student recognizes that speech does not provide an entirely reliable model for writing, a recognition that leads to his or her uncertainty about all or many parallels between speech and prose. In other words, the writer of a mixed style understands that academic writing requires more formal, more logical, and more sophisticated development than speech. But to attain these goals the writer overreaches his or her abilities, creating forms that do not exist *(to conquired)* while also trying to express ideas not fully understood. For instance:

> When a person has to go through the black market for a crime without a victim there is more of a chance he will deal with people who commit crimes with victims.

Perhaps the writer of this sentence knows what the term *victimless crime* means, but this understanding has not been conveyed to a reader. In this sense, lexical ambiguity signals the writer's failure; words and expressions are left unedited and we, as readers, must interpret them ourselves. A close reading may transform victims into partners in crime, the black market may become a shopping center to walk through ("go through"), and in this marketplace we may bargain ("deal with") people for our brand of crime. Or the writer may intend soime other meaning entirely.

Alexia and Visual Style:

In German and French, the original term for alexia was verbal blindness *(Wortblindheit, la cécité verbale)*, indicating the reader's total loss of ability to understand written words, though the reader could, of course, see them. The writer of a visual style exhibits a similar blindness to his or her own prose, and possibly to other writing, via a limited understanding of anything except the formalisms that shape meaning. This selective blindness obscures ideas by highlighting their linguistic form rather than their semantic content. As a result, the visual style often seems more substantive than a close interpretation will support.

In its worst forms, this style is nearly devoid of content, yet so inflated structurally that ten words will be used where one is enough. Paradoxically, the writer's blindness to this verbiage stems from an underlying auditory deafness. Opposite of the problems inherent to an auditory style, the writer's inner voice is completely unattuned to speech, disconnected from everything except the silent medium of prose. Lacking the constraints of spoken conversation, the writer of a visual style becomes disembodied in language, without a sense for audience or the physical limitations of readers. He or she is, in other words, deaf to the interpretive pace of reading.

The gradual development of a visual style does, however, lead to significant gains in writing ability, to more formal, more controlled uses of language. It also signals the writer's first attempts to use supporting devices like imagery, metaphor, and metynomy. In the following examples, the first two have essentially the same style as the last except for their somewhat weaker control over the form:

> This may well deserve invaluable commendings for such productivity.

> From these inventions evolved miraculous deviations in the field of transportation.... This conclusion is attainable only after examination.

> Making the handgun legal only in private residences (where it serves the act of protection of property) and in transportation by official permit only would very likely benefit the average citizen. For that citizen the handgun is a private oath insuring public freedom.

Although no example above lacks problems, the first two include lexical terms *(invaluable commendings, miraculous deviations)* that convey a sense of sophistication, though the writer may not really know what these words mean or how to use them. By contrast, the last example conveys the wrong sense of qualification but the words have the right meaning. Also, this final example shows a writer attempting to reduce abstractions to particular cases ("average citizen...that citizen"), and expanding the argument for bearing arms by the metaphor of a *private oath*.

All three writers share an intuitive sense of formality in prose, an effect they invoke unsparingly. It seems they have learned too well that formal prose can be structurally complex, stylistically impersonal, devoid of humor, and downright authoritative. This formality becomes especially apparent in later developmental stages of writing, as the writer's ideas are represented primarily in abstract forms through repeated use of deverbal nouns: *decide/decision, examine/examination, invent/invention, deviate/ deviation*, and so on.

Students who have developed a visual style will rely on Latinate vocabulary. They will also use more nouns, adjectives, and prepositions than writers of oral-based prose. These form classes often support, qualify, or expand the meaning of abstract (deverbal) nouns. This abstract diction then leads to a stative style; or vice versa, the style requires an appropriately static diction.

Unlike the writer of an auditory style who actively "points" to referents, writers of a visual style merely cite relationships, how notions X, Y, and Z, share their existence coterminously. To support this relational viewpoint, the writers avoid verbs that actively relate X to Y to Z and choose instead to state already established relations:

> As soon as there are value judgments on what a person can and can't do we have the creation of an unnecessary reaction.

> The handgun has become an important object of controversy in the aspect of crime control.

In these sentences no one actively presents the information; its existence is a *fait accompli* that obviates presentation because the writers need only recognize what is, and not how something is perceived. In other words, facts are presented as entirely self-evident.

This authoritative visual style reads like textbook prose, a likely source for students who may read little else—and never anything more carefully—than a textbook. The visual encoding of an unspoken style is most evident in the length of sentences and other features of syntax. For instance, the prose may be more grammatical (in a prescriptive sense) than one finds in mixed style, but a student's internalized command of writing conventions does not make this style easier to read. It is, instead, unnecessarily difficult to understand because the writer attends more to visual form than auditory content. Thus, disconnected from speech, a relatively simple idea becomes an elaborate formalism. The following examples demonstrate this problem:

> The most effective means used in the market is the advertisement industry where modes of human reaction are worked on.

> Using this example, vocational training has rewarded him in many ways, which has resulted in pushing forward society's intellect by perhaps one of the greatest steps in its history, all in an era of time which has now reached a maximum.

> It has been worked on constantly to have attracted the reader who is convinced of the trap that has been designed for him to fall into.

After searching through these passive constructions and subordinated clauses, a reader expects to discover something more than a well-hidden inanity, something more substantive than mere visual complexity. Obviously, no one speaks this way (at least I hope not!); the style sounds "unspeakable" because it is written in and for a passive voice. Also, the syntax of this overly-written style tends to be more complex (subordinated) and elaborate (nonredundant) than speech.

A related characteristic is the style's impersonal, third-person address:

> If one doubts these facts....

> In the course of one's journey through high school....

> If a person is not planning to attend college, chances are he will still get a good job.

In like manner, the writer adopts a pseudo-official authoritative pose, often with appeals to some documented "truth:"

> Through many documented tests and numerous research studies conducted in high school's throughout the nation, the driving motivation to continue to school, meaning at the university level, was to become highly skilled in a position that would provide money and, most important, a sense of worth and accomplishment by being productive member of society. The Truth to this classic response lies in the fact that students have indeed risen above the predominate "Working Class" found to be most common in our society today.

This is what Richard Lanham (1983a) calls an "official" style, written as if the author's objective attitude insures clarity. But the writer is more likely to create a false precision:

> Recently in the past few days... not long ago....

> Many people are not originally from Canada....

> Then as now there were imperfections that kept that period of time from being perfect.

In sum, a visual style emphasizes the formal aspects of prose, to the point of excluding speech-like features in diction, syntax, and persona. This strategy creates its own problems, in false precision, an elaborated, otiose syntax, and inappropriate uses of authority. In a positive sense, this style develops a student's control over the arbitrary rules and conventions of writing. It also exhibits the writer's nascent use of imagery, metaphor, and metonymy as appropriate support for ideas.

Melodic Style and Physical Eloquence:

When all three neurological melodies coalesce, a writer achieves the physical eloquence of a melodic style. The kinetic melody coordinates the pace of writing to match the speed of thinking. The auditory melody regulates the spoken sense of an idea with the aptness of its expression in register, cohesion, coherence, and other features of written discourse. The visual melody augments meaning through imagery, metaphor, and metonymy; it also monitors the writer's adherence to conventional uses of punctuation, spelling, grammar, and format.

In short, this style exemplifies "good" college writing. Since I have already discussed some of its stylistic counterpoints, a few summary remarks should be adequate here. In melodic style the diction varies in complexity, though it often expresses meaning through the visual devices of metaphor and imagery, as occurs in this excerpt from an essay about the high school prom:

> The hall had been transformed into a Cinderella ballroom with marble floors and a huge red carpeted staircase. Chandeliers that glistened and men at the door announcing each couple as they entered were all part of the transformation that took place in my mind.

The syntax is elaborate, but also well controlled as it combines the active description of speech-like writing with the relational emphasis of a visual style:

> My impressions of doctors had been almost totally based on the way television portrayed them in such series as "Marcus Welby" and "Emergency:" the typical nine-to-five doctor forever saving lives and performing cooly in tense situations. I always envisioned physicians as biological wizards who could easily diagnose even the most difficult problems in patients.

The writer uses personal experience rather than appealing to general authority. In this regard the prose resembles an auditory style; however, as the following examples shows, the writer also generalizes from personal experience in a way that includes the reader's experiences:

> Just about every boy says he wants to be a fireman when he grows up. I too had this fantasy when I was young. As early as I can remember the vision of me on the back of a gleaming red fire engine with sirens wailing was etched in my mind. I foresaw the life of a firefighter as that of always saving people from the viselike grip of death, just in the nick of time, and

being respected as a hero in the community. These expectations are the same in every little boy, because these are the views of firefighting as shown on the television, and in the Little Golden type of books that parents buy their children.

More than anything else, this style reads well when it is read aloud. In a metaphorical sense, it provides the equivalent of nonlinguistic cues—eye contact, body gestures, intonation—that a listener notes in speech. Since these cues are not directly available in prose, they must be added by the writer; their absence explains why other styles are relatively difficult to read aloud. By contrast, this melodic style guides a reader's interpretation as it literally transforms the writer's physical presence into a text.

Conclusion

The logic and power of a persuasive argument is not a measure of physical sophistication. Yet is is difficult to imagine a writer who can consistently and persuasively argue in prose without having first controlled the linguistic form that shapes an argument. Just as telling, knowledge of successful argumentation does not necessarily promote a concomitant fluency in writing. Since most college students have, at best, limited control over text production and its attendant melodies, and since teaching students to argue well does not make them proficient writers, it may follow that students will benefit most from a writing curriculum that leaves argumentation, critical thinking, problem solving, and related efforts at cognitive development to follow the initial achievement of physical sophistication. At the very least teachers could divide their efforts between argument and physical eloquence.

I do not want to imply some warmed-over version of 1960s rhetoric, as if self-expression is all that matters in writing. Rather, by teaching the physical sophistication of writing, we can advance a new literacy, one that trains a student's hand, eye, and ear. Personal expression is, of course, an important element in this literacy instruction, but only as it relates to the kinetic melody of creating a text, like a writer's "signature" on the rhetorical delivery of form. The rhythm, symmetry, and emphasis of text production must also be learned as part of a student's ability to generate prose. This instruction can then support a student's progressive mastery of neurological styles. In all respects, therefore, teaching students to master hand, eye, and ear is an unconventional but entirely workable program for literacy, one that distinctively addresses a student's ability to control the biology of writing.

7

Teaching the Subconscious
Acquisition of Prose

When facing a classroom of students, the writing teacher can choose to train each student's body, or, as normally happens, the teacher can ignore the body to train a student's mind. Although neither choice excludes the other, the teacher's primary emphasis—be it mental or physical—will largely determine the way writing is taught. In this chapter I will briefly explain why a literacy of physical eloquence outperforms, even deliberately undermines, a more traditional "functional" literacy that is based on formal learning and self-conscious uses of language. I will also discuss a few basic strategies for helping students to subconsciously acquire prose.

For teaching the biology of writing, we should be most concerned with this subconscious, seemingly effortless ability that all people have for acquiring a first language. Although this ability may decline somewhat after puberty, it nevertheless remains the most effective means for an adult to successfully master a second or foreign language. For college students we can anticipate the same subconscious ability to master writing.

Their success depends, as should be obvious by now, on how well a writing instructor teaches the biological functions of hand, eye, and ear. In Chapter Four I identified a maximum of six developmental stages in college writing as students begin to control the kinetic, visual, and auditory melodies. These neurological skills correspond to the linguistic registers of oral-based, mixed, and text-based prose, and they culminate, as Chapter Five explains, in the physical eloquence of spoken prose. A similar progression is described in Chapter Six, where I discuss the neurological breakdown of writing ability as aligned with three dysfunctional styles: apractic, agraphic, and alexic. When these problems are overcome, or, in developmental terms, when a writer connects all three neurological functions for the rhetorical delivery of prose, the result is a spontaneously

127

produced and neurologically melodic style. Having reviewed these biological aspects of delivery, memory, and style, I can now return to my
original arguments in the first three chapters for teaching physical
eloquence.

To meet that objective I will first redefine the terms *learning* and
acquisition as introduced in Chapter One to go beyond an exclusive
emphasis on mental states; following that redefinition, I will then discuss
the unfortunately neglected topic of how acquisition and learning can be
taught in writing courses. As a final objective, I will briefly address the
general issue of teaching the acquisition of prose throughout the writing
curriculum.

The Body and Community in Writing:
A Redefinition of Acquisition and Learning

During the 1980s the work of Stephen Krashen, a specialist in second-
language research, has increasingly influenced the teaching of writing.
Alice Horning's *Teaching Writing as a Second Language* (1987) devotes
more than a chapter to Krashen's work, especially his basic distinction
between learning and acquisition; Patrick Hartwell's article "Grammar,
Grammars, and the Teaching of Grammar" (1985) also discusses the
significance of learning versus acquisition as these terms are applied to
writing. In brief, learning results from conscious, formal attention to
language, whereas acquisition is the result of subconscious, unrehearsed
processes. Of these two options, it is acquisition that produces the best
results for students engaged in language studies.

Krashen presents his argument for the importance of acquisition in
several articles and books, notably *Second Language Acquisition and
Second Language Learning* (1981), *Principles and Practice in Second
Language Acquisition* (1982), and *The Input Hypothesis: Issues and
Implications* (1985); and he notes the relationship of second language
studies to the teaching of writing in *Writing Research, Theory and
Application* (1984). Above all, Krashen distinguishes between acquisition
and learning by noting how the mind attends to language *(Principles and
Practices)*. In this regard he defines the process of language acquisition by
the formula *input + 1*, meaning that a student subconsciously receives
input that is just one step beyond his present level of ability. If the input is
too advanced, the student will not understand it; conversely, if the input is
too simple or only at the student's present level of attainment, then there
will be no progress.

By contrast, conscious attention to language leads to explicit control
of linguistic forms; the study of grammar is the most obvious example of

this learning process as students focus their attention on mastering heuristic patterns and formal rules. Although Krashen does not make this point, nearly all writing instruction encourages students to learn consciously. For instance, traditional composition textbooks segment writing into stages of production, beginning with the thesis statement, topic sentences, controlling ideas and transitions that expand into a five-part essay arranged by the introductory paragraph, three paragraphs of development, and a concluding paragraph. More contemporary writing texts refocus a student's attention on recursive stages of the writing process, or on aspects of problem solving, or on rhetorical issues of addressing an audience. Even texts intended for writing across disciplines are primers for conscious learning as they talk *about* the differences among discourse communities.

The underlying feature of all texts is that they promote conscious learning. In other words, all composition texts formalize or encapsulate rules, ideas, advice, procedures, or some other heuristic in order to train writers. Indeed, all writing textbooks focus a student's attention on some formal aspect of written language. In a typical range of pedagogical options, practical exercises establish one kind of focus; a general discussion about the nature of writing sets another, quite different way for students to be consciously aware of their efforts.

No matter how the focus is established, textbook instruction becomes a problem as it desocializes writing. Or to make this point another way, a textbook necessarily separates language production from a community of shared values. These values, it should be added, are normally acquired without conscious attention; but the thrust of a textbook is to explain—or more often demonstrate—a value-driven use of language. Textbooks are not written for peers; rather, they initiate the uninformed, an audience that is inferior because it is putatively less capable, less informed, and less qualified than an author/teacher. One measure of this implied dominance is the textbook's reliance on monologue. No matter how well a textbook is written, it remains a one-sided conversation that socially removes the student's body from the author's implied community. While all books may do this, a textbook on writing presupposes the shared value of this physical separation between author and audience. It is more than a rhetorical question to ask why students in a writing class should endorse this apparently anti-social value.

By contrast, a physics or psychology textbook, or any kind of book that deals with a subject other than the activity of writing, merely represents the inconvenience of print as a social medium. When students read these other books, they can use them in a value-free sense, as if that use does not constitute an endorsement of written language itself. In this regard, imagine a student in another country where English is taught as a second language even though it symbolizes the legacy of former colonial rule. That student may become a proficient speaker of English, using it to advance financially or for similar reasons, while at the same time rejecting the cultural values that the English language represents. Similarly, a student can reject or "disown" written English for its seeming anti-social, monologic, isolated means of authorship, yet rationalize its uses when the preferred spoken forms of English are impractical or not available.

I do not want to suggest that students consciously reject writing because they are forced to use textbooks. Rather, most students have quite normally and subconsciously acquired the values of expressing themselves through speech. The act of writing forces students to suppress these values as it takes away the immediate satisfaction of an audience and physically removes the writer from the social community in which speech takes shape. A writing textbook not only teaches this change, but it does so the wrong way.

Above all, textbooks promote conscious learning through their emphasis on controllable aspects of writing. For students who already accept the values of written language, these textbooks may provide some service, but the overwhelming majority of students in a writing class have never acquired anything beyond the language values of speech. For these students, learning to write amounts to a rather trivial collection of rules and guidelines which they can consciously use when conditions of time and topic allow.

More problematical is their textbook model for learning to learn. As long as their coursework is focused on conscious learning, they will not have an opportunity to acquire writing or thereafter assimilate the values of print culture. Since acquisition produces the only long-term and substantive gains in a student's writing achievement, a course that does not promote acquisition essentially fails to teach writing.

Textbooks provide a valuable resource for teachers of writing because they point out what students should ultimately acquire. However, the same texts are in most respects counterproductive when students use them because the print medium is itself a problem.[1] It follows that textbooks should be removed from the writing class, perhaps stored in a reference library or designated for specific, brief, and out-of-class "learning" activities.

A writing class, on the other hand, should promote acquisition through intensive meaningful exposure to writing, exposure that also has the teacher interacting with the student *through* prose. In this way a teacher directs prose acquisition by allowing the natural ability of all students to use language to dominate. Similar to Terrell's (1977) natural method of teaching a second language, in the classroom students should express themselves exclusively and entirely in writing, at least until they have developed a sense of community and a bodily awareness of themselves in the sound of their prose.

Promoting Acquisition Through Silence

For the practical goal of teaching the acquisition of prose, I have adapted a technique from second-language instruction that essentially begins in silence (Dulay, Burt, and Krashen 1982). The first three weeks of a semester, occasionally longer, I ask students to remain silent, to use speech only in emergencies or outside the classroom. These instructions on silence are given in the syllabus, which further requires that students submit to me in writing any questions they have about the course, about grades, attendance, assignments, and so on, which I then copy, answer, and distribute for the class to read. All take-home assignments during this three-week period are voluntary; in-class writing, which normally takes up the entire period, is required.

With each assignment, students receive a separate sheet of comments that I write. This commentary deals exclusively with how I understand a student's work, a paraphrase that expresses my success or failure as a reader. No paper is marked for quality, though I do refer to specific words, sentences, or paragraphs when discussing form or content.

The first week I have students interview a partner by exchanging written questions. The second week they begin to read each other's work, usually in groups of four, followed by a voluntary exchange of written comments. Nearly all students do this voluntary work, which is modeled on the commentaries that I have written. During the third or fourth week I break this silence by having students read their work aloud. Other students are expected (but not required) to write a commentary that is given to me, copied, and returned with my remarks about the comments, one copy to the reader and another copy to the writer.

The many handouts that I distribute in each class serve as a humbling reminder of how difficult it is to write something that all students will understand. My successes and failures serve another purpose too, as they demonstrate for the class what I am asking them to do. That is, in each handout I try to explain myself as fully as possible in order to anticipate questions as I also abjure spoken clarifications. By accepting the challenge of silence, I am better prepared to understand the problems that my students will encounter. Moreover, my students can more readily accept me as someone to guide their efforts since we share the same experience.

I can only develop in this chapter a few preliminary steps towards disowning spoken English, as shown in some handouts initially distributed during the first few weeks of class. In the next chapter I will supplement this material by discussing a few teaching strategies that night be used for returning students to a silent, nascent period of language acquisition. Perhaps it is sufficient here to say that I am attempting to reproduce in the classroom an experience similar to a child's acquisition of speech, but reversed to written language and modified by the adult's slower progress yet greater efficiency in accomplishing this task.

Worksheet No. 1

Directions:

This class will be conducted in strict silence, without discussion or other forms of spoken discourse at any time during the 11:00 am to 12:15 pm class period. I will ignore spoken inquiries; I will also expect every student to refrain from talking. NOTE: If at any point during this class you have a question, then write it down. Immediately after you have written it, give the question to me. I'll either respond in writing to individual students who raise questions, or, if appropriate, I will write both the question and my answer on the chalkboard.

Please follow each step of this worksheet in the sequence indicated below. You'll find that each step (except for number 1) is timed. Adhere to these times intervals. I'll keep you posted on the chalkboard as the time elapses for each step of the worksheet.

1. If you missed class on Tuesday, come to my desk and get a copy of the syllabus. When you have finished reading the syllabus, begin working on "2" of this worksheet.
2. At the last class I requested that you carefully read the syllabus and essay topics at home. I also asked you to write down any questions about these items and then give the questions to me during this class. Some of you (perhaps most) have not come prepared with any questions. If that's the case, take a few minutes now to write down at least one question about this class. If you came prepared with a question or two, check what you have written to be sure the question is understandable.
3. After you have written and checked your question, exchange it with someone near you. Be sure your name is on the sheet you exchange. For the next five minutes answer as best you can the question(s) you received from another student. If you have more than one question to consider, choose the one that in your opinion is most important.

Please write your answer in complete sentences. If you don't know the answer to a question, begin by writing "I don't know . . ." and then finish by inventing an answer. Please try to keep these invented responses plausible.

4. Sign your name at the bottom of the paper you received from another student. Be sure your name is on this paper since I will keep attendance for this class solely from this signed paper. And please make your signature legible! Bring the paper to my desk and put it in my brief case. From my desk take a copy of the grammar diagnostic. You'll have about 40 minutes to complete this test, but most of you will be finished in half that time.
5. When you finish the grammar diagnostic, leave it at my desk and collect the homework sheet. For the remainder of this class you may choose to work on any part of the homework assignment.

Worksheet No. 5

Directions:
1. If you missed the previous class, then immediately begin writing on topic "4" as shown on your homework sheet distributed last Thursday. I have extra copies of that homework sheet on my desk. Come and collect one if you want.
2. If you did attend our last class, please take out a sheet of paper and write your name *clearly* IN LARGE LETTERS at the top of the page. Put this page where I can easily see it. I'll return your in-class essay (INC No. 2) from last class with my comments appended to it. Once you receive the essay, please begin revising it according to the suggestions I have provided. If you have any questions about my comments, write them on a separate sheet of paper and bring that sheet plus INC No. 2 to my desk.

   You'll have 35 minutes to work on this revision. I don't necessarily expect you to finish during this time, but you should make substantial progress. I will collect this revision at exactly 11:35; it will be returned to you next class with my comments and a grade. During the next class you will continue working on this revision as INC No. 3.
3. This class will be our last silent one. Before changing to a more conventional teaching style, I want your reactions to using prose as our only means of communication during class. What problems did you encounter? Why do you think I adopted this policy? For the next 15 minutes, address these and any other questions you may have that concern the silence policy.
4. For the remainder of this class I want you to write about your ability to write. You will then continue working on this topic at home and return it to me when class begins on [date]. Approximately 500 words (or about two pages handwritten) should suffice. You needn't type this assignment, but I won't object if you do.

   Consider some of these questions before you start to write: What problems or weaknesses do you have as a writer? Have you overcome any writing problems before? If so, how? If not, why not? Be specific. For example, how long do you sit at a desk before you write productively? Are you a lousy organizer when you write but not when you do other tasks? Why?

Or take a more immediate look at your writing. What are you doing right now as you start to compose? Do you pause often? When do the pauses occur? In short, analyze yourself as you write and describe your findings.

Or, as one student did recently, tell me why you like to write. How, despite the extraordinary effort, can writing be a pleasure, or at least worth the effort when the writing is done?

Obviously, you can't address all these questions, so choose a few (or make up your own too) and discuss them thoroughly. For this assignment I won't evaluate the grammar, spelling, punctuation, and other mechanical aspects of your writing as much as I will stress how thoroughly you've considered the topic. NOTE: THIS IS NOT A TAKE-HOME ESSAY. Your main responsibility continues to be essay topic No. 1 (distributed the first day of classes).

If the objectives in these handouts appear too ambitious for a single semester of writing instruction,[2] they nevertheless do help students to understand intuitively how writing and speaking differ. That understanding may even surface when I ask students to explain the purpose of the silence policy:

> I think that this policy was adopted to make us, the students, think more about what we had to say before actually saying it. The silence policy makes the relationship between the writer and the reader more personal in that everything is kept between those two people.

> Reading and writing *are* silent ventures. People today are too accustomed to TV, movies. . . .

> I think a reason why you adopted this policy is to see if we (students) can follow instructions.

> Communicating in prose is difficult because people are not accustomed to this. . . . In my opinion the silence policy is like being in training. No longer does our mouth dictate, but our mind does.

> I was surprised to read the silence policy. I at first thought it silly. . . . Having to write a question down to me is a deterrent, so I would instead try to figure it out by myself.

> I assume you adopted this policy to help us strengthen our writing skills and to show us that we should be clear and definite when writing.

> The silence policy in this class made for a very cold relationship between writer and reader. Even the best of writers would find it somewhat annoying to have to write all communication down on paper.

The only medium for communication is prose, therefore, the writer must be able to successfully relay his/her message to the reader through writing.

I am not really sure why this policy was adopted, however I can make my own guesses. I think it reintroduced me to another way of communication. It gave me a chance to communicate through my own writing and to understand through someone else's.

The problems which I encountered in silent class sessions were mainly those of convenience: it is simply easier to raise your hand and vocalize a question. Also, written communication by nature is by comparison limited in its capacity to convey meaning. To make us aware of this and to thereby show the need for succinctness and clarity in our writing is, I believe, one reason that you adopted this policy.

It's a lot easier to speak to someone than it is to write to someone.... I think that [is why] you adopted this policy....

These are typical responses to the silence policy, selected at random (every tenth one) from different sections of a freshman writing course. As these responses show, most students can state a sensible rationale for this policy; I should add, however, that a few students find the silence policy difficult to endure because, as one respondent explained, it engenders a "very cold relationship" in the class.

Certainly the experience of using prose exclusively does at first intimidate most students, but that initial awkwardness usually passes once the routine of conducting a class this way has become familiar. Moreover, when the class resumes a normal mode of instruction that includes speech, there is often an intense spirit of fellowship among the students.

After the silence policy concludes, usually during the third or fourth week, I devote the remaining 11 or 12 weeks of the semester to forms of collaborative writing and peer evaluation. In most respects these writing activities are the same as those assigned during the silent period, except that spoken questions and class discussions supplement the primary exchange of written language. Actually, once the silence policy is over, a class that emphasizes acquisition may look like any other writing class, but this apparent similarity should not disguise the distinctive characteristics of teaching acquisition.

For reasons I have already discussed, teaching the acquisition of prose begins with the subconscious desire that all people have to be understood. In other words, as students express themselves through prose, they must always strive to explain what they mean. Nothing else matters, at least not in the writing class. It follows that teachers should not spend any time lecturing about writing (or any other topic), since that effort would focus conscious attention on how writing should be used. The speech-based delivery of a lecture would also undermine the dominant role of prose for acquisition. As a simple maxim for acquisition, the more time that students have for writing only, the better they will acquire prose.

With the exit of lectures from the acquisition classroom goes the use of textbooks. In their place should be in-class writings, take-home essays, revisions, written evaluations of peers, and any other form of writing that enables students to explain themselves. Writing that concentrates on creative self-expression, as in journals, poetry, fiction, and so on, probably assists acquisition too, although the standards for evaluating these forms are difficult to establish and the response of an audience is often hard to gauge.

As a final means of promoting acquisition, I have students read their prose aloud so they will internalize a sense for the "voice" of prose, a voice that is easier to hear in spoken form than it is to recognize in silent print. This technique supplements the constant exchange of writing that would not otherwise be heard as prose.

Putting these teaching techniques aside for now, I want to re-emphasize that students acquire prose by the subconscious force of wanting to write. If speech is taboo, then prose becomes the only means for social and practical exchanges. (Nonverbal language is a factor, too, but not a feasible substitute for speech or prose.) The practical exchange begins with the syllabus—most students want to know the linguistic tortures they must endure in a writing course. The social exchange also begins, and progressively strengthens, as students become aware of their classmates *through* prose. In this regard, their voluntary participation as writers lessens the social threat of being rejected. Conversely, they must write in order to bond socially, an enticement that explains why few people choose to remain isolated for long.

There are two fundamental points I am addressing here. The first one concerns a writer's subconscious motives for using language. The second point, which addresses our normal awareness of prose, upends the discomfort we typically associate with written language by shifting the burden of formality from prose to speech. Reading aloud does this, as most students will confirm, there being no linguistic torture to outdo the self-conscious pain, the earless, almost speechless act of oral readings. Like turtles, they pull inside themselves, each reader's voice covered by a monotonic shell. And no matter how fast they read, the performance weighs down the listener until the only effect is boredom, tedium, da dum, da dum, da dum.

Why? Inexperience explains some of this problem, but not the willful contempt that even fear cannot disguise. For most students prose is alien language, especially when it enters the comfort zones of speech. They reject it, of course, just as the body would reject a transplanted organ.

Perhaps a better analogy is the bilingual child who suddenly moves to a new location where only one language is spoken. If the parents provide the only input for the first language, some children will never speak it fluently because the second language of their peers will dominate. Similarly, prose functions as a second language that competes with the first language of speech. Students use speech with their peers; they learn prose from their teachers. When the two "languages" come into conflict, students reject prose or, as happens in oral reading, they undo a linkage that would ultimately bring these languages together.

By having students read aloud, I attempt to redefine prose as a first language in the classroom. And by immersing students in prose, I try to recreate the circumstances for its successful acquisition. Having described these goals, it is important to see them in the dual perspective of acquisition *and* learning. To that end I will now discuss conscious learning as it complements the acquisition of prose.

Good and Bad Errors:
The On/Off Switch for Conscious Learning

As Mina Shaughnessy (1977), David Bartholomae (1980), Joseph Williams (1981b), and many other writing researchers have strongly emphasized, the identification of an error differs from the moral assessment of good or bad writing. Whatever qualities we attribute to good prose, these features define the end-product, the ultimate standard of achievement, but not the process of achieving that standard. A "good" error is, by contrast to static norms, transitional and subject to change. Not only does it mark present attainment, but it also helps a writer by signaling where to go, how to advance, when to attempt that advancement, even if it leads to another, "better" developmental error.

A "bad" error shifts the meaning of correctness from the writer's efforts to the written product. This perceptual change redefines *error* in the negative sense of something to be fixed and avoided. In this regard, bad errors have three characteristics—frequency, type, and degree—that establish a roughly ascending order of importance. If an error recurs throughout a text or is repeated in several essays, its frequency intensifies its negative significance, although a reader can often overlook this repetition once it becomes predictable. Certain types of errors, however, stigmatize the writer as being especially dull, or worse, as being comically inept. A single error having this effect makes it potentially more damaging than many errors of another type. But the worst error undermines sense of any kind, disrupting the normal functions of prose to such a degree that even the potential for humor stops, as a reader's interpretation of a text degenerates to pure guesswork.

From a biological perspective, these good and bad errors occur at all stages of writing development, though distributed so that writers of oral-based prose will exhibit most of the disruptive errors, writers of mixed prose will generate most of the stigmatized errors, and text-based writers will repeat the same superficial or even trivial errors. Expressed in neurological terms, a disruptive error is most often caused by a dysfunctional kinetic melody, something wrong with the basic connections between form and meaning. A stigmatized error results from a writer's inability to visualize or hear intended meanings, as happens with mixed metaphors and malaprops. Frequent errors also include the visual and auditory melodies, but divided between oral-based writers, who are most likely to transfer auditory features of speech to prose, and text-based writers, who repeat superficial and rather trivial visual errors.

By identifying the sources of these developmental errors, a teacher can focus writing tasks as a therapeutic means of aiding a student's progress. Towards that goal of physical eloquence, I have listed below some activities that a teacher might consider for dealing with each category of error.

Frequent Errors:

No one should teach writing with the exclusive goal of having students edit errors. That negative emphasis would reduce writing to a state of siege, the process itself under constant threat of attack, the doomed student always ready to concede defeat. Nevertheless, frequent errors warrant some attention, if only to let students improve their defenses.

In freshman English the most common errors are, presumably, the ones that textbook/workbook exercises are designed to fix. Maybe so. But all that really matters is the idiosyncratic prose of one student—each one having a unique set of problems. This individual attention places an enormous burden on a teacher, especially when the same error is repeated by many students. The apparent solution would be to help them as a group, yet the cause of an error varies in two ways: by the underlying process that creates it and by the context in which an error occurs.

Take the example of agreement for subject and verb, a fairly common problem when epenthesis separates them:

> *No one* I know of except perhaps for his supporters *agree* that the law clarifies this issue.

How do we evaluate this error? Obviously the writer "knows" that third-person singular subjects take an -*s* suffix, as shown in "law clarifies;" this knowledge may, however, be competing with a contiguity principle in English that allows:

> None of his supporters *know* the law well.

In this case the last element in the subject, *supporters*, dictates the plural agreement with *know*.

We could also explain the subject/verb agreement error as a performance slip, just a chance mistake that happened when the student was distracted, perhaps to answer the phone or to get some coffee. Failure to edit the prose carefully (a different type of error) underlies the mistake, even when it occurs frequently.

Or possibly the student has no firm understanding of subject/verb agreement in writing, especially when applying this rule requires a conscious knowledge of grammar. The rule itself conflates a functional category *subject*, which includes many parts-of-speech, with a taxonomic category *verb*, which describes a single part-of-speech. Divided usage between British and American English ("the committee is, are"), semantic nuance ("a glass of milk, a flock of geese: milk is, geese are"), and outright exceptions ("data is") further complicate this topic. Few students, perhaps few teachers, thoroughly study these points, raising the possibility that a student has learned incorrect or incomplete rules for subject/verb agreement.

The underlying causes of an error defy a simple analysis; in making this claim I want to reassert the importance of acquisition, for only by acquiring prose will a student permanently avoid errors. By contrast, if a student learns a rule, even a seemingly simple rule like that of subject/verb agreement, that conscious knowledge will *not* prevent mistakes; rather, a student can only apply this knowledge to "fix up" the mistake after it is written. At best, then, conscious learning is second best, a valuable resource for correcting problems but not a genuine alternative to acquired prose.

Stigmatized Errors: Humorous and Dull

It's fun to make fun of students' errors, especially the double-meanings of some freshman prose. Yet the humor is always at the writer's expense, and bringing attention to that person's work, even anonymously, has to hurt. Some teachers try to avoid this problem by saving bloopers from previous years, or by using them in classes where the author is not present. Even further removed, a teacher can find textbooks that are little more than joke books, to be politely used as whipping stocks, perhaps to show students how not to be college idiots.

I have a sense of humor, just as cruel and impossible to control as that of the next college professor; I also deeply resent the condescending, unprofessional use of stigmatized errors as a way to be funny. For sure, students must be told when an error makes them appear foolish, but not in public, and not by the derisive means of public censure. Instead, each student should have the benefit of private censure, ideally by indirect means as a teacher notes the ambiguities of a text.

Besides bloopers, which I have obviously not discussed through examples, students generate another kind of stigmatized error, one that identifies a writer at low stages of development. Less humorous than dull, these errors exhibit a full range of problems, from the most child-like generalizations (of rules, ideas, iterated prose) to the least meaningful reductions in content and form.

In order to discuss these errors, I will contrast a formal explanation for correcting mistakes with the type of commentary that I have already explained for promoting acquisition:

1. "I *sawed* the book on the desk but didn't study it."

    Commentary: I don't understand if you saw the book or if you cut it in half with a saw.

    Explanation/Correction: The verb *to see* is correctly used in the past tense as the irregular form *saw*. Unlike most verbs, which take an *-ed* past tense marker, this one has no *-ed* suffix.

2. "The Watergate man *should of* returned the money."

    Commentary: Perhaps he should've kept it. What's the moral here?

    Explanation/Correction: In the verb phrase *should of returned,* the word *of* incorrectly represents the spoken sound of the aspect marker *have* when that word is contracted and joined to the modal *should*. You should have written *should've*, although you also should know that many instructors disallow these contractions in formal writing.

3. "Doing the assignments for this course takes *alot* of time."

    Commentary: Are these assignments a whole lot of work, say, for an English course, or just a little compared to other courses? I'm not sure what you mean by *a lot*.

> Explanation/Correction: The expression *a lot* is two words, not one
> word *alot* as you have written it.

The commentary always focuses on the occasion for writing, on the author's intent or success in conveying that intention. In these examples I have tried to restate errors and then correct them without bringing notice to that objective; although students may completely ignore these corrected forms, that response is entirely acceptable—and commonplace, as every teacher of writing knows. However slow acquisition may be, it does eventually respond to a subconscious message, an alert that something has interfered with the author's desire to be understood. At some point—no one really knows when or how—the student will register the source of this interference; when that happens, the "surface" error will no longer occur, its cause having been eliminated.

As teachers of writing we can promote acquisition by these means: correct input, plenty of it, and no explicit attention to errors (unless students specifically ask for this information). I reinforce this attitude by saving *all* conscious learning for the writing lab, for conferences in my office, for assignments to be completed at home, in the library, dormitory— anywhere a student wishes, provided that the classroom remains the exclusive locale for the acquisition of prose. In that room all conscious learning stops (compare Terrell 1977).

Elsewhere the learning impulse gets full throttle. For some, perhaps most students, this drive to learn inhibits acquisition unless it has an outlet. To paraphrase Thorstein Veblen (1899), they learn to learn with a trained incapacity for anything else. So we teach them grammar because they think it speeds up the writing process, or we explain their errors for a quick-fix approach to unacquired prose.

Explanations can, of course, help. If students memorize certain errors (e.g., *alot*) and remember the correct form (*a lot*), they can *appear* to be progressing. A little success may even whet a student's appetite for more success, and so on, until genuine acquisition occurs. Although I remain skeptical of this outcome, I find the immediate value of self-correction a necessary adjunct to any theory of writing. Thus, grammar stays, as do all other topics of formal instruction that I have subsumed under this single term.

But it stays in its place, outside the classroom, where students can memorize rules, or principles of organization and development, or any textbook explanation of the writing process, provided the rule, principle or explanation is simple, brief, and understandable (Krashen 1982, 116). Of the three explanations I provided earlier, only the last one for *a lot* would seem to fit these conditions, though students with some background in English grammar or foreign languages may follow the other two without much difficulty.

Disruptive Errors: The Breakdown of Meaning

All errors potentially disrupt a writer's intended meaning, either to change how a reader understands a text or to block that understanding. The most serious errors are completely disruptive, leaving a reader bewildered, annoyed, with no incentive to continue reading. Neither commentary nor explanation helps much, since this breakdown of meaning robs us of the power to teach. At best, we can ask a student to try again, a little harder, as we remain patient witnesses to slow progress. In the worst cases, a student returns with garbled word order, random affixing, bizarre language, the kind of unintelligible prose that defies analysis.

Fortunately, this problem rarely persists. In ten years of teaching composition, and five more years of ESL, I have only met four students who, after repeated efforts, could not explain what they wrote: two from an ESL course, one deaf student, and one drug addict. The first three were using a new language and clearly had the latent ability to become proficient writers.

In all other cases the students who kept working on their prose improved it, explored it, until the unexpressed meaning came out (perhaps not as they originally intended, the discovery of what we mean being fundamental to the writing process).

Because disruptive errors need immediate attention, I treat them as special problems, too serious for the slow repair of acquisition yet too pervasive for the narrow focus of conscious learning. What to do? Rather than bring formal instruction into the classroom, I teach (in my office) what Richard Lanham (1983b) calls the "on/off" switch, the ability to look at a text for its structure then through the text to its meaning. This oscillating perspective is simple to explain, easy for students to learn, though how well they learn to apply it I cannot say.

Ideally they look *at* the text with self-conscious attention to what it means, then alternate to a *through* perspective, without any concern for the text's interpretation. I want them to edit their prose—they really have no choice if the text is otherwise unreadable. Just as important, I locate the problems without explaining them, thus aiming for a conscious awareness of prose that compensates for too little acquisition.

As word processing becomes widely available, this on/off perspective may become a simple matter of loading the right program; students can ignore most errors completely, even the disruptive ones, as they (sub-consciously) generate a text, then use an automatic editor for spelling, grammar, punctuation, rudimentary aspects of style and usage. The potential for acquisition is thus greatly enhanced, though social attitudes towards writing may ultimately preclude any positive effects of this technology.

Conclusion

To simplify my argument I have reduced traditional methods of teaching writing to what the textbooks advise (i.e., formal instruction that encourages conscious learning), and I have discussed this advice by noting its underlying assumptions: (1) students *learn* to write by conscious means, perhaps by teaching themselves to do what the textbooks say or, more likely, by doing what their writing instructors teach them, and (2) by mapping how people learn to learn, as in problem-solving tasks or other protocols of cognitive psychology, teachers can *explain* to students the writing process, even, as I understand it, the ability to think clearly.

An approach to teaching writing that is based on acquisition does not support these assumptions. What does emerge as important for the writing curriculum is the slow, basically subconscious process of language use, a process that closely resembles second-language acquisition. As an overriding goal in the teaching of writing, students should be directed to acquire prose; and by that subconscious means of language development, they can eventually come to value writing as a worthwhile manifestation of print culture. Indeed, only by this curricular plan will significant numbers of students ever achieve long-term success as writers.

8

Teaching Students *Not* To Learn:
A Practical Syllabus

For the overwhelming majority of college students, a teacher should promote the acquisition of prose by enabling students to control the biology of writing. In this chapter I will discuss ways to strengthen a student's subconscious ability to generate a text. Because this development of physical eloquence does not result from formal instruction, my advice to teachers essentially amounts to this maxim: Students should not *learn* to write. They should, instead, *acquire* the ability to coordinate hand, eye, and ear through writing that may variously emphasize kinetic, visual, or auditory functions. Actually, any writing task or exercise can serve this end, either by isolating one neurological function or by addressing all three in concert.

In recommending a few teaching strategies, I will not cite studies to support the relative merits of what I recommend. That research would not really address our concerns since it typically measures only short-term effects; in other words, only long-term studies (or longitudinal research) would aid us in identifying ways to augment the slow, developmental progress of students as they acquire prose. Unfortunately, such research simply does not exist.

In lieu of that research, I will offer the following examples as ways a teacher can try to advance a student's developmental progress towards physical eloquence, and I will leave to my readers to judge from their own teaching experience which methods are most likely to work.

Physical Eloquence and Pace:
Developing the Writer's Kinetic Melody

The ability to write depends crucially on the subconscious pace a writer adopts for producing a text. Of course many factors influence pace: type of audience and complexity of a topic; time constraints, for example, on essay exams versus take-home essays; the stage of text construction from prewriting to editing; individual differences in motivation, thinking style, and writing ability. Yet these and other factors ultimately depend on the ability to pace writing, to coordinate the observable activities of writing with the psychological and unseen act of thinking. No skill is more important for students to acquire or, unfortunately, more ignored by writing teachers and researchers.

Leaving aside the issue of more research, what I recommend for teachers of writing is more instruction that explicitly addresses pace. I will briefly mention here three among many possible techniques; indeed, almost any technique promotes this skill if, as I will insist throughout this chapter, the composition teacher's main objective is to help students *acquire* prose.

Speedwrites (Limited-Timed Writings):

In *Writing Without Teachers* Peter Elbow (1973) first introduced the now commonly used warm-up technique that has students write quickly, nonstop, for several minutes.[1] He claims this *rapid writing*, what is also called a *speedwrite* or *limited-timed writing*, helps students to flush "bad" prose from their systems—a kind of psycholinguistic laxative. Curiously, Elbow and other writers who use biological metaphors nearly always turn them back to cognitive processes, as if the physical production of a text does not have any real significance. I don't mean to criticize Elbow's recommendation—it may be worthwhile to clean the psyche. However, I do want to expand the rationale for this speedwrite technique, specifically by having students practice different speeds of text production.

In practicing this skill, students should learn to produce as many words as possible in a limited time. The criteria for time and topic can vary—two hundred words in seven minutes, one hundred words in three minutes—provided that amount of writing is the sole teaching objective. In other words, there are no errors in a speedwrite, except for the production "error" of not writing enough.

The results of several speedwrites tell an instructor (1) who edits prose automatically, with no capacity to turn the editor off; (2) who generates form automatically, not just for speedwrites but in other "wordy," unmonitored exercises; and (3) who lacks the developmental skills to generate or monitor prose. These are a few of its diagnostic uses.

As a somewhat arbitrary objective, speedwrites develop test-taking skills; students learn to produce ideas quickly but at a pace that allows them to match text production. They can also learn to recognize important correlations between writing speed and quality of writing, a point worth emphasizing since some students think twenty or thirty minutes is sufficient time for writing a take-home essay.

Slow-Writes:

Not just the opposite of a speedwrite, the *slow-write* technique trains students to analyze prose slowly, word by word, for meaning and form. Taking any essay previously written in a course, students should have ample time to revise a very small amount of text. The time spent on revision can vary depending on the time constraints of a particular class; I usually allow fifteen minutes per class for several weeks. Regardless of the schedule, during each slow-write students should produce as many different versions of a sentence (or comparably limited amount of text) as possible, choosing the "best" version by circling it and then being prepared to explain that choice. The instructor should repeatedly grade each slow-write for quality of expression and, if necessary, for the number of revisions produced.

A slow-write differs from sentence-level exercises on style and usage (e.g., Richard Lanham's *Revising Prose*, 1979, or Joseph Williams' *Style: Ten Lessons in Clarity and Grace*, 1981) in two ways. First, the slow-write develops an acquired sense for the production of prose, for the slow, interrupted, basically physiological task of getting words onto a page. As a contrast to speedwrites, this development of pace becomes an obvious skill for students to practice.

Second, and perhaps more important, a slow-write teaches students to "discover" meaning after they have already produced a text. This attitude is easier to encourage after students have experienced for themselves the enormous range of forms they can generate. One sentence can have a hundred revisions, and the best version may change repeatedly depending on the sentence that precedes or follows. In this regard, a slow-write not only allows students to discover what they mean, it also fundamentally shifts the purpose of revision from correcting mistakes to reshaping meaning.

Dictocomp:

In the *dictocomp* exercise, students produce a text that has been read aloud for several minutes, that is, long enough to prevent memorization. Without taking notes, students should concentrate on key ideas, not to replicate the formal expression of these ideas but rather to remember their significance. In this way a dictocomp provides content that is filtered through auditory recall; this input and filter then shape the particular reconstruction of a text, leaving to students the primary responsibility of selecting language—words, syntax, forms of cohesion—that are appropriate for the topic.

A dictocomp stresses form over content by supplying the basic ideas to be expressed. It also trains a student's ear for textual interpretation at a controlled pace and through a medium other than print. The ultimate objective is to have students hear their own prose, not as the silent language of print but as the public language of prose read aloud.

Physical Eloquence and Oral Reading: Developing the Writer's Auditory Melody

By having students read aloud, we can exhibit differences between speech and prose in another practical way: before an audience. We can teach students to listen for errors in their own writing; we can help them to internalize a standard for readability that is based on the reader's "pace" of interpretation; but above all, we can train a student to hear the qualities of effective writing.

By reading aloud I do not mean the trivial exercise of making noises in the airstream that correspond to words on a page. This simple recoding of print to speech occurs, as interpretation of a text, almost haphazardly. What I do mean, to paraphrase a remark by the statistician George Zipf,[2] is the almost metaphysical transition of print to a reader's retina to areas of the brain where the inanimate changes to something conscious, from one reality to another.

If the static nature of print enables someone to speedread a text out of (fleshly) existence, then reading aloud gives back to written language the body it has vaporized. Indeed, this exercise encourages the performance of words so that students can learn to read emphatically, guided by the text, yet—when necessary—alert to impose their own reading. To do this, students must ultimately understand how meaning is organized in a text, where pauses in oral phrasing should indicate semantic closure, and when to diverge from already established patterns of sound, syntax, image, and meaning.

As students read orally we can demonstrate in a practical manner how speech and prose differ. One important difference involves performance options. Even the most unemphatic, monotonic recitation conveys more information than a silent reading because it includes the ear, as well as the eye, for interpretation. In silent reading we only use a single prose channel of expression—visual print. In oral reading, however, we add a speech channel, in this case auditory, that brings with it a physiological awareness of breaks that correspond to the pauses for breathing. These breaks also highlight differences in the pace of interpreting speech or prose.[3]

A speaker must pace the delivery in relatively short breath groups that often coincide with units of meaning, or essentially complete thoughts that can be expressed in various syntactic forms. It appears that breath groups average about five stressed syllables in speech, a pattern that may represent the limits of efficiency for language processing.[4] In making this claim, I want to avoid the problem of *top-down* versus *bottom-up* theories of language processing that psycholinguists have been debating for many years now. Context (top-down) obviously determines how we read a text, that is, how much is read and how well. But language, too, controls how meaning is "packaged;" if this control were not present, then no word would convey a meaning that everyone, however vaguely, shares. The atomistic (bottom-up) view of language processing precludes a solipsistic world.

An oral reading allows us to pin words, as a lepidopterist would, for close inspections that would not be practical in the open fields of discourse and semantics. We can, for a moment, stop the reading to note style, to make students aware of ambiguities, to make them self-conscious about language before words and sounds fly away.

Besides this formal instruction, an oral reading can help students to develop an acquired sense for speech and prose as they literally merge into the same form. This new context—new for nearly everyone today since even children seldom hear prose—trains the inner voice to speak two languages, not just the monolingual English of speech but, too, the bilingual form of spoken prose. As students hear spoken prose more often, they will write more fluently, with a better understanding of how all prose sounds in a silent reading.

Most students can learn to read aloud intuitively, and rather simply, just by doing it. Reading aloud furthers the acquisition of prose by helping students to hear what they may not see. When they emphasize an "empty" word, for example, they are—when reading aloud—more likely to recognize its vacuous meaning. Or, at the very least, the oral performance highlights in sound what a printed text may not clearly emphasize. A simple example will demonstrate how this works.

The following text models the structure of spoken prose. I have modified the original version by removing all punctuation and running together clauses with sentences:

Consider the example of a nurse if she has done well in nursing school and relates well to her patients communicates effectively with doctors and other staff members and writes clear explicit patient reports she will surely be hired before a nurse who knows no more than how to inject a needle into an orange.

While I read this text aloud to set a pace for its interpretation, students mark each of my pauses, then compare results with other students. They are often surprised to find many versions of the "same" reading; in a class of twenty-five students I have had as few as three students who agreed on the occurrence of pauses (I have used a tape-recorded reading to eliminate variations in performance).

Why is this *formal* listening practice useful? Each juncture consolidates meaning, which enables a listener to interpret what has been read. To a large extent, syntax and breath group length determine the ease of this interpretation. Practice in listening to prose thus teaches students to recognize where pauses occur, a skill that develops their sense for optimal closures. This awareness then serves the writer-as-reader who monitors (aurally, though silently, by the "inner" ear) the production of a text while it is being written. In this way a student can acquire prose by just carefully listening to it.

Or this acquisition may occur for another reason, unrelated to the formal practice of listening to prose. When a student reads aloud, that performance necessarily constrains meaning by limiting it to whatever interpretation the student has chosen. Although most students try to get the miserable task done quickly, I interrupt just as quickly, sometimes after each clause to ask the reader and the class why a particular emphasis or phrasing is appropriate, why the author may have intended a different reading, even why a fast or slow pace for delivery is important. These questions force the reader(s) to consider meaning, to resolve ambiguities, ultimately to hear themselves *through* prose.

In writing classes I use this technique to develop students' awareness of how a text is subconsciously interpreted. Rather than have them analyze this process, I merely focus their attention on the meaning of a text. They do not, in other words, analyze the syntax or attempt to measure the pace of their own interpretation. Those formal perspectives would encourage students to look *at* language, to explain self-consciously how the text works rather than understand that it does without necessarily being able to explain why.

However, in advanced writing courses I shift perspectives to the formal properties of language. In these courses I find that a systematic introduction to reading aloud de-mystifies and thankfully eases the students' anxieties about the nature of style.

Teaching Style:

For the rudimentary analysis of "performance" styles, I have had advanced students consider the following sentence:

The boy is interested in enlarging his vocabulary.

This sentence can be read aloud in numerous (optional) ways that either affect its autonomous meaning or influence how we might interpret it in context. In this respect the sentence has at least five styles for getting started (the *S* and *W* markings show strong and weak stresses):

a. The boy (pause) is interested....
   W   S   W S (W) W W

b. The boy (pause) is interested....
   (W) (S)   W S (W)W W
     S   W

c. The boy is (pause) interested....
   W   S W   S (W)W W

d. The boy (pause) is (pause) interested....
   W   S   S   S (W)W W

e. The boy is interested (pause)....
   W   S W S (W)W W

In example *a* the implied meaning would be *the boy*, not the girl, man, or somebody else who wants to study vocabulary; version *b* places contrastive stress on *the*, making the boy specific in some unique way. Example *c* shifts the emphasis to *interested*, as if the boy's interest might be in question. The fourth example *d* responds affirmatively, in a strong sense, to an implied disclaimer that the boy lacks interest. The last example *e* conveys no special "extra" meaning, but it does introduce a performance ambiguity. If an oral reader conflates *boy* + *is* by running together the last phoneme of *is* /z/ with the first phoneme /i/ of *interested*, we obtain two possible interpretations:

f. The boys (who are) interested (in something). . . .

g. The boy's interested (friends). . . .

Of course the potential ambiguities of *f* and *g* are quickly resolved during subsequent reading of the sentences, but for a listener the conflated readings do raise, if only for a moment, the potential for confusion. In other examples *a* through *e* the situation is reversed, because a listener can hear intonation patterns and see other clues to meaning that a reader can only infer visually.

Returning to examples *f* and *g*, in both cases they establish an important principle for the analysis of style, the same principle underlying a definition of style as "language made strange." Someone who reads these sentences, even a careful reader, will probably suppress the ambiguous interpretations, being unaware of their existence. Most listeners, too, will anticipate a pattern of meaning that fits their "normal" expectations. If, for analyzing style, we consistently respond to language by these subconscious means, then we risk ignoring what the author has self-consciously done.

In all cases I am presuming an emphatic oral reading, one that clearly separates strong stresses from weak ones. In some cases the number of *W* syllables may vary because a word's spelling involves an underlying form that is not always pronounced. For example, *interested* can be read aloud:

interested	interested
s w w	s w w w

Either version is acceptable if, but only if, a dictionary lists them. I realize this provision excludes many elisions and reductions that characterize speech performance, but these options occur infrequently, if at all, when a text is read slowly, with emphasis. Careful readings need not always be slow, but from a teaching standpoint, it is much easier to control slow readings since they make explicit whatever performance options a reader chooses.

Style comes alive when students literally breathe into a text their performance options. Obviously, students should quickly get beyond the reading of a single sentence; the one I have just begun to describe allows thirty-one performance options, possibly more. After this close analysis of a few words, if students attend carefully to what they read, I have accomplished what this technique is meant to do.

Physical Eloquence and Revision: Developing a Writer's Visual Melody

Having students revise their prose is unremarkable in itself; like any technique for teaching physical eloquence, what matters is how the technique is used. In this case, the goal I set for a revision is that students achieve a better sense for their identity in prose. As words transform a writer's physical presence, I want the writer to see how another person might recognize him or reinterpret his ideas. A *chained essay* helps to demonstrate this revised self-identity.

Students begin writing in class for about fifteen minutes on an assigned topic. Like a slow-write, the chained essay is extended over several classes, with enough time allowed for all students to produce a few pages of text. After several classes, or until students are about midway through an essay, I have them exchange the essay with another student who must complete it. That second student is graded only for the essay's last half, though the student must keep that half consistent with the unrevised first half.

The original author receives an unmarked copy of the entire essay which he must revise for a grade. As for the other student, a grade is assigned that measures how well both halves are integrated. Given inevitable differences in writing ability, differences I do not try to ameliorate, every student has a challenge to reconstruct prose that honors two identities. Since I do not allow students to discuss these revisions with a partner, their ability to understand each other depends entirely on their writing.

The chained essay has numerous variations, depending on the point of exchange (opening paragraph, first page, and so on) or the number of students who share the same revision. For instance, as a class project I have written an initial sentence that each student has added a few lines to; I then recirculate this draft for several weeks until an entire essay is finished. From this composite essay each student revises a final version, which I collect, copy, and redistribute so that the entire class can see each student's work. If a student wants to receive a grade for this essay, it must be reviewed by all classmates who submit to me their assessments of the student's writing.

I let the class assign a student's grade, reserving the right to intervene if that grade is significantly higher or lower than I would consider appropriate. I also grade each student's evaluation, being especially concerned to find remarks about strengths and weaknesses as well as constructive advice for another revision. The original writer then receives all these evaluations, plus my comments, in order to revise the essay again. The graded evaluations are returned to other students when this final revision is done.

By grading students' advice to their classmates, I obviously intend to demonstrate my standards for evaluating their writing; but I also hope students acquire these standards—ultimately to apply them—when revising their own work. Among the simplest and most difficult of standards, I require only that they write in order to be understood. We do not discuss anything else for evaluations, and I do not hold them to any hidden measures or other standards of performance.

When a writer sees that someone else has trouble understanding him, that writer's response is often to be defensive, sometimes aggressive, and occasionally unconcerned. Yet when a revision clarifies something so that other readers begin to see what the writer means, this positive response engenders a powerful feeling of self-identity, often followed by a strong assertion: "Yes, that's what I mean!" Of course, a student who is uncertain about his or her ideas will not respond this way, unless the discovery of meaning coincides with the opportunity to revise. However it happens, most people want others to understand them, and revision offers the best opportunity for a writer to be understood.

In discussing revision, I have deliberately avoided so far the related topic of grammar. As students revise to express themselves clearly, a teacher may also have them edit the form of their writing so that it conforms to standard written English. Certainly that editing is worthwhile, but it should not become the main objective of rewriting an assignment. Even more important, formal grammar instruction should not supplant a teacher's efforts to promote the acquisition of prose.

Physical Eloquence and Grammar

Many teachers believe that teaching grammar improves—or, more cautiously stated, complements—a student's efforts to write well. This positive assessment has endured seventy-five years of contrary evidence that grammar instruction does little, if anything, to help students who are learning to write.[5] Curiously, most researchers discuss research on grammar in these strictly positive or negative terms, as if only good or bad things can happen when students learn grammar (compare Hartwell 1985; Kolln 1981 and 1983; Mellon 1979; Shook 1983). Yet this blindspot for "neutral" effects may actually tell us why grammar is worth teaching and why it is unrelated to the acquisition of prose.

Students who receive no grammar instruction will ultimately write as well as students who are taught grammar in traditional or transformational forms, as an adjunct to a writing course or as part of that course. To explain these results we need only compare forms of instruction. Grammar provides students with quick, formal knowledge of English, with rules that can be used to edit prose or even pre-edit inner language before something is written. But knowing these rules does not really help students to generate prose, and even then the rules can only be applied to a tiny fraction of English, a limitation defined by a grammarian's incomplete knowledge of English, by a teacher's secondary knowledge of theoretical grammar, and by a student's inability to understand, memorize, and apply every rule presented in grammar lessons.[6]

The opposite problem creates essentially the same result for acquired prose. Students who receive no formal grammar instruction must rely on the slow, developmental pace of acquisition. This subconscious process limits "correct" forms because the student has not yet acquired the fluency to generate them. Yet the student can acquire more prose than a formal introduction to language would provide, and by this means the student will generate more written language that is "correct."

From a teacher's vantage, formal grammar instruction enables students to fix errors, perhaps not frequently or effectively, but the *appearance* of this editing skill will reinforce the belief that students can help themselves if they know some grammar. Perhaps the practical experience of teachers confirms this impression well enough to support grammar as a temporary, initial aid for developmental writers. But the same practical experience may also explain why other teachers view grammar another way, as worthless ultimately, since the editing skills a student learns are quickly forgotten, and worse, frequently viewed as all-important.

In defense of grammar, some teachers cite the pedagogical advantage of using grammatical terms for correcting a student's essay. But this argument essentially ignores the issue of a student's performance; if students do not benefit from grammar instruction, then why should ease of citing grammatical terms be a justification for teaching grammar? Why should students learn to recognize the metalanguage of an irrelevant topic?

One answer is that any exchange between student and teacher promotes acquisition, provided the discourse focuses on meaningful uses of prose. For the discourse to be meaningful, students must learn to "speak" grammar. But two points follow. Teachers who recognize the value of grammar potentially confuse its value with the more fundamental process of acquisition. Students must learn grammar, not because grammar itself is helpful, but because any meaningful exchange, regardless of topic, helps a student to acquire prose. The second point undercuts the first one. If students must learn to "speak" grammar, they have a double burden as language learners, first to develop their writing and then to understand the teacher's response to their writing. Paradoxically, a teacher may see the importance of grammar because students who do not understand grammatical terms cannot understand the teacher's grammar-based comments.

Another reason often cited for teaching grammar is the acuity it gives to students for editing prose since they learn to see problems that would not be evident to a naive student of writing. In a positive sense, they can also analyze style by noting distinctive and sophisticated uses of language. In *Analyzing Prose*, Richard Lanham (1983) calls this ability *sprezzatura,* a term he borrows from the Italian Renaissance writer Castiglione. By self-conscious attention to prose, a writer develops the *sprezzatura* to make artifice into something that appears natural; even more, a writer learns to use it effortlessly.

In fairness to Lanham, no one should expect students to become master stylists after one semester of instruction. But his claims for self-conscious writing are not usefully relevant to developmental writers who, despite their relative incompetence, may exhibit a reverse *sprezzatura*, a self-conscious, mannered, almost painfully artificial style, produced with great reluctance and unlimited effort. Perhaps for these students the inability to "display" language explains their frustrations, not only to improve their writing but, in a more fundamental sense, to obtain the input that would enable them to acquire prose.

Other students can learn to fix their prose, in small ways and for a limited time, by editing it. Grammar instruction thus helps some students improve their writing, at least for the final product that a teacher sees, and for this reason a teacher may view grammar as important, indeed central to the teaching of writing, as Martha Kolln argues in "Closing the Books on Alchemy" (1981).

We need to remember, however, that rules a student learns for editing prose, for fixing the grammar or improving the style, remain *post hoc* additions to the writing process. These rules do not generate prose; they probably do not "filter" into the subconscious after a student has learned them; they do not really contribute to the writing process until a writer is ready to acquire them, and that acquisition would occur regardless of the writer's conscious ability to use a rule.[7]

In any case, most students quickly forget rules for grammar and style. A perfect memory would not help much, either. If a student memorized every rule in a handbook and rhetoric, there remains the problem of knowing when and how to apply these rules. If this knowledge could somehow be learned, then a student would still be limited to the imperfect, relatively context-free and finite quality, application, and range of these rules.

Having noted these problems, a teacher could still argue that *some* grammar instruction is helpful, if only to supplement the acquisition of prose. Yet for developmental students even a little (very little) formal training will give them the wrong access to writing—above all, they need to control the biology of writing, they need to coordinate the neurological functions hand, eye, and ear, and they need the opportunity to develop physical eloquence before they need the quickly learned, relatively easy, and utterly superficial skills of editing a text. Most college students are, it is well to remember, developmental writers in this biological sense.

More advanced writers can profitably use their conscious knowledge of rules to repair a text, to rearrange elements for stylistic emphasis, to do whatever is needed to please a reader. But these students represent a small percentage of those who now attend college.

Grammar for Teachers:

A little grammar instruction, preferably outside the composition class and in the writing lab, may help some advanced students to write a little better. For teachers, though, a sophisticated understanding of English will do much more. Grammar is, in this regard, a powerful diagnostic tool but not necessarily a pedagogical aid for the teaching of writing. In the same way, a doctor might use X-rays to diagnose a fracture, yet no one would presume that a developed X-ray, if shown to a patient, would then heal the fracture.

Like the X-ray in relation to the fracture, grammar may have no direct teaching application to the classroom. It may also, like still photos of the healing process, change a dynamic event into a series of disconnected images, easy to misinterpret when read separately or out of order. In this regard, a student may perform poorly on a test of usage and mechanics yet, when writing an essay, the same student will produce the same test items without error. Conversely, a student who can pass a grammar diagnostic will not necessarily demonstrate that knowledge in a writing exercise.

A grammar test reveals a student's *conscious* knowledge of prose; it may even measure acquired prose, but not fully (no grammar test is comprehensive enough) and not consistently enough to separate above-average from below-average writers. Its power as a diagnostic tool is found in the extremes of very good and very poor writers, a significant correlation since the top 4 percent can often rely on acquired prose when formal learning fails them, whereas the bottom 8 percent have almost no resources—acquired or learned—to assist them.[8]

The diagnostic value of grammar might be strengthened by having tests measure the "twin" grammars of speech and prose. These tests would include interviews and tape-recorded passages along with the standard pencil and paper format of current exams. They would be used to evaluate a student's understanding of contrasts between speaking and writing at all levels of discourse, from breath group length to relationships between pauses and punctuation to differences in register, style, and forms of cohesion. At the simplest level a student would be asked to identify and then assign contexts for speech-like versus prose-like utterances. A more ambitious test would gauge a student's ability to produce speech/prose contrasts.

In their present form, grammar tests measure only half of written language—the half that is derived from a declining print culture. Because few students acquire this half of written language, they can only bring to the classroom a rudimentary sense of forms in prose that are used primarily in speech. What they don't necessarily know—nor should they be expected to know in a formal sense—is the overlap between speaking and writing. A grammar test should be designed to augment this knowledge by clearly distinguishing the forms of spoken and written language.

By ignoring these forms, the authors of grammar tests (often the same authors who write handbooks for freshman English) have cut students off from their intuitions about written language. No small problem. What these tests measure is basically a "foreign" grammar as if it were based on a native language, in this case on a false equivalence between speech and prose.

In concert with handbooks, tests of grammar overwhelmingly fail to distinguish between a student's familiar spoken grammar and the less familiar written grammar being measured. They presume to test one form of English without connecting it to the form(s) that students already know intuitively. To the extent that speech and prose share the same grammars, students can trust their intuitions, yet when these forms of language diverge—in some cases quite markedly—students cannot (or should not) trust a speech-based intuition for prose. A grammar test that does not measure this awareness tells us exactly what seventy-five years of grammar research already shows: nothing that is significant.

Acquired Grammar:

As numerous studies have shown, grammar instruction does nothing that significantly enhances a student's writing. Instead, significant progress occurs through largely subconscious means, that is, without a formal understanding of grammar, without texts, handbooks, or any checklist of linguistic forms.

Nevertheless, outside a classroom the teaching and testing of grammar may help some students, even some teachers who cannot give up what Shirley Brice Heath (1987) calls the "myth" of formal learning. To supplement the many workbooks and exercise routines already available for grammar instruction, one technique offers a practical and common-place way to focus attention on language while also preserving the social and biological dynamics that encourage language acquisition.

Most teachers are familiar with the *cloze procedure*; like any technique, it only serves the pedagogical end that is assigned to it. Merely having students fill in the blanks is not the point of this exercise; nor is the goal to make grammar instruction more "fun," say, than ordinary handbooks or grammar drills would allow. One purpose it could serve would be as a diagnostic measure of speech/prose grammars. It can also be used to promote acquisition:

English is the international _____ of science and _____, and, in this _____, it symbolizes Western _____. When developing countries adopt English as the _____ for gaining access to Western _____, they implicitly endorse the _____ of Western culture: individualism, material _____, progress—these are values directly linked to modern _____. And English is linked similarly.

In the above paragraph, a single part-of-speech (nouns) has been deleted, with enough of the meaning still evident so that students can fill each blank with an appropriate word. All that matters here is the student's ability to provide a *meaningful* answer for each blank, a response that measures a student's intuitive understanding of grammar, or more specifically, what linguists call the "nouniness" of words.

Students should be told that one blank may sometimes allow several answers. Their job is to choose from among the "best" answers at least one word that makes sense within the context of the entire paragraph.

To relate this exercise to spoken grammar, the passage can be read aloud as a dictation. After students copy the dictation, they fill in the blanks and return their copies to the teacher. Before the next class meets, the teacher evaluates their clozes, records their errors (if any), and returns their copies exactly as they were written, unmarked and without a grade.

At the next class, the teacher should also return a typewritten version of the cloze, with the blanks unfilled. Working in groups of four, the students then discuss the best answer for each blank, defending their own choices and, if necessary, marking several answers on the typewritten cloze when no one agrees on the same word. Because each group works at its own pace, it is helpful to have other activities ready for students who finish early.

When everyone is done, one student should record the group's answers; using a blackboard or overhead projector, the teacher then reviews the collective answers of each group. For particularly difficult clozes, a reward keeps students striving to be the "winning" group; that reward can be reduced homework, a special credit in the grade book, any prize that is finally more show than substance. The game-like approach of this technique is often reward enough for most students.

As the class discusses each group's work, the teacher should note the justification for a group's answers and whether or not they have agreed on a single word per blank. Matching the original text is not important, nor even possible always, but students should provide an entire text that coheres. At no point should the teacher discuss grammatical terms that would characterize a deleted word; all that matters is the meaningful use of language in the written text.

What makes this technique worthwhile is the social occasion for using language, for discussing meaning by the contexts that shape it. The students are, in other words, making sense of grammar by using it rather than studying it, not only by talking about words but also by fitting them into larger segments of discourse, by noting their ambiguities and how they affect other students in the classroom. In this paradoxical way, students acquire the grammar of prose because they are not learning it.

Conclusion

Published in 1974, Richard Lanham's *Style: An Anti-Textbook* thoroughly debunked the texts for their special authority to be wise, for their *reductio ad absurdum* of style, and most tellingly, for their advice to students on being clear, brief, and sincere.[9] I don't see much that has changed over the years as far as textbooks are concerned, although we now have more of them, as many texts it seems as there are people who also study writing (and who promptly publish their own text as the *sine qua non* of name recognition). Certainly the texts have changed somewhat, being less concerned now with product than process, and most recently going backwards to rediscover new trends: for critical thinking, for cross-disciplinary writing, for basic writing, and with the aid of computers, for self-paced teaching. In another decade this list will undoubtedly change without really becoming new.

What will change is the status of textbooks, handbooks, and rhetorics. Commenting on their future role in our profession, W. Ross Winterowd joins Jacques Derrida in pronouncing "the end of the [text]book." Their use will be devalued as "the reaction against the authority of accepted texts will be doubled and quadrupled. . . ." In effect, "composition will increasingly become a textbookless class" (1986, 92).

It bears repeating that textbooks merely symbolize a way of teaching, a formal approach supported by a long tradition. Although I have advocated a different tradition, one sometimes (and mistakenly) labeled the *natural method*, my purpose in criticizing textbooks is only to diminish their presence rather than to eliminate them entirely. Indeed, textbooks on style and sophisticated features of writing have a legitimate place in advanced composition courses. But for most freshmen, textbooks of any kind promote the wrong—conscious, formal—access to language. As a result, students fail to develop the subconscious and spontaneous eloquence to physically control the biology of writing.

As for the "natural" method, I see a closer affinity between the student in freshman English and beginning Spanish than the same student compared to an infant acquiring its first words. This perceptual shift is important because the natural method is traditionally associated with principles of first-language acquisition, whereas I have stressed the adult's ability to acquire a second language, an ability that parallels the attempts of a college student to master prose.

Besides the contributions of second-language studies, I must acknowledge genuine progress in all areas of composition research. To a large extent the textbooks incorporate these gains, but my argument against textbooks (and the print culture they represent) essentially obviates their use as an *effective* tool for teaching the biology of writing. It simply doesn't matter that textbooks have up-to-date theory in their pages. Neither does it matter that a student learns something *about* writing from a text.

What does matter is how a student acquires the ability to write without formal instruction. In this regard, textbooks offer the wrong principle of instruction since they direct a student's attention to conscious knowledge of the writing process. Workbooks introduce a similar problem, focusing attention on language itself and thereby fundamentally changing the occasion for using English. So what should writing teachers do?

Above all, they should engage their students in dialogue, written or spoken, and they should design their courses to promote this exchange. Neither textbooks nor workbooks can talk or write to students except in the inert language of pre-packaged monologue. Similarly, a teacher who lectures students by, for example, discussing strategies of invention or characteristics of "good" prose, becomes a talking textbook, very much the person whom students listen to but the wrong person for them to hear. Even a lively discussion, however defined, does little more than make a teacher feel good if the discussion is disengaged from the writing that students have actually done.

Students need a teacher—on that point I want to be thoroughly understood because teaching begets successful writing. All that really matters for this instruction to succeed is that teachers help their students to subconsciously control an essentially unknown biological process.

I realize that circumstances do not always allow the best possible instruction. Special problems may arise with new writing teachers or those, like many of my literature colleagues, who teach composition infrequently and without much previous training, prior success, or current enthusiasm.

They are the ones least likely to resist the lure of textbooks, undoubtedly because these texts provide some security for doing things right. For new instructors especially, a textbook may also be required as part of a prescribed syllabus. Although there may be no alternative to this arrangement, with a little ingenuity a teacher can often subvert the most rigid curriculum by teaching what is required while changing how students are expected to learn.

The key to this change is to counteract formal learning by not doing anything that would promote a conscious knowledge of writing. For example, if a teacher expects students to identify or produce thesis statements, topic sentences, controlling ideas, and so on, these teaching objectives will promote formal learning. In effect, students will be expected to know the metalanguage for talking about writing. Rules of correct usage, rhetorical patterns for organizing an essay, tips for getting started, strategies of problem-solving, and guidelines for clear thinking are also overwhelmingly based on a pedagogy of formal learning.

On the other hand, a teacher can assist students in acquiring prose by exclusively teaching the biological functions of hand, eye, and ear. This instruction depends entirely on the physical identity in prose that reader and writer share. In this respect, the teacher-as-reader should focus only on meaning in order to discover that identity, to understand what a student means and, conversely, to have a student-as-writer explain that meaning. This reader/writer dialogue may include others besides the teacher, but only the teacher can set the appropriate standard for improvement within the context of each student's ability.

Absolute standards for writing quality, the kind of pre-cooked *A* through *F* evaluations that some texts provide, are necessarily poor substitutions for a teacher's own judgments based on the real strengths and weaknesses of a writing class. Just as students change from year to year, so do standards of quality from school to school; it is pointless to resist these changes, to be the cultural Tom Thumb who will plug all the leaks in qualitative standards—as if normal differences in topic and audience would not reshape these standards anyway.

Absolute norms are, in any case, impossible to define so that everyone (even just the Tom Thumbs) will accept them. Differences in standards simply reflect the variations in taste that characterize social classes and historical periods. In a fairly stable and cohesive society (e.g., eighteenth-century Japan or twelfth-century Persia), most people will share the same standards, or at least think they do. In a society as diverse as ours, however, the only standards we can generally agree on are the slow-to-change trivialities of language shape, like spelling and punctuation.

It makes sense to enforce rules governing these shapes, since without them a writer inevitably confounds the dialogue with a reader, but to teach these rules for their own sake presupposes that students will value the exchange with a teacher or whomever else reads their work. Indeed, how can they learn to value something, except as a way to keep the teacher happy, if they lack the personal experience to understand its importance? This question applies equally to all levels of writing instruction, from rules of discourse to motives of eloquence, because our students have almost no opportunity to experience for themselves why they should write.

No textbook, no matter how well it is written, can provide this experience; rather, a student acquires it only through the biological motive of writing for a response, of writing for the primary reason of being understood, and, without being formally taught, of writing for someone— like a teacher—who values standards of correctness and taste. To some extent every writing class provides this experience, which I think explains the small but consistent gains that students show after they complete a writing course. But this improvement needs more support than we normally provide.

9

The Morality of Physical Eloquence

In the Platonic ideal made eloquent by the *Phaedrus*, a writer is like a lovesick person imbued with qualities of truth and justice that serve a greater good. Without debunking this divine sickness, I would suggest a humbler apotheosis of prose, one closer to personal and biological experience than the godly kind, yet one our students might accept as being almost eloquent or even acceptably sublime.

For teachers, this literacy of physical eloquence is a way of motivating students, of promoting a healthy attitude of play with language, of having them write for the pleasure of being understood, while also being expressive and daring enough to risk their identity in prose. Thus, for students, a literacy of physical eloquence serves as the ultimate measure of self-identity, a measure that allows unlimited effort and reward.

Without this literacy, a student returns to the functionalism of a declining print culture. Indeed, for most students the opportunity to improve as writers stops when they leave a writing class or, at best, is only preserved awhile until they leave the university. To offset this problem, which is really a manifestation of larger social attitudes towards writing, I have recommended in this book a curricular design that tracks the best students through four years of intensive writing instruction. This program does not detract from the literacy instruction all other students receive; by requiring that the specially trained students serve as peer instructors and by adjusting class sizes, all students receive better training as writers. Indeed, my basic goal is to promote long-standing gains in literacy while also cautioning against quick-fix solutions that are always in vogue.

This book brings together theory and application from many sources, but I do not claim to have presented here anything unique about writing. In a profession where everything that is sensible has been discussed somewhere, sometime, in the last 2,500 years, a claim for uniqueness would be nothing less than stating my ignorance. Rather, in this book I have offered

165

my views on the biology of writing as it shapes the development of writing ability and is expressed in kinetic through melodic styles. From this biological perspective I have also recommended teaching eloquence as a literacy skill, while also giving this idea a modern sense that is consistent with its origins in education and rhetoric.

As the first rhetoricians claimed, eloquence is a gift of nature conferred at birth, a special talent that instruction may refine but not create. In the seminal works of Isocrates, reiterated by Aristotle, then emphasized by Cicero and Quintilian, eloquence is above all performance, a matter of voice, effective gesture and pose in the orator's delivery. In subsequent history of rhetoric, eloquence becomes a sixteenth-century garden of tropes and schemes; in this Edenic sense, as Henry Peacham understands it, eloquence is a divine gift to be recovered after the Fall by careful and mundane study. Given this moral point of view, it should not surprise us to learn that students four hundred years ago were whipped and bullied towards a state of literary refinement, of purity, grace, and eloquence that few achieved despite the other-worldly incentives for that achievement.

Today, to be even slightly eloquent is a remarkable act of defiance, an unnatural act almost, that few college students would emulate for any writing teacher's sake. How could they? Too often our schools at all levels of instruction teach a literacy of plainness and utilitarian discourse, so that whatever gifts a writer is born with stay wrapped up, permanently covered by the bland functionalism of what needs to be taught.

Of course the schools express a social attitude that no teacher can work alone to overcome; a gift with words arouses the typical American's fear of language, a fear deeply felt though casually expressed by the "you know" assertions that substitute for genuine meaning. Because language empowers us to see ourselves, it makes a teacher's job a matter of saying to students, "I don't know what you mean." But that's not enough. Like schoolmasters of four hundred years ago, if we look merely to dictate the students' use of language, most will suffer our peculiar tastes for as long as the temporary world of writing instruction has them at risk.

Rather than forcing students to learn the peculiar values of our print tradition, a tradition that most students are ill-disposed either to understand or to accept, I have recommended in this book a much more basic program of instruction, one that begins with the biological acquisition of language and culminates in the writer's subconscious drive for personal eloquence.

By the time they reach college, most students have become writers without a personal style, without the ability to write well or even the desire to be more than competent writers. What they experience in college, in freshman English and in most other courses that teach writing, is the utilitarian end of prose: it will help them to think clearly, help them to study for other courses, help them to get decent jobs, and once this help has been provided, the practical value of learning to write comes to an end.

By setting a utilitarian goal for literacy, we motivate the successful writer to stop improving. By contrast, a literacy of physical eloquence sets a personal goal, one that encourages students to write for the same biological and largely subconscious reasons that motivate them to speak. We all need to socialize, if only to express ourselves so that others will understand us. To be slightly eloquent is the writer's means of socializing well—or well enough to keep on trying. Actually, since no writer achieves a skill that obviates refinement, a literacy of eloquence has no practical limit: a writer can always strive to be more eloquent.

Teachers of writing can promote this goal without really knowing they are, as much by upholding various standards for quality as by conveying to students a genuine love of language. But teachers can do more, of course, than merely serve as role models; and one means I have recommended is to teach physical eloquence as something not learned from a textbook.

Not only will students improve as writers, but they will retain their writing skills longer and at a higher level of ability if they are encouraged *not* to learn. The best way for teachers to measure this negative definition of teaching is to ask if their students are encouraged to acquire prose. Nearly all students can acquire prose despite themselves, despite a trained incapacity to do anything except learn language through formal instruction. The alternatives I have most often recommended are based on second-language teaching, although any technique from any field of language instruction could be modified to promote the acquisition of prose.

In choosing a second-language approach to the teaching of writing, I have emphasized the "foreignness" of prose, as if writing were a foreign language that students are neither familiar with nor especially anxious to know. The decline of print culture insures that writing teachers will be devalued, too; our success as representatives of an almost alien language and culture depends in large measure on our willingness to rethink who we are, whom we teach, how they are taught, and why.

I have argued in this book for a self-assessment that begins with the biology of writing. Above all, teachers must recognize the physical constraints of hand, eye, and ear, and they must learn to assist students in mastering these neurological functions. Measures of style also give teachers evidence of a students' progress towards physical eloquence as they move through the stages of development from a kinetic, auditory, and visual style to the neurological sophistication of a melodic style.

No checklist of linguistic features will adequately identify in one writing sample the developmental stages that lead to physical eloquence. Nevertheless, a teacher can intuitively assess several examples of a student's work, first by attending to speech-like versus prose-like constructions, and then by reading a text to gain a general impression of a student's writing ability. Once a teacher becomes adept at this two-part evaluation, it proceeds quickly and efficiently. Moreover, as the appendix to this chapter shows, when several teachers join together in doing this work, the results they obtain can be used for many important purposes besides diagnostic evaluation of individual students. At the very least, measures of physical eloquence, whether obtained for political or scholarly reasons, show that students ultimately benefit from writing instruction.

The Future of Literacy

Only in another book could I begin to describe an emerging oral literacy as it is now and as it will likely develop in contrast to traditional written literacy. Perhaps the writing produced by most of our future students will be more recursive than linear in organization; it may also depend more on associational rather than critical reasoning. Whatever these changes may be, I do not want to imply that a radical change will occur, as if literacy in its oral forms differs fundamentally from its written forms. Rather, I do want to stress a change in *values* associated with the decline of print literacy and the emerging ascendancy of spoken literacy.

Before I continue, I must acknowledge that making predictions about the future of literacy is not a safe or perhaps even responsible endeavor. Nevertheless, the persistent though largely unsubstantiated alarms about the "literacy crisis," and the reprehensible denigration of students' use of language, strongly implies that a basic change in values is taking place. This change not only frightens many people, it also prompts them to rally in support of traditional print literacy while they also demean the shortcomings of modern students' writing.

We can proceed on one of three assumptions: that college students write with the same proficiency now as they did at any time during this century; that students' writing has markedly declined or improved by comparison to some prior standard of ability; or that students neither write the same nor better or less capably but instead write differently than they may have in previous decades. It is impossible to prove any of these assumptions, but I can ask my readers to judge for themselves which is more likely.

Regarding the first assumption, teachers and other people concerned with literacy have an almost visceral reaction to students' writing, a reaction that is hard to explain if students are unchanged as writers, or if the people evaluating students have failed to keep pace with changes. As for the second assumption, whose standard should we use? The very choice of a standard reflects social values about writing that may not fairly measure a particular cultural group or even the same group across time. In other words, standards of performance change as much as writing does because both are imbued with evolving social values. (Imagine a student who writes about censorship as Milton does in "Aeropagitica." The teacher's comments at the end of the paper might read something like: "No paragraph sentences, please. Why do you make all these vague references to popular culture? Take care to avoid ambiguous pronoun references. Can you get to the point more directly?")

The third assumption obviates the other two. In one sense, students' writing probably is *relatively* the same as it has always been. In another sense, their writing has perhaps declined or improved by comparison to some older, inappropriate standards of performance that we inevitably carry with us. In both cases, if we accept as axiomatic that any language will serve the needs and purposes of its users, then students are writing today as well as they need to.

The problem of illiteracy is not in our students but, unfortunately, in us. As educators we need to accept the changing values of a society that is moving away from print literacy and towards a literacy of oral expression. A slow evolution perhaps, but whatever the pace of change, I do not wish to repress our students' use of language. Instead, I see the only ethical way to teach writing as the teaching of physical eloquence. I would encourage other teachers of writing to do the same.

APPENDIX TO CHAPTER 6:

Review of Neurolinguistic Research
on Writing Disorders

Aphasiologists often compare their patients' language to the speech or prose of normal subjects, a comparison that shows relative differences between both groups. Dubois writes in "La Neurolinguistique" about the problems of making this comparison, since "at the very start of his work the neurolinguist is confronted with the delicate and difficult task of defining what is normal and what is pathological language behavior" (1967, 18). American, German, and British neurologists have all expressed similar concerns.

Despite this concern for defining normal and abnormal language, surprisingly few researchers have examined similarities between language impairment and stages of language development.[4] When researchers have studied this relationship, they have nearly always restricted their attention to the speech of infants and children, as the work of Teuber and Rudel demonstrates (1967), or to the related issues of cerebral plasticity and recovery rates after brain injury, as found in Lenneberg's *The Biological Foundations of Language* (1967).

In what follows I examine previous research on agraphia to explore relationships between the developmental writing of normal adults and the impaired writing of adults who have suffered a neurological injury. Considering the novelty of this study as it compares normal developmental progress versus abnormal neurological failures, I have tried to be especially cautious in obtaining and stating results.

As one constraint I have limited my review of agraphia studies to research conducted before 1980, in order to concentrate on findings that have been corroborated over several decades, and in some cases for more than a century. By this procedure I hope to avoid discussing evidence that is merely topical or fashionable. Of course, by limiting my review this way I necessarily omit more recent work by Michael Gazzaniga, David Caplan, Alfonso Caramazza, Andre Lecours, to name just a few of the more prominent researchers now studying language and the brain. But their work remains untested for its lasting value, so I have chosen to emphasize the "classical" studies only.

As another way to strengthen this review, I have included studies from the French, German, English, and American research traditions to note convergences across time (the mid-1800s to 1980) and across linguistic and cultural perspectives. In other words, since the literature on this subject is vast and often speculative, I have tried to summarize the main findings.

Neurological Disorders in Writing

The four disorders I will discuss are apraxia, aphasia, agraphia, and alexia. Having focused this discussion on impaired writing, I will begin with the central disorder of agraphia, which can then be compounded with the others to produce these terms: *apractic agraphia, productive agraphia* (like Broca's aphasia), *receptive agraphia* (like Wernicke's aphasia), and *agraphia with alexia.*

Agraphia:

Researchers have long debated the existence of agraphia in a pure form, which would be complete loss of writing ability (but not the ability to copy) without any other language impairment. In 1884, Pitres' article "Considération sur l'Agraphie" cited the first case of pure agraphia, but as Chedru and Geschwind ("Disorders," 1972) have subsequently evaluated the evidence, Pitres' subject actually could write with the nondominant hand and suffered from other language-related disorders. This reinterpretation is partly a matter of definition, since Brain *(Speech Disorders)* allows that patients with pure agraphia are "usually, but not always, able to write with the left [nondominant] hand" (1963, 134). Other researchers have taken similar latitude in defining this disorder.

Besides the ambiguity of this term, another important factor in defining pure agraphia has been the attempt to locate a center for writing, called *Exner's center*, named after the author of the book *Untersuchungen über die Lokalisation der Funktionen in der Grobhirnrinde des Menschen* (1881). Although various locations for Exner's center have been proposed by researchers from many countries and over several decades, including Gordinier (1899), Bastian (1898), Henschen (1922), Nielsen (1946), and Brain (1965), no site has proven to be tenable, a shortcoming that has been well documented by opponents of this idea, who also represent diverse countries and many research periods: Dejerine (1891), Wernicke (1903), Russell and Espir (1961), Hécaen, Angelergues, and Douzenis (1963), and Luria (1970b).

Today, researchers have largely abandoned the search for Exner's center, and many have rejected the similar effort to identify cases of pure agraphia. In summarizing this viewpoint, Chedru and Geschwind note that writing is a delicate, fragile task, barely encoded by the average person. As a result, isolated writing disorders can occur from diffuse brain dysfunctions. In any case, as Geschwind points out, "The neural circuits employed in writing are not known in detail" (1982, 115). Among those researchers who take a more moderate position, Dubois, Hécaen, and Marcie argue in "L'Agraphie 'Pure'" (1969) that pure agraphia exists as the extreme manifestation of writing disorders, but they also acknowledge that other language disorders may accompany this "pure" form.

A more promising way to classify agraphia divides it into two main types corresponding to the left and right hemispheres. Although this distinction has become part of popular folklore during the last two decades, its importance has been noted by diverse researchers throughout this century: Wernicke (1903), Foix (1922), Kleist (1922), Leischner (1948), Hécaen (1962), and above all Joseph Bogen

(1969) for his seminal two-part article "The Other Side of the Brain." Related studies confirm that lesions in the right hemisphere typically produce an apractic agraphia, or the inability to construct writing, as defined by Kleist (1934), Nielsen and Raney (1938), Critchley (1953), and Alajouanine and Lhermitte (1960). Other researchers follow Weisenberg and McBride (1964) in referring to this condition as *spatial agraphia*; still others adopt Russell and Espir's (1961) term of *motor aphasia*. These different usages, which bedevil many terms in aphasiology, are more annoying than significant; as a practical solution I will use only one term and not hereafter refer to its alternate forms.

Lesions in the left hemisphere cause nearly all other forms of agraphia, including agraphia with productive or receptive disorders and agraphia with alexia. Although I will not review all these left hemisphere varieties, those I do discuss will follow a review of the right hemisphere disorder.

Apractic Agraphia:

According to Hécaen and Albert, "Apraxia produces agraphia by impairing the ability to form formal graphemes, inversions and distortions appearing in their stead" (1978, 65). In most cases this disorder also affects a person's ability to spell or to compose words with alphabet blocks. According to Bogen (1969) its most salient characteristic is a patient's loss of the "memory" to form letters, although words may be spelled aloud correctly. Russell and Espir (1961) note two milder versions of this disorder: (1) micrographia, the production of tiny, carefully drawn letters, and (2) the opposite condition of macrographia, which is the production of letters in oversize script. In either case a patient's control of text production is aberrant because the normal size and shape of written language is distorted.

Although Weisenberg and McBride (1964) and Hécaen, Angelergues, and Douzenis (1963) have questioned the linguistic basis of apractic agraphia, this disorder does affect linguistic output and, for that reason, it belongs in a classification of writing disturbances. As Bogen notes, apractic agraphia is a linguistic problem to the extent that a patient cannot translate verbal comprehension into action. Similarly, Geschwind's major article "Disconnexion Syndromes in Animals and Man" (1965) clearly links the cause of apractic agraphia to the linguistic nature of this disorder, since it results from "the absence of engrams" for language in the right hemisphere, a loss perhaps attributable to disconnections between the two hemispheres.

The aggregate of evidence about apractic agraphia shows that it severely limits a writer's ability to generate forms, as exhibited in poor muscle control when writing and the limited amount of text actually written. Causing these symptoms of apractic agraphia are two key neurological dysfunctions: a malformed kinetic melody "blocks" writing, or a deficient visual melody deforms the size and arrangement of letters.

Compared to normal writing, this disorder most closely resembles an oral-based style, especially as both disrupt the kinetic melody of text production. Developmental problems with handwriting, mostly in manuscript, also link the least capable oral-based writers to someone with apractic agraphia. This similarity is based on their inability to control the neurophysiology of writing; they may differ, of course, as to the breakdown of this control versus the absence of its prior development.

Productive and Receptive Agraphias:

Most agraphias result from an injury to the left hemisphere (LH) and are often characterized by a writer's disoriented thinking or even complete breakdown of ideational processes. Although the severity of these agraphias varies widely, as does the location of a cerebral injury, the four LH agraphias that I will discuss do represent a typical though not comprehensive inventory of productive and receptive writing problems.

According to Agranowitz and McKeown (1968), a patient with *amnesic agraphia* can shape single letters correctly but cannot join them into sensible words. Kinsbourne and Rosenfield explain this problem in "Agraphia Selective for Written Spelling" (1974) as the patient's lack of an engram to visualize an entire word. Yet, as they further establish, the patient retains the engram for shaping individual letters. In effect, the kinetic melody remains intact, enabling a patient to write graphic forms, but the patient's memory of these forms has been partially obstructed for their visual interpretation and fully disconnected from the inner voice of prose comprehension. Significantly, the same patient may have no difficulty understanding speech or spelling a word aloud.

A similar problem, labeled *paragraphia* by Agranowitz and McKeown and by Hécaen and Albert (1978), disrupts the writer's ability to join words syntactically so as to construct a meaningful clause. The patient may know the meaning of a word in isolation, and may spell the word correctly in a sentence, but that sentence will also include nonsense words (albeit sensibly spelled) and other words that are substituted out of context. Like amnesic agraphia, this disorder apparently does not affect a writer's ability to generate words, and neither does it completely disrupt the visual melody of spelling. However, the patient's inner voice cannot regulate the construction of sentences or convey ideas in a meaningful sequence.

Ideokinetic agraphia differs from the first two examples in that a writer must go through an elaborate warm-up phase, and, in some cases, must repeat this ritual to create each mark on a page. Brain (1965) describes a patient with this disorder who starts writing by adopting an appropriate posture, grasping a pen or pencil, and then bringing it to a page, as if the writer initiates an elementary stage of prewriting in order to slow down all aspects of text production. If this serialized ritual enables the writer to control the kinetic melody as a step-by-step process, then it may also provide enough time for the writer to control the other neurological melodies.

As a nearly opposite problem, *jargonagraphia* characterizes a writer almost out of control, who generates fixed expressions automatically, at a normal and sometimes faster than normal speed. Kinsbourne and Warrington further note in "Jargon Agraphia" (1963) the writer's lack of linguistic control, which is signaled by neologisms and other words used out of context (paragraphias), and by asyntactic constructions that are well-formed in some places but not throughout a sentence, paragraph, or larger unit of written discourse.

Jargonagraphia potentially disrupts all three neurological melodies, though the evidence for an impaired kinetic melody is debatable to the extent that an abnormally fast pace of writing represents a production problem. Since relatively few patients exhibit this accelerated writing, Dubois, Marcie, and Hécaen do not refer to it when they classify jargonagraphia in their "Description et Classification des Aphasies" (1967) as the loss of visual and auditory functions, a loss so severe that it often disconnects meaning from writing.

In sum, agraphia exhibits a broad range of symptoms, from production errors in words and sentences, and unusually slow or fast speeds of text construction, to receptive problems of recognizing nonsense words or unscrambling a random, confused syntax. The three neurological functions create these respective symptoms: the kinetic melody disrupts the pace of text production, the visual melody is "blind" to neologisms and paragraphias, and the inner voice of the auditory melody does not hear asyntactic prose. Since these dysfunctions differ significantly from one case to another, it is probably best to regard agraphia as a mix—rather than a pure example—of language disorders. In this sense, agraphia also subsumes the productive and receptive disorders of Broca's and Wernicke's aphasias.

Normal writing exhibits many of these "disorders" throughout later stages of an oral-based style and in all aspects of a mixed style. Developmental progress apparently has the same variety of neurological connections that a writer must control as there are breakdowns in these connections that result in agraphias.

Agraphia with Alexia:

As an isolated research topic, alexia has traditionally received far more attention than agraphia. For that reason I will begin with a review of alexia research only, and then broaden this review to include instances of agraphia with alexia.

In a richly documented article on alexia, "Les Analyses Neuropsychologiques et Neurolinguistiques de l'Alexie," written in 1976, Dubois-Charlier reviews research from 1838 to 1969. From the earliest periods of this research (1838 to 1890), she cites six fundamental findings:

1. In the most severe cases of alexia, a patient cannot read his or her own handwriting or that of another person, yet can occasionally read printed texts, especially newspaper and magazine titles. In less severe cases the patient can read individual letters but not entire words.
2. The incapacity to read isolated letters can be overcome when a patient traces the letters in the air or on a page. Grasping a pen or pencil seems to help the patient, as if a strong association between writing implements and reading re-establishes the visual melody.
3. When the disorder has stabilized, a patient may speak normally, although sometimes the alexic's speech will include irrelevant or nonsense words (paraphasias). The relative absence of other speech problems suggests that an alexic's auditory melody remains largely intact.
4. A form of "verbal amnesia" may persist long after the onset of other

symptoms. This forgetfulness occurs most often in spontaneous speech, but it can also include written words.

5. In most respects the ability to produce writing is unimpaired, consistent with a patient's writing ability prior to an injury. However, during the onset of alexia, a patient will often misspell words, producing errors that suggest some disruption of the kinetic melody (i.e., the patient can recognize correct spellings but cannot produce them).

6. Quantitative skills are unaffected as shown by a patient's ability to do simple arithmetic. In other words, alexia is properly classified as a linguistic disorder, since a patient's "blindness" does not extend beyond verbal forms.

These six symptoms of alexia have been subsequently accepted by most researchers, but differences regarding the interpretation of these symptoms have long been debated. One common source of disagreement has been the effort to identify precise locations of brain injuries that correspond to forms of alexia and agraphia. Opposed to this largely French school of localizationists is the German tradition of associationism, which emphasizes the interrelatedness of brain functions. As a direct consequence, associationists rejected the idea of a writing center, believing instead that writing is a cerebrally integrated skill. Wernicke stands out as a leading exponent of this viewpoint.

By contrast, during the first part of this century most French researchers followed the lead of Dejerine (1891) and Marie (1926), who tried to find a specific location in the brain for writing. As I noted earlier, although researchers have now rejected the idea of a writing center, Dejerine did show the existence of alexia with agraphia, a finding which has subsequently been confirmed by Hécaen, Angelergues, and Douzenis (1963).

Patients with this combined disorder will exhibit problems that are directly related to word length. A three-letter word, for instance, will take longer to read or write than shorter words; this difference may also correspond to word type, since most function words are shorter than substantives. Predictably, as word length increases, a patient experiences greater difficulty in recognizing a word or using it correctly. Howes (1962) finds that the same pattern may apply to all forms of aphasia.

Marshall and Newcombe (1966) provide additional evidence that word type, including a word's shape, meaning, and derivation, directly correlates with three types of alexia. In the first type, patients will reverse single letters or entire words, substituting a backwards sequence for the intended form (*dug* for *bug*, or *gub* for *bug*). The second type includes patients who confuse the grapheme/phoneme correspondence of similar looking forms *(barge, bargain)*. This problem could also be explained as a partial breakdown of auditory and visual connections. The final type of disorder has two characteristics, one being a patient's confusion of derivational forms *(truth, true)*, and the other is a related problem with producing or interpreting abstract nouns. In this regard, work by Richardson (1975) and Shallice and Warrington (1975) indicates that even severely dyslexic patients will read and write concrete nouns more easily than any other lexical items, perhaps because the concrete nouns are more "imagistic."

A similar analysis of alexias with agraphias has been proposed by Dubois-Charlier in "A Propos de l'Alexie Pure" (1972). Based on the earlier work of Hécaen and other French researchers, she identifies three forms of alexia. In cases of *verbal alexia*, a patient can decode graphemes and spell short words accurately. Problems arise due to word length and the relative infrequency of a word's occurrence in ordinary discourse. Most often a patient will have trouble with the end of long, unusual words, a difficulty that is apparently related to the Latinate vocabulary of much written language. Normal readers and writers similarly tend to neglect the terminal part of a word, inferring the whole from its initial components; or expressed in a positive sense, Dunn-Rankin asserts that "the beginning letter . . . of a word is the dominant visual characteristic" (1982, 135). Because this contextualized reading depends on informed guesswork, a successful reader must have an underlying memory of written language and its arcane lexicon. Loss of this memory, even partial loss as is usually the case for patients with alexia and agraphia, will significantly impede the production and interpretation of writing. The same point applies to normal but developmental readers and writers. Lacking an extensive memory of prose, they make uninformed guesses, and, as a result, they will make "basic" errors.

A second category of alexia represents a patient's loss of grapheme recognition as shown in problems with reading individual letters or even naming them. Yet a patient's ability to read and understand entire words remains largely intact. Called *literal alexia*, it demonstrates the patient's use of a "global strategy" when reading or writing a word, rather than an atomistic procedure of analyzing each letter (Dillon 1981 reviews the related issue of top-down versus bottom-up language processing). Context may play an important role in assisting these patients as they read and write. One could argue, as Dubois-Charlier (in "Les Analyses") does, that patients can infer from the identification of some letters the probable spelling and meaning of an isolated word. Yet a patient's ability to recognize whole words may simply indicate that they are neurolinguistically stored as complete units. Also, the patient may have had engrams for graphemes and word recognition but at some time lost the former. Context does become an advantage, however, when words are used in meaningful sentences.

Alexia of the phrase or sentence is the last form that Dubois-Charlier identifies. Patients with this disorder can read isolated letters without difficulty, but they do have problems with whole words, frequently deleting a word's last part. Moreover, they have their greatest difficulty reading words in context, being unable to recognize syntactic organization or failing to understand semantic clues when words are grouped together.

This three-part classification reveals a general characteristic of agraphia with alexia that is supported by most other research. Above all, there is a complex network of interdependent functions regulating the task of reading and writing. As connections within this network go awry, problems develop at every linguistic level, from the smallest correspondence between phoneme and grapheme to the largest relationships of extended discourse. Except for the most extreme instances of language disorders, as described in Weigl's "Neuropsychological Experiments on Transcoding Between Spoken and Written Language Structures" (1974), most patients can eventually manage to re-establish these connections, perhaps not fully, but at least to some extent through compensatory use of intact systems.

In sum, alexia with agraphia represents a breakdown of the networks that connect the three neurological functions. Although a person may write fluently, the visual melody does not function to edit spellings, especially at the ends of Latinate words. This selective focus also characterizes the writer's auditory melody, which relies on context to signal meaning, apparently because the writer has difficulty hearing or analyzing the content of individual words.

Like the text-based style of normal writing, this disorder "blinds" a writer's ability to see prose as others would read it. This similarity can be stated in opposite relationship too, since the text-based writer invokes a visual melody that is largely unavailable to someone with alexia with agraphia.

Summary of Evidence:

How does this review of language disorders explain differences in the styles of normal adult writers? When neurological functions of hand, eye, or ear are disrupted, the resulting linguistic problems are strikingly similar to the developmental problems of college writers. Whether due to cerebral injury or lack of neurophysical encoding, failure to write effectively can be characterized by a range of styles with distinctive linguistic features.

By studying these kinetic, visual, and auditory features, it is possible to reconstruct the biology of writing as a normal writer develops from one stage of ability to the next. This development continues until a writer achieves the neurological maturity and stylistic sophistication of physical eloquence.

APPENDIX TO CHAPTER 9:

A Five-Year Evaluation of Writing Performance

Teachers do make a difference in improving students' writing. That claim is supported by five years of evidence obtained by composition teachers at the University of Maryland Baltimore County (UMBC). This evidence shows the progress of freshman writers and other students in a range of composition courses. Besides the intrinsic value of knowing that writing instruction works, these results offer evidence of a practical kind that all teachers should learn to take advantage of. Although we may understand the slow, developmental advances of our students, too few people outside the writing profession have the same insights. Not just colleagues in other departments, or even administrators who allocate the money for writing courses, but the general public as well needs to understand the fragile, relatively slight, but nevertheless significant gains that occur because of writing instruction.

Since 1981 teachers in the UMBC Writing Program have been measuring the writing abilities of college students who take a composition course. The results for each year confirm these trends: (1) that students become better writers after completing a composition course, (2) that this improvement is modest but consistent for all courses, and (3) that skills formally learned in a writing course erode rather quickly unless writing practice is combined with writing instruction so that students can acquire prose. I will discuss these points briefly as they apply to each year of the five-year study.

In 1981, as for each subsequent year, this basic question was asked: Would students enrolled in freshman English and related courses improve their writing skills? In 1981 slightly more than one-half did. That is, 54 percent of the students improved, 25 percent remained at the same level, and 22 percent declined. These findings, though hardly spectacular, represented a significant ($p = \leq .05$) change from the first to the last week of classes.

The ratings for each study were based on a six-point scale (1.0 was the highest rating and 6.0 the lowest). At the end of each semester, composition teachers rated students' writing from other teachers' classes, and they did not know whether they were rating a students' pretest or posttest essay. The teachers' ratings were highly consistent ($r = .88$).

On the pretest essay, the "average student" received a score of 3.6 (see Chart 9.1). The posttest scores increased by .5 of a point to 3.1. This increase, though slight, is greater than the average .3 of a point improvement shown by students in a developmental writing course, ENGL 99 (pretest $\bar{x} = 4.3$ and posttest $\bar{x} = 4.0$).

Similarly, students in freshman English (ENGL 100) who had formerly completed ENGL 99 improved by only .35 of a point (pretest $\bar{x}$ = 3.95 and posttest $\bar{x}$ = 3.6). These results underscore the slow progress of students with long-standing problems as writers. Certainly it is unreasonable to expect these students to become fluent in Standard Written English after completing only one or two writing courses. The biology of writing does not heal itself so quickly.

Chart 9.1: **Mean ($\bar{x}$) Scores for Pretest and Posttest Essays**

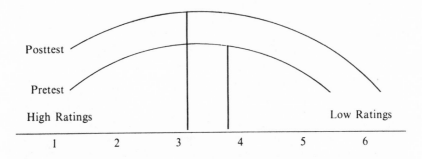

The results for 1982 were *identical* to those obtained the previous year. Although it may appear unimpressive that only 54 percent of the students for these two years improved, that result is actually quite good.

Several points need to be considered when interpreting these results. First, the students' performance is measured on one of four topics about the relationship between a student's education and a career. Regardless of how well these topics have been chosen and constructed, they cannot encompass the interests of all students or insure against special advantages for some students with personal experience relating to a topic. Second, in-class writings differ from other essay assignments, especially ones completed at home after several days or even weeks of writing. With this additional time, a student can edit the form and revise the content of a take-home essay, whereas the student writing a timed essay in class has little opportunity to mask weaknesses or emphasize strengths in writing. As a final point, if it were possible to redo an evaluation with the same students but having them complete a different pre- and posttest essay, the overall results of this second evaluation would closely resemble those of the first evaluation, but the performance of each student would potentially vary because of the change in topic, date of the test, and personal well-being of the test taker. That is, in retesting these students, a different group would comprise the majority who improve, those who decline, and those who remain unchanged. These differences in individual performance occur whenever a large number of people are tested for writing. Considering that many students do quite well on posttest essays, this performance suggests that writing teachers prepare their students to write effectively even under adverse conditions.

As Table 9.2 shows, freshman writers have gradually improved over the five-year period since their writing was first evaluated.

Chart 9.2: **Percentage of Improvement by Course and Year**

Year:	1981	1982	1983	1984	1985
Course:					
ENGL 99	58%	60%	65%	82%	83%
ENGL 100	54%	54%	64%	64%	69%

Beginning in 1984, students in ENGL 100—about 64 percent—show a .56 gain in their writing performance after completing this course. In effect, they begin the semester (Spring or Fall, 1984) writing *C-* prose and finish the semester with a *C*. Students in ENGL 99 start with a *D+* and conclude with a *C-/D+*, or a gain of .25. Although this rate of improvement is slight, just half that of ENGL 100 students, a very high percentage of ENGL 99 students (82 percent in 1984 and 83 percent in 1985) show some gain (18 percent higher than ENGL 100 in 1984 and 11 percent higher in 1985).

In 1984 the improvement for ENGL 99, a developmental writing course, is unusually good, a result that may indicate the importance of a fourth hour of instruction that was added to that course and, in 1985, to special sections of freshman English (referred to below as ENGL 100A). This interpretation is strengthened, as Table 9.3 shows, by a slight drop in ENGL 99 pretest scores after 1983.

Chart 9.3: **Pretest and Posttest Scores by Course and Year**

Year:	1981		1982	1983		1984		1985	
	Pre	Post	Pre-Post	Pre	Post	Pre	Post	Pre	Post
Course:									
ENGL 99	4.3	4.0	4.4 4.2	4.0	3.5	4.21	3.95	4.48	3.65
ENGL 100	4.0	3.6	4.1 3.6	3.6	3.1	3.60	3.04	3.40	3.02
ENGL 100A								3.39	2.82

Two questions underlie these results: Why was the fourth hour of writing instruction added, and how did this change affect the performance of freshman writers? The answer to the first question is that members of the Writing Program wanted to gauge the overall success of having students exposed to more writing instruction than they would normally receive in a course meeting three hours each week. The second question can be answered this way: approximately 150 students who comprise sections of ENGL 99 each year achieved an 82 percent rate of improvement in 1984 and a 83 percent rate in 1985 (see Table 9.2), or about 120 of these students become significantly better writers, while only 12 declined and 18 remained unchanged. These figures compare to the 65 percent rate of improvement for 1983 or preceding years (58 percent in 1981 and 60 percent in 1982). Although not as large a gain occurred in the four credit sections of freshman English (ENGL 100A), which enroll about 20 percent of the 1,400 freshmen eligible for ENGL 100, there is a pattern showing higher posttest scores in the experimental sections versus the regular three credit sections of that course.

For advanced writing courses (ENGL 391, Intermediate Exposition, and ENGL 393, Technical Writing) the value of more exposure to writing instruction becomes especially clear. In Table 9.4 I have listed the pretest scores for both advanced courses and, compared to the evidence in Table 9.2, these results show the initial writing ability of juniors and seniors at or below the pretest scores for entering freshmen. Even worse, the 3.39 exit score for ENGL 393 merely returns students to the 3.39 pretest level of ENGL 100!

Chart 9.4: **Pretest and Posttest Scores for Advanced Composition**

Course:	ENGL 391	ENGL 393
Pretest:	3.50	3.85
Posttest:	2.85	3.39

As an immediate response to these scores we could say that students decline in writing ability after several years in college, but that generalization would grossly simplify the evidence. In fact, students who do write frequently in other courses exhibit a similar drop in performance (a decline of .56 from their freshman English posttest scores to the advanced composition pretest scores). Although part of the decline shown in Table 9.4 can be explained as lack of writing practice, that explanation is not by itself sufficient to account for the overall decline of all students taking advanced composition. Indeed it appears that students can only maintain (or improve) their writing skills when practice is combined with instruction, especially when that instruction is provided by experienced teachers of writing.

If the results of Table 9.4 are compared to results from previous years, we can infer another reason for the drop in 1985 pretest scores. From 1981 to 1984 the pretest scores in advanced composition courses have averaged 2.9. But in 1985 the initial score for ENGL 391 and 393 averages 3.68, or a drop of .78 from the average for previous years. This decline coincided with increasingly large numbers of transfer students taking advanced writing courses.

This comparison is particularly important because the writing ability of entering freshmen during this five-year period consistently improved. Table 9.5 shows the gains over the last five years for ENGL 100, beginning with 1981 pre- and posttest scores of 4.0/3.6 and concluding with 1985 scores of 3.39/2.91. The average gain during the five years is .61 for pretests and half a letter grade better than 1981 freshmen.

Chart 9.5: **Five-Year Summary of ENGL 100 Pretest and Posttest Scores**

Year:	1981	1982	1983	1984	1985
Pretests:	4.0	4.1	3.6	3.60	3.39
Posttests:	3.6	3.6	3.1	3.04	2.91
Gain:	+.4	+.5	+.4	+.56	+.48

Although 1985 freshman writers score somewhat better on the pretests (3.39) than freshmen from previous years, they nevertheless average about the same degree of gain on their posttests (.48). By contrast, students taking advanced writing courses are considerably less capable writers than when they began college, in some cases dropping below the ability they exhibited as freshmen on their pretest scores.

These results strongly endorse an approach to teaching writing that aims for lasting gains. Students who acquire prose—those who are taught to subconsciously master the biology of writing—are the only ones who remain capable writers throughout their college years. They are also the only students who may ultimately achieve the physical eloquence to use writing as a learning aid in their other courses.

In a course that emphasizes the biology of writing, evaluation assumes a crucial role in shaping the syllabus and justifying the open-endedness of instruction. Without a textbook, the instructor begins a course with a "silent" method for diagnosing each student's abilities, in part to develop a student's intuition for the "inner voice" of writing, but in equal part to establish, demonstrate, and promote the appropriate standards for measuring progress in that course. Measurement, in this sense, is based on a standard of developmental progress and not on *a priori* judgments as to what constitutes "good" or "bad" writing. In other words, the quality of a student's writing is less important than his or her biological fluency.

Obviously, a teacher can teach this fluency and still have students complete work in textbooks; but each exercise from a text or any work that encourages formal learning of writing will take time away from teaching students to acquire prose, and to have them subconsciously internalize norms by which essays are evaluated and grades are assigned. The more time devoted to this goal, as shown in the results of the five-year study just cited, the more completely students will develop their writing abilities.

In an important political sense, evaluation confirms the effectiveness of writing instruction, perhaps as a measure of teaching ability when several instructors are compared over many semesters of teaching, but most appropriately when an entire program is tested to determine the progress of students from the beginning to end of any semester. Results can show rate of improvement (how many students improve) and the complementary measure of relative gains in performance (or essentially by how much students improve). With this information, instructors have solid evidence of their own contributions to students' literacy, evidence of practical value when they must deal with administrators, and evidence that the general public should certainly know about.

NOTES

Chapter One

1. In "Creating a Literate Environment in Freshman English: Why and How," Patrick Hartwell (1987) has labeled the conventional view of literacy as "dumb," in that theorists like Walter Ong (1982) and Thomas Farrell (1984) make too sharp a distinction between orality and literacy, and they essentially ignore multiple forms of literacy. Citing the metaphor of an iceberg, Hartwell argues that little is really known about literacy since much of this phenomenon is submerged in social and individual nuance. While I fully agree with this critique, I would prefer a different metaphor, if only because the top of an iceberg isn't really much different from the invisible bulk.

A more suitable metaphor is the geological deposits of oil, which may vary in quality, amount, and location. To discover productive oil fields, a geologist typically surveys the topography, isolates promising areas from which rock samples are obtained and tested. And if the signs are right, a few exploratory wells are drilled. Anybody who studies written literacy for long may eventually feel like an unlucky geologist who keeps testing for signs of oil. We study the surface features, make some informed guesses, explore a few promising leads—but the big strike, if there ever can be one, continues to elude us.

2. Stephen Toulmin's *The Uses of Argument* (1958) and *An Introduction to Reasoning* (1979) are two representative works that show his concern for the irrelevance of formal argumentation to practical reasoning. Chaim Perelman's collaborative work with Lucie Olbrechts-Tyteca, *The New Rhetoric: A Treatise on Argumentation* (1969), and his more recent *The Realm of Rhetoric* (1982), demonstrate his concern for a "new rhetoric" that would emphasize rationality over style. Both Toulmin and Perelman have strengthened modern rhetorical theory, but their work has had the negative consequence of a "mind-only" perspective.

3. Stanley Fish's first and perhaps most telling attack on linguistic style studies appeared in the English Institute articles of 1973 ("What Is Stylistics and Why Are They Saying Such Terrible Things About It?"). At that time he used the term *affective stylistics* to mean what has subsequently been called his reader-response theory.

4. Much of the work on prewriting deserves praise too; in criticizing it I mean only to show its relative neglect of physical processes that underlie brainstorming,

networking, tree-building, listing, and other innovative—mental, cognitive—aspects of writing. For a brief review of prewriting as it is related to physical aspects of writing, see James D. Williams' *Preparing To Teach Writing*, 1989, 41-43.

5. This mind-only attitude towards writing is succinctly reviewed by Richard L. Larsen in "The Writer's Mind: Recent Research and Unanswered Questions" (1983).

6. Rod Ellis' *Classroom Second Language Development* (1984) provides a thorough critique of Krashen's work (see especially Chapters Five and Seven). Barry McLaughlin's "The Monitor Model: Some Methodological Considerations" (1978) is an early example of criticism; his more recent *Theories of Second Language Learning* (1987) is an extended attack of Krashen's research methodology. Michael Long's "Input and Second Language Acquisition Theory" (1985) gives a more sympathetic reading of Krashen's work in light of second-language theory.

7. Krashen does allow that a teacher's "simplified talk" can be comprehensible input, but he remains unclear as to the possibility of learning introduced by a teacher and leading to acquisition. These problems are briefly noted in Paolo Balboni's "Review of *The Input Hypothesis: Issues and Implications*" (1988). My view of teaching parallels that of Manfred Pienemann, one of Krashen's critics, who maintains that acquisition can be "guided" and that a teacher's efforts can have "an accelerating effect on acquisition for learners who are ready for it" ("Is Language Teachable?" 1989, 61). In most other respects, however, I follow Krashen's views and not those of his critics.

Chapter Two

1. Another part of the explanation for these differing figures on illiteracy is that the term is poorly understood and therefore popularly used without adequate caution. As Francis Kazemek explains in "Necessary Changes: Professional Involvement in Adult Literacy Programs" (1988):

> Literacy is a relative phenomenon, one that is both personal and social; it occurs in different contexts, situational as well as cultural; it depends upon the reader's and writer's purposes and aims for engaging in literacy acts; and it varies according to the nature of the text. Finally . . . literacy is an ethical endeavor that has as its goal the liberation of people for intelligent, meaningful, and humane action in the world. (1988, 467)

Kazemek goes on to note that estimates of illiteracy in America range from 27 million adults to 64 million, but these figures are misleading because they undoubtedly represent a continuum along the lower range of zero literacy to low or moderate literacy. In any case, the type of literacy we identify may well require different standards or levels of language performance, making any comprehensive measure of illiteracy a dubious undertaking. A report recently issued by the National Assessment of Educational Progress (Kirsch and Jungeldut, 1986) makes a similar claim, as does Graff's influential book *The Legacies of Literacy: Continuities and Contradictions in Western Culture and Society* (1987).

2. For a thorough discussion of the "literacy myth," see Harvey Graff (*The Legacies of Literature*), who essentially discounts the prevalence of illiteracy and the importance of being literate. For the opposite viewpoint that a "literacy crisis" does indeed exist, see E.D. Hirsch, Jr.'s, *Cultural Literacy* (1987).

3. Gilbert Austin's *Chironomia*, published in 1806, may be the most extensive textbook ever devised for teaching delivery. For a full discussion of this work, see Mary Margaret Robb and Lester Thonssen, eds., *Chironomia or A Treatise on Rhetorical Delivery by Gilbert Austin* (1966). Not long after Austin's book was published, the rhetorician Richard Whately wrote in the last chapter of his *Elements of Rhetoric* (1828) that the Elocutionists had confounded the teaching of delivery with the prescriptive use of rules. By this observation Whately anticipates the difference between learning and acquisition, though he does not specifically refer to these terms.

4. The two most prominent examples of cultural revisionism are E.D. Hirsch, Jr.'s, *Cultural Literacy* (1987) and Allan Bloom's *The Closing of the American Mind* (1987). In citing these authors I certainly do not intend to endorse their views; rather, I am merely identifying an "extreme" view of literacy. For a review of this extremist position and its dangers, see Stanley Aronowitz and Henry Giroux, "Schooling, Culture, and Literacy in the Age of Broken Dreams: A Review of Bloom and Hirsch" (1988).

5. In Gregory Bateson's *Steps to an Ecology of Mind* (1972), he refers to two kinds of schismogenesis, regenerative and degenerative, a distinction explained this way:

> The terms *regenerative* and *degenerative* are borrowed from communications engineering. A regenerative or "vicious" circle is a chain of variables of the general type increase in *A* causes increase in *B*; increase in *B* causes increase in *A*. Such a system, if provided with the necessary energy sources and if external factors permit, will clearly operate at a greater and greater rate of intensity. A degenerative or "self-corrective" circle differs from a regenerative circle in containing at least one link of the type: "increase in *N* causes decrease in *M*." ... In many instances the same material circuit may be either regenerative or degenerative.

In this chapter I consider language learning to be a combination of both cycles. I also distinguish it from cybernetics. The latter circuit is analogous to the wall switch of a house light. Schismogenesis is the whole system of lights and switches, circuit breakers and fuses, and so on.

Chapter Three

1. As noted in Chapter One, no figure is entirely accurate since the term *literacy* allows diverse interpretations. In a study of college students' "errors," (1988) Robert Connors and Andrea Lunsford found that students today make essentially the same number of errors in their writing as students did in 1917 and 1930. One way of interpreting the data is to discount the hysteria about a "literacy crisis." However, one could also say that the teaching of writing may be no more effective today than in previous decades, since teachers past and present have probably stressed formal instruction over subconscious acquisition. That approach to teaching writing has not been notably successful, at least not when measured by frequency of students' errors.

2. This 65 percent failure rate includes a large percentage of students who are just marginally below the passing score of *3* (or the grade of *C*). That is, about three-fifths of the students who score below *C* on the pretest essay are within one standard deviation of the mean.

3. These findings were reported in a paper I read at the 1986 Penn State Conference on Writing and Rhetoric. The paper was titled "The Case Against Writing Across the Curriculum."

4. A more recent variant of this argument posits a different, broader purpose for literacy instruction that would have students master "the concept of discourse itself." In other words, multi-disciplinary writing teaches students the value-free ability to use all forms of writing for all occasions. As advocated by Patricia Bizzell, "The most important thing for students to master is not necessarily academic discourse itself, but rather the concept of discourse, the idea that language use in any social context is formed into a regular discourse by the collaborative efforts of the people who have worked and are working in the discourse" (1986, 45).

Missing from Bizzell's argument is the possibility that students may already possess this insight from their knowledge of registers in speech. Or, if they lack it, Bizzell could nevertheless explain why students might feel compelled to master the concept of discourse. If we can agree that students already feel indifferent towards most writing, then why would they master an all-embracing concept of discourse, unless that discourse has some practical use? From *écriture* to mundane prose, few students read, admire, and imitate a text for its self-evident worth. The unlimited discourses championed by Bizzell offer students nothing to value except what they already consider worthwhile, and in terms of popular culture, that worth is measured in practical uses. Why should a biology major, for instance, want to "collaborate" in learning the discourses of history, English, philosophy, music, art, and other humanistic disciplines, not to mention those in social sciences, unrelated professions, and especially the "pure" sciences?

5. Among reviews of research that cite this relationship are Stephen Krashen, *Writing Research, Theory and Application* (1984) and Vivian Zamel, "Teaching Composition in the ESL Classroom: What We Can Learn From Research in the

Teaching of English" (1976). Examples of original research include Hunting, "Recent Studies of Writing Frequency" (1967); Richard Braddock, Richard Lloyd-Jones, and Lowell Schoer, *Research on Written Communication* (1963); Paul Dressel, John Schmid, and Gerald Kincaid, "The Effect of Writing Frequency Upon Essay-Type Writing Proficiency at the College Level" (1952).

George Hillocks, Jr.'s, summary article "What Works in Teaching Composition" (1984) and the more comprehensive report in *Research in Written Composition* (1986) strongly imply that writing instruction is an essential component of students' progress as writers. Although Hillocks does not directly address the issue of instruction versus practice, his findings show that an "environmental" method of instruction, which promotes student inquiry that is guided by a teacher, by far surpasses any other form of instruction, including a "natural" method that would have students essentially practice writing.

6. One could argue that mediocre writers might give other mediocre writers something better, approaching "a zone of proximal development" as Vygotsky (1978) would have phrased this point. The same argument might also be extended to the least capable writers. Nevertheless, I have reserved the tutorial role for the best writers because they are the only ones who have achieved the personal literacy to counteract other, more functional or educational motives for writing. Also, the politics of higher education make it far more plausible to give excellent writers stipends or other institutional rewards.

Chapter Four

1. B. Thomas and J. Richter report this relationship between speaking and writing disorders in "Psychological Inquiries Regarding the Handwriting of Stutterers" (1972).

2. Andre Lecours discusses this problem in "Serial Order in Writing: A Study of Misspelled Words" (1967).

Chapter Five

1. From the 1920s until recently, most language theorists have followed Leonard Bloomfield by dismissing writing as a trivial recoding of speech. Not until Josef Vachek's *Written Language* (1973) was this view seriously challenged. In a review of Vachek's book, Robert Hall (1975) presents the "traditional" perspective in support of speech as a primary system (he refers to this traditional perspective as "correlationist").

The primacy of speech has also been accepted by many persons concerned with teaching writing. Zoellner's "Talk-Write: A Behavioral Pedagogy for Composition" (1969) may represent the most direct application of this view, though many authors of rhetoric texts, perhaps most, have also advised students to write as they talk: use your own voice, model your writing on the art of conversation, read your prose aloud to check its spoken qualities).

Among the more recent attempts to study the differences between speaking and writing, I will list here only a few representative articles: David Olson, "From Utterance to Text: The Bias of Language in Speech and Writing" (1977); John C. Schafer, "The Linguistic Analysis of Spoken and Written Texts" (1981); Deborah Tannen, "Oral and Written Strategies in Spoken and Written Narratives" (1982); F. Niyi Akinasso, "On the Differences Between Spoken and Written Language" (1982).

For a brief review of speech/prose contrasts, see Jeanne W. Halperin's "Differences between Speaking and Writing and Their Implications for Teaching" (1984). In the same issue of *CCC* Sarah Leggett also provides an annotated bibliography of research on speaking and writing: "The Relationship Between Speaking and Writing: An Annotated Bibliography" (1984).

2. Kenneth Bruffee provides an overview of the anti-foundational approach to language and knowledge in his article "Social Construction, Language, and the Authority of Knowledge: A Bibliographical Essay" (1986). On the other hand, George Hillocks, Jr., has implicitly endorsed the foundational position in the first chapter of his book *Research On Written Composition* (1986).

3. Michael Frede distinguishes between two forms of skepticism, the classical and the dogmatic ("The Sceptic's Two Kinds of Assent," 1984). The *classical skeptic* realizes that any position or perspective is tenable, even the view that some things may be known for certain. The *dogmatic skeptic*, on the other hand, asserts that nothing can be known for certain. I have assumed that Bizzell accepts this dogmatic form of skepticism; however, since she is not explicit about this distinction, I have characterized her position as *radical skepticism*.

4. There is an extensive body of research on pauses in language production; for readers unfamiliar with this topic, Freida Goldman-Eisler's *Psycholinguistics: Experiments in Spontaneous Speech* (1968) is a good place to start. For composition research, Ann Matsuhashi's work deserves special notice, perhaps most of all "Explorations in the Real-Time Production of Written Discourse" (1982). A more recent study is James Williams' "Covert Linguistic Behaviors During Writing Tasks" (1987).

5. Over the last ten years I have analyzed more than four thousand placement and exit essays from a total of forty thousand that were written by college students who attended two-year and four-year public and private schools on both coasts. During the last five years I have compared my analysis of these randomly selected four thousand essays to all forms of writing assigned in all departments at one school, the University of Maryland Baltimore County. A partial review of this study is provided in the appendix of the final chapter.

6. I am using the term *style* without attempting to distinguish it from related terms like *register, usage,* and *manner of speech.* By conflating these terms, I hope to circumvent the myriad problems of defining what *style* means exactly. For example, does *style* inhere in the text as evidence of a writer's linguistic choices, or does it inhere in us as we perceive a text, not simply as a matter of readability but more generally as the cultural biases we all bring to interpretation? On this latter

point, Joseph Williams claims in *Style and Variables in English*:

> no analysis or explanation of style can precede a sensitive and dis-
> criminating reading of the text and an articulate understanding of how
> that text determines our experience of it. We might analyze various
> features of the text so that we might better understand it. We might
> modify what we think we experienced on the basis of that better
> understanding. But ultimately, our explanation of a text rests on our
> understanding of how we as readers relate to it (1981, 215).

For a significantly different view of style, see Richard Lanham's *The Motives of
Eloquence* (1976, 20-32), especially the discussion of *rhetorical releasers*. For a
standard but nevertheless problematic definition of style, see James D. Williams'
Preparing to Teach Writing (1989).

7. I should distinguish here between amplitude of subvocalized speech and the
amount of muscular activity related to speech production. While beginning writers
will subvocalize near the threshold of audible speech, they will actually exhibit less
overall motor activity than accomplished writers. This difference corresponds to
the relatively greater neurophysical demands of an accomplished writer's physical
eloquence. The beginning writer simply does not invoke as many neuromuscular
controls for the hand, eye, and ear. Research that would seem to support this
distinction includes Daiute's "Do Writers Talk to Themselves?" (1985); Liberman
and Mattingly's "The Motor Theory of Speech Perception Revisited" (1985); and
Williams' "Covert Linguistic Behavior During Writing Tasks" (1987).

8. Barry Kroll has developed a similar four-part model of writing development, as reported in "Developmental Relationships Between Speaking and
Writing" (1982). He claims that "speaking and writing progress through four
principal relationships: separate, consolidated, differentiated, and integrated.
Each principal relationship defines, in turn, a phase of development" (p. 39). At the
first stage a child learns handwriting, conventions of spelling, and a vocabulary
that is based on ordinary speech. At the second stage a child "strengthens writing by
drawing on . . . oral language competence" (p. 39). The penultimate stage occurs
when students recognize the distinctive contrasts between speech and prose.
During the last stage (if it is achieved at all) a student integrates speaking and
writing in ways that complement both language systems.

As an important qualification to this model, Kroll notes that the four phases
"are somewhat artificial, since the boundaries between phases will be imprecise, and
since there will be large individual differences both in the timing and duration of
progress through the phases" (p. 40). This qualification applies as well to the inner
language model that I have proposed.

9. Citing the problem of joining thinking to writing, Joseph Harris questions
the writer-based/reader-based distinction as it implies that many students lack an
important cognitive ability ("Rethinking the Pedagogy of Problem-Solving,"
1988). Summarizing criticisms of cognitivist theory, Harris claims that "our

students lack not an ability to reason but a sense of how to use the conventions that shape academic writing" (157). While I accept this basic argument for a student's inherent ability to reason, I nevertheless assume that a student's "sense" for writing is acquired developmentally. For that reason I will only use the terms *reader-based/writer-based* by way of transition to the developmental terms *oral-based, mixed, text-based,* and *spoken-prose.*

10. This simplified means of increased production speed may also have two measurable effects: (1) less "covert linguistic behavior" as shown in muscular activity (Williams 1983; 1987); and (2) fewer pauses for planning ahead, or less efficient use of these pauses (Witte 1985).

11. John Oxenham's *Literacy: Writing, Reading and Social Organization* (1980) discusses the social aspects of literacy, especially as it is acquired. The first chapter of E.D. Hirsch, Jr.'s, *Cultural Literacy* (1987) notes some of the economic consequences of illiteracy.

12. As Piaget (1964) expresses it, "Language serves to translate what is already understood" (5).

13. I have discussed the relationship between rhythm and cognition in the first chapter of *Rhythm and Writing,* 1989.

14. Language researchers' neglect of similarities between speaking and writing has been stressed by F. Niyi Akinasso in "On the Similarities Between Spoken and Written Language" (1985).

15. In a comprehensive summary of writing research, George Hillocks, Jr., reports that grammar instruction has no meaningful impact on a writer's development (*Research On Written Composition,* 1986). Besides the lack of empirical support for grammar instruction, Patrick Hartwell argues on several theoretical grounds against the use of grammar for teaching writing ("Grammar, Grammars, and the Teaching of Grammar," 1985). However, in both cases these researchers are describing a non-contrastive form of grammar.

Chapter Six

1. Following the usage adopted by most aphasiologists, including Hécaen, Angelergues, and Douzenis in their classic study "Les Agraphies" (1963), I will subsume degrees of language impairment under a single term. Thus, agraphia will refer to complete loss of writing ability as well as partial loss.

2. A strictly linguistic analysis produces four styles: oral-based, mixed, text-based, and spoken. In effect, the oral-based style subsumes kinetic and auditory functions; the remaining classifications are equivalent to mixed, visual, and melodic styles.

3. As noted in other chapters, I have analyzed thousands of students' in-class essays as well as take-home essays. The evidence I have reported in this chapter is

based primarily on in-class writing—there could be no question as to who wrote these papers, and the peculiar time constraints of an in-class assignment, in this case a forty to forty-five minute limit, may well highlight problems in text production that might not otherwise be apparent in take-home essays. Of course, the related risk of using these samples is that they may not represent the normal processes of text production. If they do not, I presume the differences are relatively minor.

4. A notable exception would be David Shapiro's *Neurotic Styles* (1965), a work that is based on psychiatric principles rather than biological analysis.

Chapter Seven

1. The overwhelming presence of textbooks on writing must send a negative message to students too, as if anything goes in a composition class because almost anything is taught. David Kaufer and Gary Waller express a similar point in "To Write Is To Read Is To Write, Right?" (1985). As they put it, "One of the great deceptions foisted upon our students is perpetrated through the sheer bulk and quantity of textbooks on grammar and style" (p. 80).

2. Since 1980 I have measured the progress of all students taking a writing course at the University of Maryland Baltimore County. These measures are based on pre- and posttest essays given at the start and finish of each semester. Working in pairs, at least two experienced writing teachers have rated these essays, not knowing when they were written, the student who wrote them, nor the score of a prior rating.

One result of these ratings is the evidence of consistent though slight progress for the majority of students in writing courses. Thus, a single semester of writing appears to improve a student's writing ability, but not dramatically (i.e., the average gain is the equivalent of half-a-grade improvement, typically from *C* to *C*+).

Another result shows that most students routinely backslide after one semester away from a writing course, but those students who completed a writing course that emphasized acquisition show no evidence of backsliding. These results may confirm the frequently made claim in second-language studies that acquisition produces lasting gains whereas conscious learning produces only temporary gains.

Chapter Eight

1. Elbow advises students to do freewriting exercises regularly: "The idea is simply to write for ten minutes (later on, perhaps fifteen or twenty). Don't stop for anything. Go quickly without rushing. Never stop to look back, to cross something out, to wonder how to spell something, to wonder what word or thought to use, or to think about what you are doing" (1973, 3). Another composition teacher, John Trimble, takes this exercise considerably further. He suggests that students quickly write several drafts for all their writing: "Instead of writing a single rough draft, which is what most novices do, I strongly recommend that you *scribble off two or*

three quick rough drafts in the same amount of time it would normally take you to write one good draft" (1975, 9).

2. This paraphrase is from Zipf's *Psycho-Biology of Language* (1935, 301), one of the first studies that seriously considered writing as a biological activity.

3. Freida Goldman-Eisler reports in *Psycholinguistics: Experiments in Spontaneous Speech* (1968, 97) that nearly one-third of breathing pauses occur at clause junctures in speech, but in oral readings all breathing pauses coincide with clause junctures. Most research on pause/clause junctures has focused on spontaneous speech; a brief review of the few studies on writing can be found in Black's "Psycholinguistic Processes in Writing" (1982).

4. I have extrapolated this—necessarily speculative—figure from research on speech pauses (e.g., Butterworth and Goldman-Eisler, "Recent Studies on Cognitive Rhythm," 1979), from studies of word and sentence perception (e.g., Vellutino, "Theoretical Issues in the Study of Word Recognition: The Unit of Perception Controversy Reexamined," 1982), from the seminal article by Miller, "The Magic Number Seven, Plus or Minus Two" (1967), and from the equally important article on rhythm by Martin, "Rhythmic (Hierarchical) Versus Serial Structure in Speech and Other Behavior" (1972). Other relevant studies that deal directly with writing include Williams' "Covert Linguistic Behavior During Writing Tasks" (1987), Matsuhashi's "Pausing and Planning" (1981), Flower and Hayes' "The Pregnant Pause" (1981c), and Witte's "Pretext and Composing" (1987).

5. This claim should be understood to include the positive and negative results of some studies. John Mellon has made a similar claim in "A Taxonomy of Compositional Competencies," in *Perspectives on Literacy* (1979, 242-272).

6. This limitation has been fully discussed by Stephen Krashen in *Principles and Practice of Second Language Acquisition* (1982, 91-94). See also Patrick Hartwell's "Grammar, Grammars, and the Teaching of Grammar (1985, 118).

7. The research supporting this view is briefly reviewed in Dulay, Burt, and Krashen's *Language Two* (1982, 62-65).

8. I have based these percentages on my informal studies of freshman prose, which are presented in the appendix to Chapter Nine. The top 4 percent of freshman writers correspond to the spoken or melodic styles; the bottom 8 percent are related to oral-based or auditory-kinetic styles.

9. For readers who are familiar with Richard Lanham's *Revising Prose* (1979), *Revising Business Prose* (1981), or *Analyzing Prose* (1983) it may be surprising to learn that he attacks conventional textbooks in his fascinating work *Style: An Anti-Textbook*. However, in taking on these books, Lanham objects foremost to their definitions of clarity; he does not, in other words, recommend tossing textbooks out of the writing classroom, as I do, but recommends instead that their message change.

BIBLIOGRAPHY

Agranowitz, Aleen and Mildred R. McKeown. *Aphasia Handbook for Adults and Children.* Springfield, Illinois: C.C. Thomas, 1968.

Akinasso, F. Niyi. "On the Differences Between Spoken and Written Language." *Language and Speech* 25 (1982): 97-125.

———. "On the Similarities Between Spoken and Written Language." *Language and Speech* 28 (1985): 323-359.

Alajouanine, T. and F. Lhermitte. "Les Troubles des Activites Expressives du Langage dans l'Aphasie, Leurs Relations avec les Apraxies." *Revue Neurologique* 102 (1960): 604-629.

Alexander, T.V. "Meaning of Handwriting Opinions." *Journal of Police Science Administration* 5 (1977): 43-47.

Aristotle. *The "Art" of Rhetoric.* (Trans. by John Henry Freese). Cambridge, Massachusetts: Harvard University Press, 1926.

Aronowitz, Stanley and Henry A. Giroux. "Schooling, Culture, and Literacy in the Age of Broken Dreams: A Review of Bloom and Hirsch." *Harvard Educational Review* 58 (1988): 172-194.

Atkins, G. Douglas and Michael L. Johnson (eds.). *Writing and Reading Differently.* Lawrence, Kansas: University of Kansas Press, 1985.

Austin, Gilbert. *Chironomia.* In Mary M. Robb and Lester Thonssen (eds.). Carbondale, Illinois: Southern Illinois University Press, 1966.

Bailey, Richard W. and Robin M. Fosheim (eds.). *Literacy for Life: The Demand for Reading and Writing.* New York: Modern Language Association, 1983.

Balboni, Paolo. "[Review of] The Input Hypothesis: Issues and Implications." *Language Learning* 38 (1988): 149-56.

Bartholomae, David. "The Study of Error." *College Composition and Communication* 31 (1980):253-69.

———. "Inventing the University." In Mike Rose (ed.), *When a Writer Can't Write.* New York: Guilford Press, 1985.

Bastian, H.C. *Aphasia And Other Speech Defects.* London: H.K. Lewis, 1898.

Bateson, Gregory. *Steps to An Ecology of Mind*. New York: Ballantine, 1972.

Bernstein, Basil. *Class, Codes, and Control (Vol. 1)*. London: Rutledge and Kegan Paul, 1971.

Bizzell, Patricia. "College Composition: Initiation into the Academic Discourse Community," *Curriculum Inquiry* 12 (1982): 191-207.

———. "Foundationalism and Anti-Foundationalism in Composition Studies," *PRE/TEXT* 7 (1986): 37-56.

———. "Literacy in Culture and Cognition." In Theresea Enos (ed.), *A Sourcebook for Basic Writing Teachers*. New York: Random House, 1987.

Black, John. "Psycholinguistic Processes in Writing." In S. Rosenberg (ed.), *Handbook of Applied Psycholinguistics*. Hillsdale, New Jersey: 1982.

Bleich, David. *Subjective Criticism*. Baltimore: Johns Hopkins University Press, 1978.

———. "Cognitive Stereoscopy and the Study of Language and Literature." In Bruce T. Petersen (ed.), *Convergences: Transactions in Reading and Writing*. Urbana, Illinois: National Council of Teachers of English, 1986.

———. *Double Perspective: Language, Literacy, and Social Relations*. New York: Oxford University Press, 1988.

Bloom, Allan. *The Closing of the American Mind*. New York: Simon and Schuster, 1987.

Bloomfield, Leonard. *Language*. New York: Holt, Rinehart and Winston, 1933.

Bogen, Joseph E. "The Other Side of the Brain: Dysgraphia and Dyscopia Following Cerebral Commissurotomy." *Bulletin of the Los Angeles Neurological Societies* 34 (1969) 73-105 (I); (1969) 135-162 (II); (1969) 191-219 (III).

Braddock, Richard, Ricard Lloyd-Jones, and Lowell Schoer. *Research on Written Communication*. Urbana, Illinois: National Council of Teachers of English, 1963.

Brain, R. *Speech Disorders*. London: Buttersworth, (2nd ed.) 1965.

Brandt, Deborah. "The Message Is the Massage: Orality and Literacy Once More." *Written Communication* 6 (1989): 31-44.

Britton, James, Tony Burgess, Nancy Martin, Alex McLeod, and Harold Rosen. *The Development of Writing Abilities (11-18)*. London: Macmillan Education, 1975.

Broca, Paul. "Remarques sur le Siège de la Faculté du Langage Articulé, Suives d'une Observation d'Aphémie (Perte de la Parole)." *Bulletins de la Société Anatomique* 6 (1861): 330-57.

————. "Sur le Siège de la Faculté du Langage Articulé." *Bulletins de la Société d'Anthropologie de Paris* 6 (1865): 377-93.

Bruffee, Kenneth A. "Collaborative Learning and the 'Conversation of Mankind.'" *College English* 46 (1984): 635-52.

————. "Social Construction, Language, and the Authority of Knowledge: A Bibliographical Essay." *College English* 48 (1986): 773-90.

————. "Writing and Reading as Collaborative or Social Acts." In Theresa Enos (ed.), *A Sourcebook for Basic Writing Teachers*. New York: Random House, 1987.

Burke, Kenneth. *Language as Symbolic Action*. Berkeley, California: University of California Press, 1968.

————. *Philosophy of Literary Form*. Berkeley, California: University of California Press, 1969.

————. *Permanence and Change*. Indianapolis, Indiana: Bobbs-Merrill, (1st ed.) 1965, (2nd ed.) 1972.

Butterworth, Brian and Freida Goldman-Eisler. "Recent Studies on Cognitive Rhythm." In Aron W. Siegman and Stanley Feldstein (eds.), *Of Speech and Time*. Hillsdale, New Jersey: Lawrence Erlbaum, 1979.

Caillois, Roger. *Man, Play, and Games*. New York: Free Press, 1961.

Caplan, David (ed.). *Biological Studies of Mental Processes*. Cambridge, Massachusetts: Massachusetts Institute of Technology Press, 1980.

————. "Prospects for Neurolinguistic Theory." *Cognition* 10 (1981): 59-64.

Caplan, David., Andre Lecours, and A. Smith (eds.). *Biological Perspectives on Language*. Cambridge, MA: MIT Press, 1984.

Cappa, Stefano F., Giuseppina Cavallotti, and Luigi A. Vignolo. "Jargon-agraphia: Clinical and Neuropsychological Correlates." *Brain and Cognition* 25 (1987): 281-86.

Caramazza, Alfonso. "The Logic of Neuropsychological Research and the Problem of Patient Classification in Aphasia." *Brain and Language* 21 (1984): 9-20.

Caramazza, Alfonso, Gabriele Miceli, Giampero Villa, and Cristina Romani. "The Role of the Graphemic Buffer in Spelling: Evidence from a Case of Acquired Dysgraphia." *Cognition* 25 (1987): 59-76.

Castiglione, Baldesar. *The Book of the Courtier*. (Trans. by Charles S. Singleton.) New York: Doubleday, 1959.

Celce-Murcia, Marianne and Frances Hinofotis. "ESL Composition Techniques

Applicable to Remedial Composition Classes." Paper read at UCLA Chancellor's Conference on Composition, Los Angeles, December 2, 1978.

Chafe, Wallace L. "Linguistic Differences Produced by Differences Between Speaking and Writing." In D.R. Olson, N. Torrance, and A. Hildyard (eds.). *Literacy, Language and Learning: The Nature and Consequences of Reading and Writing.* Cambridge, Massachusetts: Cambridge University Press, 1985.

Chatman, Seymour (ed.). *Literary Style: A Symposium.* London: Oxford University Press, 1971.

Chedru, F. and Geschwind, N. "Disorders of Higher Cortical Function in Acute Confusional States," *Cortex* 8 (1972): 395-411.

Churchland, Patricia Smith. *Neurophilosophy: Toward a Unified Science of the Mind/Brain.* Cambridge, MA: MIT Press, 1986.

Cole, Michael and Barbara Means. *Comparative Studies of How People Think: An Introduction.* Cambridge, Massachusetts: Harvard University Press, 1981.

Cole, Michael and Sylvia Scribner. *Culture and Thought: A Psychological Introduction.* New York: Wiley, 1974.

Connors, Robert J. and Andrea A. Lunsford. "Frequency of Formal Errors in Current College Writing, or Ma and Pa Kettle Do Research." *College Composition and Communication* 39 (1988): 395-409.

Corder, S. Pit. *Error Analysis and Interlanguage.* London: Oxford University Press, 1981.

Critchley, Macdonald. *The Parietal Lobes.* London: E. Arnold and Co., 1953.

Cullen, Robert J. "Writing Across the Curriculum: Adjunct Courses." *Association of Departments of English Bulletin* 80 (1985): 15-17.

Daiute, Colleen. "Psycho-Linguistic Foundations of the Writing Process." *Research in the Teaching of English* 15 (1981): 5-22.

———. "Do Writers Talk to Themselves?" In S. Freedman (ed.), *The Acquisition of Written Language: Revision and Response.* Norwood, New Jersey: Ablex, 1985.

———. "Physical and Cognitive Factors in Revising: Insights from Studies with Computers." *Research in the Teaching of English* 20 (1986): 141-59.

Davies, Martin. "Literacy and Intonation." In B. Couture (ed.), *Functional Approaches to Writing Research Perspectives.* London: Frances Pinter, 1986.

Davis, H. and P. Davis. "The Electrical Activity of the Brain: Its Relation to Physiological States of Impaired Consciousness." In F. Kennedy, A. Frantz, and

C. Hare (Eds.), *The Interrelationship of Mind and Body, A.R.N.M.D. 19.* Baltimore: Williams and Wilkins, 1939.

Dejerine, J. "Sur un Cas de Cécité Verbale avec Agraphie, Suivi d'Autopsie." *Memoires de la Societe de Biologie 3* (1891): 197-201.

Derrida, Jacques. *Of Grammatology.* Baltimore: Johns Hopkins University Press, 1976.

Dillon, George. "Clause, Pause, and Punctuation in Poetry." *Linguistics* 169 (1976): 5-20.

———. *Constructing Texts.* Bloomington, Indiana: Indiana University Press, 1981.

Dinklage, K.T. "The Inability to Learn a Foreign Language," In G. Blaine and C. McArthur (eds.), *Emotional Problems of the Student.* New York: Appleton-Century-Crofts, 1971.

Dreman, S. "A Review of Directionality Trends in the Horizontal Dimension as a Function of Innate and Environmental Factors." *Journal of General Psychology* 96 (1977): 125-134.

Dressel, Paul, John Schmid, and Gerald Kincaid. "The Effect of Writing Frequency Upon Essay-Type Writing Proficiency at the College Level." *Journal of Educational Research* 46 (1952): 285-292.

Dubois, Jean. "Présentation." *Langages* 5 (1967a): 3-5.

———. "La Neurolinguistique." *Langages* 5 (1967b): 6-17.

Dubois, J., P. Marcie, and H. Hécaen. "Description et Classification des Aphasies." *Langages* 5 (1967): 18-36.

Dubois, J., H. Hécaen, and P. Marcie. "L'Agraphie 'Pure'." *Neuropsychologia* 7 (1969): 271-286.

Dubois-Charlier, Francoise. "Approche Neurolinguistique du Problème de l'Alexie Pure." *Journal de Psychologie* 1 (1971): 39-68.

———. "A Propos De L'Alexie Pure." *Langages* 25 (1972): 76-94.

———. "Les Analyses Neuropsychologiques et Neurolinguistiques de l'Alexie: 1838-1969." *Langages* 44 (1976): 20-67.

Dulay, Heidi, Marina Burt, and Stephen Krashen. *Language Two.* New York: Oxford University Press, 1982.

Dunn-Rankin, Peter. "The Visual Characteristics of Words." In *Scientific American: Human Communication: Language and Its Psychobiological Bases.* San Francisco: W.H. Freeman and Company, 1982.

DuPasquier, J. "Handwriting and Fantasy: Death of the Father and Handwriting." *Pratique des Mots* 15 (1974): 7-15.

Early, G.H. "Cursive Handwriting, Reading, and Spelling Achievement." *Academic Therapy* 12 (1976): 67-74.

Elbow, Peter. *Writing Without Teachers.* New York: Oxford University Press, 1973.

Elley, W.B., I.H. Barham, and M. Wyllie. "The Role of Grammar in a Secondary School English Curriculum." *Research in the Teaching of English* 10 (1976): 5-21.

Ellis, Rod. *Classroom Language Development.* Oxford: Pergamon Press, 1984.

Emig, Janet. *The Composing Processes of Twelfth Graders.* Urbana, Illinois: National Council of Teachers of English, 1971.

———. "Writing as a Mode of Learning." *College Composition and Communication* 28 (1977): 122-128.

———. "Hand, Eye, Brain: Some 'Basics' in the Writing Process." In Charles R. Cooper and Lee Odell (eds.), *Research on Composing: Points of Departure.* Urbana, Illinois: National Council of Teachers of English, 1978.

———. *The Web of Meaning: Essays on Writing, Teaching, Learning, and Thinking.* Upper Montclair, New Jersey: Boynton/Cook, 1983.

Exner, S. *Untersuchungen über die Lokalisation der Funktionen in der Grobhirnrinde des Menschen,* Vienna: W. Braumuller, 1881.

Farrell, Thomas J. "IQ and Standard English." *College Composition and Communication* 35 (1984): 469-78.

Fergusson, J. and F. Boller. "A Different Form of Agraphia: Syntactic Writing Errors in Patients with Motor Speech and Movement Disorders," *Brain and Language* 4 (1977): 382-389.

Fish, Stanley. "What Is Stylistics and Why Are They Saying Such Terrible Things About It?" In Seymour Chatman (ed.), *Approaches To Poetics: Selected Papers from the English Institute.* New York: Columbia University Press, 1973.

Flesch, Rudolph. *The Art of Readable Writing.* New York: Harper and Row, 1949.

Flower Linda. "Writer-Based Prose: A Cognitive Basis for Problems in Writing." *College English* 41 (1979): 19-37.

———. *Problem-Solving Strategies.* New York: Harcourt, Brace, Jovanovich, (2nd ed.) 1985.

Flower, Linda and John R. Hayes. "A Cognitive Process Theory of Writing." *College Composition and Communication* 32 (1981a): 365-87.

———. "Plans that Guide the Composing Process." In Carl H. Frederiksen and Joseph F. Dominic (eds.), *Writing: Process, Development, and Communication.* Hillsdale, New Jersey: Lawrence Erlbaum, 1981b.

———. "The Pregnant Pause: An Inquiry Into the Nature of Planning." *Research in the Teaching of English* 15 (1981c): 229-243.

Fodor, Joseph. *The Modality of Mind.* Cambridge, Massachusetts: Massachusetts Institute of Technology Press, 1983.

Foix, C. "Sur une Variétié des Troubles Bilatéraux de la Sensibilité par les Unilatérale du Cerveau," *Revue de Neurolinguistique* 29 (1922): 322-31.

Frede, Michael. "The Skeptic's Two Kinds of Assent and the Question of the Possibility of Knowledge." In Richard Rorty, J.B. Schneewind, and Quentin Skinner (eds.), *Philosophy in History.* Cambridge: Cambridge University Press, 1984.

Freedman, Sarah Warshauer (ed.). *The Acquisition of Written Language: Response and Revision.* Norwood, New Jersey: Ablex, 1985.

Freeman, Donald, (ed.). *Linguistics and Literary Style.* New York: Holt, Rinehart and Winston, 1970.

Friedman, Rhonda B. and Michael P. Alexander. "Written Spelling Agraphia." *Brain and Language* 36 (1989): 503-17.

Fulwiler, Toby. "Showing, Not Telling, at a Faculty Workshop." *College English* 43 (1981): 55-63.

———. "Writing: An Act of Cognition." In C. Williams Griffin (ed.), *Teaching Writing in All Disciplines.* San Francisco: Jossey-Bass, 1982.

———. "How Well Does Writing Across the Curriculum Work?" *College English* 46 (1984): 113-125.

———. "The Argument for Writing Across the Curriculum." In Art Young and Toby Fulwiler (eds.), *Writing Across the Disciplines: Research Into Practice.* Upper Montclair, New Jersey: Boynton/Cook, 1986.

———. *Teaching With Writing.* Portsmouth, New Hampshire: Boynton/Cook, 1987.

Fulwiler, Toby and Art Young (eds.). *Language Connections: Writing and Reading Across the Curriculum.* Urbana, Illinois: National Council of Teachers of English, 1982.

———. *Writing Across the Disciplines: Research Into Practice.* Upper Montclair, New Jersey: Boynton/Cook, 1986.

Gardner, Robert. *Social Psychology and Second Language Learning.* London: Edward Arnold, 1985.

Gardner, Robert and Wallace Lambert. *Attitudes and Motivation in Second Language Learning.* Rowley, Massachusetts: Newbury House, 1972.

Gass, Susan M. and Carolyn G. Madden (eds.). *Input in Second Language Acquisition.* Rowley, Massachusetts: Newbury House, 1985.

Gazzaniga, Michael S. "Right Hemisphere Language Following Brain Bisection: A 20-Year Perspective." *American Psychology* 38 (1983): 525-37.

————. *The Social Brain.* New York: Basic Books, 1985.

Geschwind, Norman. "Disconnexion Syndromes in Animals and Man. *Brain* 88 (1965): 237-94, 585-644.

————. "The Organization of Language and the Brain," *Science* 170 (1970): 940-44.

————. "Language and the Brain." *Scientific American* 226 (1972): 76-83.

————. "Apraxia and Agraphia in a Left-Hander." *New England Journal of Medicine* 289 (1973): 530-541.

————. "The Alexias." In *Selected Papers on Language and the Brain.* Dordrecht, Holland: D. Reidel, 1974a.

————. "Writing Disturbances in Acute Confusional States." Dordrecht, Holland: D. Reidel, 1974b.

————. *Selected Papers on Language and the Brain.* Dordrecht, Holland: D. Reidel, 1974c.

————. "Specializations of the Human Brain." *Scientific American: Human Communication: Language and Its Psychobiological Bases.* San Francisco: W.H. Freeman and Company, 1982.

Gibson, E. "Learning to Read." *Science* 148 (1965): 1066-72.

Gibson, E. and H. Levin. *The Psychology of Reading.* Cambridge, Massachusetts: Massachusetts Institute of Technology Press, 1975.

Ginsberg, Herbert and Sylvia Opper. *Piaget's Theory of Intellectual Development.* Englewood Cliffs, New Jersey: Prentice Hall, 1969.

Givón, Talmy. *On Understanding Grammar.* New York: Academic Press, 1979.

Goffman, Erving. *The Presentation of Self in Everyday Life.* New York: Anchor Press, 1959.

Goldblum, Marie-Claire. "Analyse Des Réponses de Dénomination Chez les Aphasiques." *Langages* 25 (1972): 66-75.

Goldman-Eisler, Frieda. *Psycholinguistics: Experiments in Spontaneous Speech.* London: Basil Blackwell, 1968.

Goody, Jack. *The Domestication of the Savage Mind.* Cambridge: Cambridge University Press, 1977.

Gordinier, H.C. "A Case of Brain Tumor at the Base of the Second Left Frontal Circonvolution." *American Medical Science* 117 (1899): 526-535.

Graff, Harvey, J. *The Literacy Myth.* New York: Academic Press, 1979.

———. *The Legacies of Literacy: Continuities and Contradictions in Western Culture and Society.* Bloomington, Indiana: Indiana University Press, 1987.

———. "Critical Literacy Versus Cultural Literacy—Reading Signs of the Times?" *Interchange.* 20 (1989): 46-52.

Gregg, K.R. "[Review of] *The Input Hypothesis: Issues and Implications.*" *TESOL Quarterly* 20 (1986):116-22.

Griffin, C.W. "Programs for Writing Across the Curriculum: A Report." *College Composition and Communication* 36 (1985): 398-403.

Hall, Robert. "[Review of] *Written Language.*" *Language* 51 (1975): 461-65.

Halpern, Jeanne W. "Differences Between Speaking and Writing and Their Implications for Teaching." *College Composition and Communication* 35 (1984): 345-357.

Harris, Joseph. "Rethinking the Pedagogy of Problem-Solving." *Journal of Teaching Writing* 7 (1988): 157-164.

Hartwell, Patrick. "The Writing Center and the Paradoxes of Written-Down Speech." In Gary A. Olson (ed.), *Writing Centers: Theory and Administration.* Urbana, Illinois: National Council of Teachers of English, 1984.

———. "Grammar, Grammars, and the Teaching of Grammar." *College English* 47 (1985): 105-127.

———. "Creating a Literate Environment for Freshman English: Why and How." *Rhetoric Review* 6 (1987): 4-20.

Havelock, Eric. *Preface to Plato.* Cambridge, Massachusetts: Harvard University Press, 1963.

———. *The Origins of Western Literacy.* Toronto: Ontario Institute for Studies of Education, 1976.

Heath, Shirley Brice. "The Literate Essay: Using Ethnography to Explode Myths." In Judith A. Langer (ed.), *Language, Literacy, and Culture: Issues of Society and Schooling.* Norwood, New Jersey: Ablex, 1987.

Hécaen, Henri. "Clinical Symptomology in Right and Left Hemisphere Lesions." In V.B. Mountcaste (ed.), *Interhemispheric Relations and Cerebral Dominance*, Baltimore: Johns Hopkins University Press, 1962.

————. "Aspects Sémiotiques des Troubles de la Lecture (Alexies) au Cours des Lésions Cérébrales en Foyer." *Word* 23 (1967): 265-87.

————. *Introduction a la Neuropsychologie.* Paris: Larousse, 1972.

Hécaen, Henri and Martin Albert. *Human Neuropsychology.* New York: Wiley, 1978.

Hécaen, H., R. Angelergues and J.A. Douzenis. "Les Agraphies." *Neuropsychologia* 1 (1963) 179-208.

Hendrick, C., J. Vincenzo, and C. Nelson. "Formality of Signature as an Index of Subject Motivation in the Psychological Experiment." *Social Behavior and Personality Bulletin* 3 (1975): 1-4.

Henschen, S.E. *Klinische und Anatomische Beiträge zur Pathologie des Gehirns.* Stockholm: Nordiske Bokhandeln, 1922.

Herrington, Ann J. "Writing to Learn: Writing Across the Disciplines." *College English* 43 (1981): 379-87.

————. "The First Twenty Years of *Research in the Teaching of English* and the Growth of a Research Community in Composition Studies." *Research in the Teaching of English* 23 (1989): 117-138.

Hillis, Argye, and Alfonso Caramazza. "The Graphemic Buffer and Attentional Mechanisms." *Brain and Language* 36 (1989): 208-235.

Hillocks, George, Jr. "Inquiry and the Composing Process." *College English* 44 (1982): 659-76.

————. "What Works in Teaching Composition: A Meta-Analysis of Experimental Treatment Studies." *American Journal of Education* 93 (1984): 133-70.

————. *Research in Written Composition: New Directions for Teachers.* Urbana, Illinois: National Council of Teachers of English, 1986.

Hinschelwood, J. *Letter, Word, and Mind-Blindness.* London: H.K. Lewis, 1900.

Hirsch, E.D., Jr. *The Philosophy of Composition.* Chicago: Chicago University Press, 1977.

————. *Cultural Literacy.* Boston: Houghton Mifflin, 1987.

Holdaway, Don. *The Foundations of Literacy.* Exeter, New Hampshire: Hienemann, 1979.

Holland, Norman. *Five Readers Reading.* New Haven: Yale University Press, 1975.

Horning, Alice S. *Teaching Writing as a Second Language.* Urbana, Illinois: National Council of Teachers of English, 1987.

Howes, D. "An Approach to the Quantitative Analysis of Word Blindness." In J. Money (ed.), *Reading Disability*. Baltimore: Johns Hopkins University Press, 1962.

Huck, S.W. and W.G. Bounds. "Essay Graders: An Interaction Between Handwriting Clarity and the Neatness of Examination Papers." *American Educational Research Journal* 9 (1972): 279-283.

Hunting, J. "Recent Studies of Writing Frequency." *Research in the Teaching of English* 29 (1967): 29-40.

Jeeves, M.A. and G. Baumgartner. "Editorial: Methods of Investigation in Neuropsychology." *Neuropsychologia* 24 (1986): 1-4.

Jorgenson, D. "Signature Size and Dominance: A Brief Note." *Journal of Psychology* 97 (1977): 269-70.

Kaufer, David and Gary Waller. "To Write Is To Read Is To Write, Right?" In G. Douglas Atkins and Michael L. Johnson (eds.), *Writing and Reading Differently*. Lawrence, Kansas: University of Kansas Press, 1985.

Kazemek, Francis E. "Necessary Changes: Professional Involvement in Adult Literacy Programs." *Harvard Educational Review* 58 (1988): 464-487.

Kinsbourne M. and D.B. Rosenfield. "Agraphia Selective for Written Spelling." *Brain and Language* 3 (1974): 215-25.

Kinsbourne, M. and Elizabeth K. Warrington. "Jargon Aphasia." *Neuropsychologia* 1 (1963): 27-37.

Kirsch, I.S. and A. Jungeblut. *Literacy: Profiles of America's Young Adults*. Princeton, New Jersey: National Assessment of Educational Progress and Educational Testing Service (Report No. 16-PL-02). Princeton: Educational Testing Service, 1986.

Kirsch, Gisa. "Writing Across the Curriculum: The Program at Third College, University of California at San Diego." *Writing Program Administration* 12 (1988): 47-55.

Kitzhaber, Albert R. *Themes, Theories and Therapy: The Teaching of Writing in College*. New York: McGraw-Hill, 1963.

Kleist, K., In O. Schjernings (ed.), *Handbuch der Argblichen Erfahrungen*. Leipzig: Barth, 1922.

———. *Gehirnpathologie*. Leipzig: Barth, 1934.

Koch, Carl and James M. Brazil. *Strategies for Teaching the Composition Process*. Urbana, Illinois: National Council of Teachers of English, 1978.

Kolln, Martha. "Closing the Books on Alchemy." *College Composition and Communication* 32 (1981): 139-151.

———. "Reply to Ronald Shook." *College Composition and Communication* 34 (1983): 496-98.

———. *Writing and Language.* New York: Macmillan, 1984.

Krashen, Stephen. "Lateralization, Language Learning, and the Critical Period: Some New Evidence." *Language Learning* 23 (1973): 63-74.

———. *Second Language Acquisition and Second Language Learning.* Oxford: Pergamon, 1981.

———. *Principles and Practice of Second Language Acquisition.* New York: Pergamon, 1982.

———. *Writing Research, Theory and Application.* New York: Pergamon, 1984.

———. *The Input Hypothesis: Issues and Implications.* London: Longman, 1985.

Kroll, Barry. "Developmental Relationships Between Speaking and Writing." In Barry Kroll and Roberta J. Vann (eds.), *Exploring Speaking-Writing Relationships: Connections and Contrasts.* Urbana, Illinois: National Council of Teachers of Writing, 1982.

Kurfiss, Joanne. "Do Students Really Learn From Writing?" *Writing Across the Curriculum Newsletter* 3 (1985): 3-4.

Kutz, Eleanor. "Between Students' Language and Academic Discourse: Interlanguage as Middle Ground." *College English* 48 (1986): 385-396.

Laine, Tarmo and Reijo J. Martilla. "Pure Agraphia: A Case Study." *Neuropsychologia* 19 (1981): 311-16.

Langer, Judith A. (ed.). *Language, Literacy, and Culture: Issues of Society and Schooling.* Norwood, New Jersey: Ablex, 1987.

Lanham, Richard. *A Handlist of Rhetorical Terms.* Berkeley, California: University of California Press, 1969.

———. *Style: An Anti-Textbook.* New Haven, Connecticut: Yale University Press, 1974.

———. *The Motives of Eloquence.* New Haven, Connecticut: Yale University Press, 1976.

———. *Revising Prose.* New York: Scribners, 1979.

———. *Revising Business Prose.* New York: Scribners, 1981.

———. *Analyzing Prose.* New York: Scribners, 1983a.

———. *Literacy and the Survival of Humanism.* New Haven, Connecticut: Yale University Press, 1983b.

Larsen, Richard L. "The Writer's Mind: Recent Research and Unanswered Questions." In Janice N. Hays, Phyllis A. Roth, Jon R. Ramsey, and Robert D. Foulke (eds.), *The Writer's Mind: Writing as a Mode of Thinking.* Urbana, Illinois: National Council of Teachers of English, 1983.

Lashley, Karl S. *Brain Mechanisms and Intelligence.* Chicago: University of Chicago Press, 1929.

Lauer, Janice, and J. William Asher. *Composition Research: Empirical Designs.* New York: Oxford, 1988.

Lecours, Andre R. "Serial Order in Writing: A Study of Misspelled Words in 'Developmental Dysgraphia.'" *Neuropsychologia 4* (1967): 221-41.

Lecours, Andre R., Jacques Mehler, and Maria A. Parente (et al.). "Illiteracy and Brain Damage: 1. Aphasia Testing in Culturally Contrasted Populations (Control Subjects)." *Neuropsychologia* 25 (1987a): 231-45.

———. "Illiteracy and Brain Damage: 2. Manifestations of Unilateral Neglect in Testing 'Auditory Comprehension' with Iconographic Materials." *Brain and Cognition* 6 (1987b): 243-65.

———. "Illiteracy and Brain Damage: 3. A Contribution to the Study of Speech and Language Disorders in Illiterates with Brain Damage." *Neuropsychologia* 26 (1988): 575-89.

Leggett, Sarah. "The Relationship Between Speaking and Writing: An Annotated Bibliography," *College Composition and Communication* 35 (1984): 334-344.

Leischner, A. "Über die Aphasie der Mehrsprachigen," *Archives of Psychiatry* (LPZ), 118 (1948): 731-775.

Lenneberg, Eric. *Biological Foundations of Language.* New York: Wiley and Sons, 1967.

Liberman, Alvin M. and Ignatius G. Mattingly. "The Motor Theory of Speech Perception Revisited." *Cognition* 21 (1985): 1-36.

Lindemann, Erika. *A Rhetoric for Writing Teachers.* New York: Oxford, (2nd ed.) 1987.

Long, Michael. "Input and Second Language Acquisition Theory." In Susan M. Gass and Carolyn G. Madden (eds.), *Input in Second Language Acquisition.* Rowley, Massachusetts: Newbury House, 1985.

Luria, Aleksandr R. *Traumatic Aphasia: Its Syndromes, Psychology, and Treatment.* The Hague: Mouton, 1970a.

———. "The Functional Organization of the Brain." *Scientific American* 3 (1970b): 66-78.

———. *The Working Brain: An Introduction to Neuropsychology.* New York: Basic Books, 1973.

Luria, Aleksandr R. and F. Yudovich. *Speech and the Development of Mental Processes in the Child.* Harmondsworth, England: Penguin, 1971.

Maimon, Elaine P. "Writing Across the Curriculum: Past, Present, and Future." In C. Williams Griffin (ed.), *Teaching Writing in All Disciplines,* 1982.

———. "Maps and Genres: Exploring Connections in the Arts and Sciences." In Winifred Byran Horner (ed.), *Composition and Literature: Bridging the Gap,* 1983.

Maimon, Elaine P., Barbara F. Nodine, and Finbarr W. O'Connor (ed.). *Thinking, Reasoning, and Writing.* New York: Longman, 1989.

Margolin, D.I. "The Neuropsychology of Writing and Spelling: Semantic, Phonological, Motor and Perceptual Processes. *Quarterly Journal of Experimental Psychology* 36A (1984): 459-89.

Marie, P. *Travaux et Memoires.* Paris: Masson et Cie, 1926.

Marrou, Henri. *A History of Education in Anitquity.* (Trans. by George Lamb). New York: Sheed and Ward, 1956.

Marshall, John. "The Description and Interpretation of Aphasic Language Disorder." *Neuropsychologia* 24 (1986): 5-24.

Marshall, J.C. and F. Newcombe. "Syntactic and Semantic Errors in Paralexia," *Neuropsychologie* 4 (1966): 169-76.

Marshall, J. and J.M. Powers. "Writing Neatness, Composition Errors, and Essay Grades." *Journal of Educational Measurement* 6 (1969): 97-101.

Martin, James. "Rhythmic (Hierarchical) Versus Serial Structure in Speech and Other Behavior." *Psychological Review* 79 (1972): 487-509.

Matsuhashi, Ann. "Pausing and Planning: The Tempo of Written Discourse Production." *Research in the Teaching of English* 15 (1981): 113-34.

———. "Explorations in the Real-Time Production of Written Discourse." In Martin Nystrand (ed.), *What Writers Know: The Language, Process, and Structure of Written Discourse.* New York: Academic Press, 1982.

Mayher, John S., Nancy Lester, and Gordon M. Pradl. *Learning to Write/Writing to Learn.* Portsmouth, New Hampshire: Boynton/Cook, 1983.

McCarthy, Lucille. "A Stranger in Strange Lands," *Research in the Teaching of Writing* 21 (1987): 233-265.

McGuigan, F. Covert Oral Behavior as a Function of Quality of Handwriting." *American Journal of Psychology* 83 (1970): 377-88.

McLaughlin, Barry. 1978. "The Monitor Model: Some Methodological Considerations." *Language Learning* 28 (1978): 309-32.

———. *Theories of Second Language Learning*. London: Edward Arnold, 1987.

McLeod, Susan. "Defining Writing Across the Curriculum." *WPA: Writing Program Administration* 11.1-2 (1987): 19-24.

———. *Strengthening Programs for Writing Across the Curriculum* (New Directions for Teaching and Learning No. 36). San Francisco: Jossey-Bass, 1988.

McQueen R., A.K. Murray, and F. Evans. "Relationships Between Writing Required in High School and English Proficiency in College." *Journal of Experimental Education* 31 (1963): 419-423.

Mead, George H. *Mind, Self, and Society: From the Standpoint of a Social Behaviorist*. Chicago: University of Chicago Press, 1934.

Mellon, John C. "Round Two of the National Writing Assessment—Interpreting the Apparent Decline of Writing Ability: A Review." *Research in the Teaching of English* 10 (1976): 66-73.

———. "A Taxonomy of Compositional Competencies." In Richard Beach and P. David Pearson (eds.), *Perspectives on Literacy*. Minneapolis: University of Minnesota College of Education, 1979.

Miller, George. "The Magic Number Seven, Plus or Minus Two." In *The Psychology of Communications*. New York: 1967.

Moffett, James. "Writing, Inner Speech, and Meditation." *College English* 44 (1982): 231-246.

Morais, Jose, Luz Cary, Jesus Alegria, and Paul Bertelson. "Literacy Training and Speech Segmentation." *Cognition* 24 (1986): 45-64.

Nickerson, R.S. "Speech Understanding and Reading: Some Differences and Similarities." In Ovid J. Tzeng and Harry Singer (eds.), *Perception of Print: Reading Research in Experimental Psychology*. Hillsdale, New Jersey: Lawrence Erlbaum, 1981.

Nielsen, J.M. *Agnosia, Apraxia, Aphasia: Their Value in Cerebral Localization*. New York: Hoeber, (2nd ed.) 1946.

Nielsen, J.M. and Raney, R.B. "Symptoms Following Surgical Removal of Major (Left) Angular Gyrus." *Bulletin of the Los Angeles Neurological Society* 3 (1938): 42-46.

Ochsner, Robert S. *Rhythm and Writing*. Troy, New York: Whitston Press, 1989.

Ogle, J.W. "Aphasia and Agraphia in St. George's Hospital," *Reports of the Medical Research Council (London)* 2 (1867): 83-122.

Ohmann, Richard. "Literacy, Technology, and Monopoly Capital." *College English* 47 (1985): 675-689.

Olson, David. "From Utterance to Text: The Bias of Language in Speech and Writing." *Harvard Educational Review* 47 (1977): 257-281.

———. (ed.). *Understanding Literacy.* Toronto: Ontario Institute of Studies in Education, 1987.

Olson, David R., Nancy Torrance, and A. Hildyard (eds.). *Literacy, Language and Learning: The Nature and Consequences of Reading and Writing.* Cambridge: Cambridge University Press, 1985.

Ong, Walter J. *Interfaces of the Word.* Ithica, NY: Cornell University Press, 1977.

———. *Orality and Literacy: The Technologizing of the Word.* New York: Metheun, 1982.

Ormrod, Jeanne E. "Learning to Spell: Three Studies at the University Level." *Research in the Teaching of English* 20 (1986): 160-173.

Ornstein, R. *Multimind.* Boston: Houghton Mifflin, 1986.

Oxenham, John. *Literacy: Writing, Reading and Social Organization.* London: Routledge and Kegan Paul, 1980.

Patterson, Karalyn, and Alan Wing. "Processes in Handwriting: A Case for Case." *Neuropsychologia* 6 (1989): 1-23.

Pattison, Robert. *On Literacy.* New York: Oxford University Press, 1982.

Perelman, Chaim. *The Realm of Rhetoric.* (Trans. by William Kluback) Notre Dame, Indiana: University of Notre Dame Press, 1982.

Perelman, Chaim and Lucie Olbrechts-Tyteca. *The New Rhetoric: A Treatise on Argumentation.* (Trans. by John Wilkinson and Purcell Weaver). Notre Dame, Indiana: University of Notre Dame Press, 1969.

Perl, Sondra. "The Composing Process of Unskilled College Writers." *Research in the Teaching of Writing 13* (1979): 317-339.

Piaget, Jean. *The Language and Thought of the Child.* Cleveland: Meridan Books, 1955.

———. "Cognitive Development in Children." In R.E. Ripple and V.N. Rockcastel (eds.), *Piaget Rediscovered: A Report of the Conference on Cognitive Studies and Curriculum Development.* Ithaca, New York: Cornell University Press, 1964.

Piaget, Jean and Bärbel Inhelder. *The Psychology of the Child.* New York: Basic Books, 1969.

Piattelli-Palmarini, Massimo. "Evolution, Selection and Cognition: From 'Learning' to Parameter Setting in Biology and in the Study of Language." *Cognition* 31 (1989): 1-44.

Pienemann, Manfred. "Psychological Constraints on the Teachability of Languages. *Studies in Second Language Acquisition* 6 (1984): 186-214.

————. "Is Language Teachable? Psycholinguistic Experiments and Hypotheses." *Applied Linguistics* 10 (1989): 52-79.

Pirozzollo, F. and M. Wittrock. *Neuropsychological and Cognitive Processes in Reading.* New York: Basic Books, 1981.

Pitres, A. "Considération sur l'Agraphie: A Propos d'une Observation Nouvelle d'Agraphie Motrice Pure." *Revue Medicine* 4 (1884): 855-73.

Plato. *The Phaedrus.* New York: Bollingen Foundation, 1961.

Posteraro, Lucio, Patrizia Zinelli, and Anna Muzzucchi. "Selective Impairment of the Graphemic Buffer in Acquired Dysgraphia: A Case Study." *Brain and Language* 35 (1988): 274-86.

Quintilian. *The Institutio Oratoria of Quintilian* (Books X-XII). Cambridge, Massachusetts: Harvard University Press, 1922.

Resnick, Daniel P. and Lauren B. Resnick. "The Nature of Literacy: An Historical Exploration." *Harvard Educational Review* 47 (1977): 370-85.

Richardson, J.T.E. "The Effect of Word Imageability in Acquired Dyslexia." *Neuropsychologia* 13 (1975): 281-88.

Robb, Mary M. and Lester Thonssen (eds.). *Chironomia or a Treatise on Rhetorical Delivery by Gilbert Austin.* Carbondale, Illinois: Southern Illinois University Press, 1966.

Roeltgen, David P., and David M. Tucker. "Developmental Phonological and Lexical Agraphia in Adults." *Brain and Language* 35 (1988): 287-300.

Roeltgen, David P. and Karl Heilman. "Review of Agraphia and a Proposal for an Anatomically-Based Neuropsychological Model of Writing." *Applied Psycholinguistics* 6 (1984): 205-30.

Rorty, Richard. *Philosophy and the Mirror of Nature.* Princeton: Princeton University Press, 1979.

————. *Consequences of Pragmatism.* Minneapolis: University of Minnesota Press, 1982.

Rose, Mike. "Rigid Rules, Inflexible Plans, and the Stifling of Language: A Cognitivist Analysis of Writer's Block." *College Composition and Communication* 31 (1980): 389-401.

————. *Writer's Block: The Cognitive Dimension.* Carbondale, Illinois: Southern Illinois University Press, 1984.

————. "Narrowing the Mind and Page: Remedial Writers and Cognitive Reductionism." *College Composition and Communication* 39 (1988): 267-302.

Rudolph, Frederick. *Curriculum.* San Francisco: Jossey-Bass, 1978.

Russell, W.R. and M.L. Espir. *Traumatic Aphasia.* London: Oxford University Press, 1961.

Schafer, John C. "The Linguistic Analysis of Spoken and Written Texts," in Barry Kroll and Roberta Vann (eds.), *Exploring Speaking-Writing Relationships: Connections and Contrasts.* Urbana, Illinois: National Council of Teachers of English, 1981.

Schnitzer, Marc L. Toward a Neurolinguistic Theory of Language." *Brain and Language* 6 (1978): 342-61.

Scholes, Robert J. and Brenda J. Willis. "Invisible Speech—Oral Language Skills in Braille Readers." *Interchange* 20 (1989): 1-13.

Schumann, John. "Social Distance as a Factor in Second Language Acquisition." *Language Learning* 25 (1977): 135-143.

————. "Social and Psychological Factors in Second Language Acquisition." In J.C. Richards (ed.), *Understanding Second Language Learning.* Rowley, Massachusetts: Newbury House, 1978.

Schwartz, Sybil. "Spelling Disability: A Developmental Linguistic Analysis of Pattern Abstraction." *Applied Psycholinguistics* 4 (1983): 303-16.

Scovel, T. "The Ontogeny of the Ability to Recognize Foreign Accents." In C. Henning (ed.), *Proceedings of the Los Angeles Second Language Research Forum.* Los Angeles: University of California at Los Angeles, 1977.

Scribner, Sylvia and Michael Cole. *The Psychology of Literacy.* Cambridge, MA: Harvard University Press, 1981.

Searle, John R. *Speech Acts: An Essay in the Philosophy of Language.* Cambridge: Cambridge University Press, 1969.

Sebeok, Thomas (ed.). *Style in Language.* Cambridge, Massachusetts: Massachusetts Institute of Technology, 1964.

Selinker, Larry. "Interlanguage." *International Review of Applied Linguistics* 10 (1972): 209-31.

————. "The Current State of IL Studies: An Attempted Critical Summary." In Alan Davies, C. Criper, and A P.R. Howatt (eds.), *Interlanguage.* Edinburgh: Edinburgh University Press, 1984.

Shallice, T. and E.K. Warrington. "Auditory-Verbal Short-Term Impairment and Conduction Aphasia." *Brain and Language* 4 (1977): 479-91.

Shapiro, David. *Neurotic Styles.* New York: Basic Books, 1965.

Shaughnessy, Mina. *Errors and Expectations.* New York: Oxford University Press, 1977.

Sheils, M. "Why Johnny Can't Write." *Newsweek* 86 (1975): 58-62.

Shook, Ron. "Response to Martha Kolln." *College Composition and Communication* 34 (1983): 491-5.

Sokolov, A.N. *Inner Speech and Thought.* New York: Plenum Press, 1972.

Spolsky, Bernard. "Formulating a Theory of Second Language Learning." *Studies in Second Language Acquisition.* 7 (1985): 269-88.

Stockwell, Robert P. "Contrastive Analysis and Lapsed Time." In James E. Alatis (ed.), *Monograph Series on Languages and Linguistics. Nineteenth Annual Round Table: Contrastive Linguistics and Its Pedagogical Implications.* Washington, D.C.: Georgetown University School of Languages and Linguistics, Georgetown University Press, 1968: 11-26.

———. *Foundations of Syntactic Theory.* Englewood Cliffs, New Jersey: Prentice-Hall, 1977.

Stockwell, Robert, Donald Bowen and J. Martin. *The Grammatical Structures of English and Spanish.* Chicago: University of Chicago Press, 1965.

Swanson, B., and R. Price. "Signature Size and Status." *Journal of Social Psychology* 87 (1972): 319.

Swanson-Owens, Deborah. "Identifying Natural Sources of Resistance: A Case Study of Implementing Writing Across the Curriculum." *Research in the Teaching of English* 20 (1986): 69-97.

Tannen, Deborah. "Oral and Written Strategies in Spoken and Written Narratives." *Language* 58 (1982a): 1-21.

———. "The Myth of Orality and Literacy." In William Frawley (ed.), *Linguistics and Literacy.* New York: Plenum Press, 1982b.

———. "The Orality of Literature and the Literacy of Conversation." In Judith A. Langer (ed.), *Language, Literacy and Culture: Issues of Society and Schooling.* Norwood, New Jersey: Ablex, 1987.

Taylor, Donna. *Family Literacy: Young Children Learning to Read and Write.* Exeter, New Hampshire: Heinemann, 1983.

Terrell, Tracy. "A Natural Approach to Second Language Acquisition and Learning." *Modern Language Journal* 61 (1977): 325-337.

Teuber, H.L. and R. Rudel. "Behavior After Cerebral Lesions in Children and Adults." *Developmental Medicine and Child Neurology* 4 (1967): 3-20.

Thomas, B. and J. Richter. "Psychological Inquiries Regarding the Handwriting of Stutterers." *Psychiatrie, Neurologie und Medizinische Psychologie* 24 (1972): 201-209.

Torrance, Nancy, and David Olson. "Development of Metalanguage and the Acquisition of Literacy." *Interchange* 18 (1987): 136-47.

Toulmin, Stephen. *The Uses of Argument.* New York: Cambridge University Press, 1958.

Toulmin, Stephen, Richard Rieke, and Allan Janik. *An Introduction to Reasoning.* New York: Macmillan, 1979.

Tremaine, R. *Syntax and Piagetian Operational Thought.* Washington, D.C.: Georgetown University Press, 1975.

Trimble, John. *Writing With Style.* Englewood Cliffs, New Jersey: Prentice-Hall, 1975.

Vachek, Josef. *Written Language.* The Hague: Mouton, 1973.

Van Bergejik, W. and David, E. "Delaying Handwriting." *Perceptual and Motor Skills* 9 (1959): 347-357.

Van Dijk, Tuen A. *Text and Context: Explorations in the Semantics and Pragmatics of Discourse.* London: Longman, 1977.

Veblen, Thorstein. *The Theory of the Leisure Class.* New York: Penguin, 1979.

Vellutino, F.R. "Theoretical Issues in the Study of Word Recognition: The Unit of Perception Controversy Reexamined." In S. Rosenberg (ed.), *Handbook of Applied Psycholinguistics.* Hillsdale, New Jersey: Lawrence Erlbaum, 1982.

Vygotsky, Lev. *Thought and Language.* (Trans. by E. Hanfmann and G. Vakar.) Cambridge, Massachusetts: Massachusetts Institute of Technology Press, 1962.

———. *Mind in Society: The Development of Higher Psychological Processes.* Cambridge, Massachusetts: Harvard University Press, 1978.

Weaver, Richard. *The Ethics of Rhetoric.* Chicago: Henry Regnery, 1953.

Weigl, Egon. "Neuropsychological Experiments on Transcoding Between Spoken and Written Language Structures." *Brain and Language* 1 (1974): 227-40.

Weisenberg, T. and K.E. McBride. *Aphasia: A Clinical and Psychological Study.* New York: Hafner, 1964.

Wernicke, Carl. "Ein Fall von Isolierter Agraphie." *Mtschr. Psychiat. Neurol.* 13 (1903): 241-265.

Whately, Richard. *Elements of Rhetoric.* Carbondale, Illinois: Southern Illinois University Press, 1963.

White, William Allen. *The Autobiography of William Allen White.* New York: Macmillan, 1966.

Whitehead, Alfred. *The Aims of Education.* New York: Free Press, 1957.

Williams, James D. "Covert Language Behavior During Writing." *Research in the Teaching of English* 17 (1983): 301-312.

―――. "Covert Linguistic Behaviors During Writing Tasks: Psychophysical Differences Between Above-Average and Below-Average Writers." *Written Communication* 4 (1987): 310-28.

―――. *Preparing to Teach Writing.* Belmont, California: Wadsworth, 1989.

Williams, Joseph. *Style and Variables in English.* Cambridge, MA: 1981a.

―――. "The Phenomenology of Error." *College Composition and Communication* 32 (1981b): 152-168.

―――. *Style: Ten Lessons in Clarity and Grace.* Glenville, Illinois: Scott, Foresman and Co., (1st ed.) 1981, (2nd ed.) 1984.

Winterowd, W. Ross. *Composition/Rhetoric: A Synthesis.* Carbondale, Illinois: Southern Illinois University Press, 1986.

Witte, Stephen P. *Evaluating College Writing Programs.* Carbondale, Illinois: Southern Illinois University Press, 1983.

―――. "Revising, Composing Theory, And Research Design." In Sarah W. Freedman (ed.), *The Acquisition of Written Language.* Norwood, New Jersey: Ablex, 1985.

―――. "Pre-Text and Composing." *College Composition and Communication* 38 (1987): 397-425.

Wright, J. and E. Allen. "Ready to Write." *Elementary School Journal* 75 (1975): 430-35.

Zaidel, Eran. "Concepts of Cerebral Dominance in the Split Brain." In P. Buser and A. Rougeul-Buser (eds.), *Cerebral Correlates of Conscious Experience.* Amsterdam: Elsevier, 1977.

Zamel, Vivian. "Teaching Composition in the ESL Classroom: What We Can Learn From Research in the Teaching of English," *TESOL Quarterly* 10 (1976): 206-221.

Zipf, G. *The Psycho-Biology of Language: An Introduction to Dynamic Philology.* Cambridge, Massachusetts: Massachussetts Institute of Technology, 1935.

Zoellner, R. "Talk-Write: A Behavioral Pedagogy for Composition." *College English* 30 (1969): 267-320.

INDEX